Learn Lua for iOS Game Development

Jayant Varma

Apress

Learn Lua for iOS Game Development

ISBN-13 (pbk): 978-1-4302-4662-6

ISBN-13 (electronic): 978-1-4302-4663-3

Trademarked names, logos, and images may appear in this book. Rather than use a trademark symbol with every occurrence of a trademarked name, logo, or image we use the names, logos, and images only in an editorial fashion and to the benefit of the trademark owner, with no intention of infringement of the trademark.

The use in this publication of trade names, trademarks, service marks, and similar terms, even if they are not identified as such, is not to be taken as an expression of opinion as to whether or not they are subject to proprietary rights.

President and Publisher: Paul Manning
Lead Editor: Michelle Lowman
Development Editor: Richard Carey
Technical Reviewers: Mekha Shrestha and Yujan Shrestha
Editorial Board: Steve Anglin, Mark Beckner, Ewan Buckingham, Gary Cornell, Morgan Ertel, Jonathan Gennick, Jonathan Hassell, Robert Hutchinson, Michelle Lowman, James Markham, Matthew Moodie, Jeff Olson, Jeffrey Pepper, Douglas Pundick, Ben Renow-Clarke, Dominic Shakeshaft, Gwenan Spearing, Matt Wade, Tom Welsh
Coordinating Editor: Brigid Duffy
Copy Editor: Damon Larson
Compositor: SPi Global
Indexer: SPi Global
Artist: SPi Global
Cover Designer: Anna Ishchenko

Distributed to the book trade worldwide by Springer Science+Business Media, LLC., 233 Spring Street, 6th Floor, New York, NY 10013. Phone 1-800-SPRINGER, fax (201) 348-4505, e-mail orders-ny@springer-sbm.com, or visit www.springeronline.com.

For information on translations, please e-mail rights@apress.com, or visit www.apress.com.

Apress and friends of ED books may be purchased in bulk for academic, corporate, or promotional use. eBook versions and licenses are also available for most titles. For more information, reference our Special Bulk Sales–eBook Licensing web page at www.apress.com/info/bulksales.

The information in this book is distributed on an "as is" basis, without warranty. Although every precaution has been taken in the preparation of this work, neither the author(s) nor Apress shall have any liability to any person or entity with respect to any loss or damage caused or alleged to be caused directly or indirectly by the information contained in this work.

The source code for this book is available to readers at www.apress.com.

To my loving parents and my son, Mihir

Contents at a Glance

Contents

About the Author

Jayant Varma is the executive director of OZ Apps, an Australian-based consultancy focused on assisting local and international businesses in mobile product enhancement strategies and specialized services for mobile development and training. He has several apps on the Mac App Store to his credit.

Jayant has an MBA-MIT and is an IT veteran with over 20 years of rich and varied experience in several countries, in sectors including automotive and higher education. Following on with his passion for teaching, he has lectured and developed subject outlines at the James Cook University.

His mobile development journey started in early 2000 with the Microsoft Pocket PC (Compaq iPaq) and has continued to Apple's iOS today. His fascination with technology and games goes back to when he started writing games on his first computer, the ZX Spectrum.

Jayant has been an active member of ACS (Australian Computer Society) and is part of the executive board for the local chapter. He is a founding chairman of the first local YIT (Young IT) chapter. He has conducted iOS development workshops for the AUC (Apple University Consortium) and is enthusiastic with mentoring and advising young developers. He also helps other developers via his blogs on topics related to development.

You can follow Jayant on Twitter at @ozapps, on the blogs at http://howto.oz-apps.com and http://reviewme.oz-apps.com, and the Lua blogs http://dev.oz-apps.com and @LearnLua.

About the Technical Reviewers

Mekha Shrestha and **Yujan Shrestha** are founders of the software development company M.Y. Developers, which develops advanced tools for software and game development.

Yujan Shrestha completed his education in biomedical engineering at the University of Texas in Austin, and Mekha Shrestha studied neuroscience at Baylor University. After working on various projects in college, they decided to work together on some innovative projects for research on autism disorders conducted at the University of Texas Medical School at Houston. Following their research, they worked on making simple strategic games. Their first game project was Space Conquest, which is an adventure/action game with realistic physics that enables the player to experience strategic game play. During its development, they recognized the need for tools that improved the quality of game development for indie and professional developers alike, which lead to the making and designing of various tools for Corona SDK—namely, Corona Profiler and Corona Ultimote. They also developed an acclaimed Lua-based IDE called Lua Glider for various platforms, including Corona SDK, Moai SDK, Gideros SDK, and LÖVE 2D.

As a team they aim to develop and improve tools that will enhance the experience of software and game development.

Patrick Meehan is the Founder and CEO of Zipline Games, Inc and the architect of Moai SDK.

http://www.linkedin.com/in/patrickmeehan

Atilim Çetin: Studied at METU Computer Engineering department during 1996–2001. He worked as a software specialist at Makrosam Software, Tübitak UEKAE and Meteksan System companies. During 2006–2009 he worked as a specialist software engineer, technical group leader and three dimensional software group leader in various simulation projects at KaTron Defense, Space and Simulation Technologies company in Koç Group. In 2010 he founded Gideros Mobile and is the design architect and technical leader of the Gideros Studio. He is the author of the book entitled Computer Graphics (ISBN: 975 347 104 0) and also one of the authors of "Three Dimensional Computer Graphics" and "Animation" titles in the Turkish Informatics Encyclopedia.

Acknowledgments

This is an important section for me, because without the help of these people, this book would not have been possible at all. Andrei Buta, a talented graphic designer from the United Kingdom, introduced me to this opportunity with Apress. Michelle Lowman helped with outlining a couple of concepts around iOS development, and the book idea was born. During the entire process, Brigid Duffy from Apress was an immense support and helped to keep up with the deadlines. From there on, because of the variety of topics and frameworks, writing the book was a challenging task. I received a lot of support from Michael Hartlef from Whitesky Games, Atilim Çetin from Gideros Mobile, Patrick Meehan from Zipline Games (Moai), Simeon Nasilowski from Two Lives Left (Codea), and Mekha and Yujan Shrestha from M.Y. Developers—all of whom helped with the completion of the book and checking the technical details and content.

I would also like to acknowledge two prominent personalities: Steve Jobs of Apple for the iOS platform, and Roberto Ierusalimschy of Tecgraf for the Lua language. I would also like to thank the companies that have made the various frameworks covered in the book; each framework has a wonderful set of features that is constantly being updated.

On a personal note, I would also like to thank my family and friends for all of their support during the writing this book—especially Monica Sharma and Agnikrit Sharma. It would not have been possible without their understanding and support.

Lastly, I'd like to thank you, the reader—the most integral part of this equation—for believing in this book and reading it. I hope it helps you in your journey toward development.

I would like to include everyone that has been part of this book in some way and I hope that I have been able to do that. Thank you all.

Chapter 1

Introduction to Lua

Apple has been issuing checks to developers, and the 2012 figures indicate that it has so far been to the tune of $5 billion. In the past, it used to be desktops with Microsoft-based products that were raking in money for developers, with Visual Basic, or earlier with database products such as dBase and FoxPro. While the major share of this revenue goes to larger companies such as EA, Chillingo, Gameloft, Rovio and even Disney, a lot of indie developers and smaller companies vie for a share of that big pie. Who knows what idea might just become the money-spinner for a developer. Robert Nay, a 14-year-old, made the game Bubble Ball while he was learning to code, and it went viral, with over 8 million downloads. And no one knows what the next top game will be.

As a person that has an interest in development, you have made the first step in this journey. You could be a student that has never developed before, or you could be a guru developer who can whip up an enterprise app in minutes. The point is that whatever your background, you are for some reason drawn to this strange-sounding language, Lua (pronounced *LOO-ah.*).

What Is Lua?

Lua is a programming language that has a small footprint, works across several platforms, and is quite flexible and extensible. Further, Lua is a game changer for developers that want to write apps for the mobile devices. It has powered a lot of apps and games in the Apple App Store, and it has been spoken about by the late Steve Jobs. It has even been linked with one of the most advanced self-replicating and mutating viruses, the Flame. Despite all of that, Lua remains to be a language that seems more like plain English than a cryptic programmer's language, making it a language with a smaller learning curve.

The History of Lua

While knowing the history of Lua will not change anything in terms of making anyone a better programmer, it important to get an idea of why you'd want to use Lua.

Lua was created at the Pontifical Catholic University of Rio de Janeiro, Brazil, by Roberto Ierusalimschy, Luiz Henrique de Figueiredo, and Waldemar Celes, who were members of the

Computer Graphics Technology Group (TeCGraf). Generally, funding for university research is provided by industry, which also expects solutions to some problems that they face. Petrobas, a Brazilian oil company, one of the clients this group was helping them resolve issues related to data entry. Operations of a petroleum company are large, and a large number of data transactions were to be processed on a daily basis. They approached the group to devise a graphical front end that would help eliminate errors in data entry, especially when working with legacy code from fixed-format files.

TeCGraf looked at the whole series of screens that were provided to them and tried to find some form of uniformity to help find a solution. For this they came up with a simple and unified data entry language (DEL), which was used to describe the data in each data entry task. I think a good parallel would be that of XML, but without the multitude of tags that make it confusing to understand. That way one could define the entities and the restrictions or rules. This became very popular, as it was easy to define entities and create records that would help validate the data.

With popularity came feature requests, so the users that were using DEL now required more functionality, which was pushing DEL from being a descriptive language to a programming language with requests such as loops, conditional control, and so on. If you were a software developer in the '90s, you will realize that one of the aspects that many developers spent time on was changing the color and font of the data entry screens. The group created another specialized description language that allowed for setting these attributes. This was called Simple Object Language (SOL), as it allowed the user to create an object and manipulate the color, font, and other characteristics of the object. (*Sol* also means *sun* in Portuguese.)

The architecture of this language was made more like that of a compile-and-run-type of language than that of an IDE-type application. The API was implemented as a C library and linked to the main program. Each type could have a callback function that functioned as the constructor (i.e., the function is called when an object of a particular type is created). In 1993, the creators realized that DEL and SOL could both be combined into a single more powerful language. This led to a proper programming language that would have it all: assignment, control structures, subroutines, functions, and so on. However, it would also work with the basic requirement to be able to offer data-description facilities like those of DEL or SOL. They wanted it to be an easy–to-use language without cryptic syntax and semantics, as the end users weren't expected to be professional programmers. Lastly, they wanted it to be portable to run on any and every platform (if required).

Because it was a modified version of SOL, the creators called this new program *Lua* (which mean moon in Portuguese).

Lua Timeline

As of this writing, Lua is in version 5.2.1. It has undergone quite a few changes and has been used extensively in many projects for enterprise, entertainment, games, and apps. For many of us, it might come as a surprise that Lua is used in South American homes practically on a daily basis. It powers their interactive televisions. Universities use Lua in their research to allow for quick processing and results.

In 1996, Lua got exposure internationally after an article in *Dr. Dobbs*. Following the article, there were e-mails from developers. In a paper, Roberto narrates about how Bret Mogilefsky, who was the lead programmer at LucasArts (of Grim Fandango fame), wanted to replace their scripting language SCUMM with Lua. This drew interest from other developers, and Lua started to appear on newsgroups.

Starting with Lua

One important point that I'll make throughout the book is that, with Lua, it doesn't matter what framework you use; what's important is the glue that holds it all together: Lua. In the '90s, Microsoft was pushing client-server and three-tier architecture (similar to what Apple has been pushing as MVC [Model-View-Controller]). The idea behind MVC is that it involves three distinct portions: a *model*, which takes care of the data; a *view*, which displays the data from the model and provides interaction with the user; and a *controller*, which communicates between the model and the view, as these two do not have any idea of each other's existence. The controller is the broker that helps the two talk to each other. The most usual way to work with MVC is to use a framework, which takes care of a lot of the details for you.

In this book, I shall cover a few frameworks: CoronaSDK, Gideros Studio, Moai, Codea, and LÖVE. All of these except LÖVE help develop and run apps on the iOS platform. The architecture of a Lua-based mobile app is simple, as the diagram in Figure 1-1 shows.

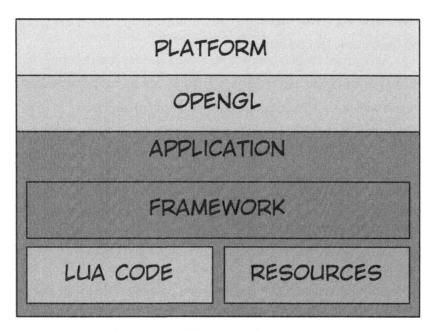

Figure 1-1. The architecture of an app using Lua on a mobile device platform

An application is made up of all the resources graphics, music, text, etc.), which are compiled into the application, with the Lua code along with the framework stub. When run, the framework or the engine creates an OpenGL surface on which all of the graphics are displayed. This is how all of the frameworks work, and this is how they can offer cross-platform compatibility. The limitations on the framework are imposed mainly due to either the limitations of OpenGL or the framework engine.

The MVC pattern discussed earlier holds true in this architecture. If we write our code with this in mind, we can create not only cross-platform applications, but cross-framework ones. The controller code that we write in Lua will change to cater for the other framework, but the rest of the code will be the same.

In the next section, we shall focus on Lua and how to use it. After that, we'll look specifically at the frameworks and integrate some of the things that you've learned.

Setting Up Lua

If we need to work with Lua, we need to have Lua. Since most of the frameworks use Lua 5.1.4, we shall use that version for compatibility. Lua can be obtained as a precompiled binary or source code that you can compile. It is also available for a variety of platforms, including Windows, Mac, *nix, iOS, and Android.

Online Lua Shell

This is perhaps the easiest way to test out the Lua code, and involves no installation or setup of any kind. You can simply navigate to www.lua.org/demo.html.

Windows, Mac OS X, and *nix

You can download the binaries for Lua version 5.1.4 from http://sourceforge.net/projects/luabinaries/files/5.1.4/Executables/.

You can choose lua5_1_4_Win32_bin.zip or lua_5_1_4_Win64_bin.zip as per your version of Windows.

For the Mac, there are versions for Tiger, Leopard, Snow Leopard, and Lion.

For *nix, they are based on the kernel version; in this case, it's easier to download Lua from the app catalog in each of the distributions.

iOS

There are two apps that I know of that allow for running Lua code interactively. Unlike the other Lua offerings mentioned, these are not free.

- *iLuaBox*: This app uses the newer version of Lua 5.2 and costs about $2.99 in the App Store.
- *Lua Console*: This app works with Lua 5.1.4 and costs $1.99 in the App Store.

Of the two, iLuaBox has some advanced functionality in terms of managing files and directories.

Features of Lua

Lua is implemented as a library written in C. It does not have a main program, as there is no need to invoke something automatically; it works as in embedded mode and calls the embedding program. This code can invoke other functions, assign variables, and read and write the data. Having been written in C, it can also be extended; however, the official release will only add features that have been approved by a committee.

Variables

In simple computing terminology, a *variable* is a location that holds a value and can be accessed by giving it a name. Think of it as a filing cabinet in a company's HR department. It can hold many files with details on the employees. When you need to access data from one of them, you can look it up via the file's name tag. If you have two employees with the same first and last names, there need to be two files and the name tag would require some form of identification to distinguish between the two. Just as you cannot have two files with the same tag, you cannot have two variables with the same name. There has to be some point of differentiation (e.g., `tag1` and `tag2` instead of just `tag`).

The names given to the variables can be a series of letters, digits, and underscores; however, they cannot begin with a digit. The names are case sensitive, so there is a difference between `T` and `t`. In addition to variables, Lua also uses *keywords*, which cannot be used for variable names, as Lua identifies them as commands for the code, not variable names. Here's the list of system keywords, which cannot be used as variable names):

```
and
break
do
else
elseif
end
false
for
function
if
in
local
nil
not
or
repeat
return
then
true
until
while
```

Hello World, the Variable Way

To begin with, we need to start Lua in interactive mode for the purpose of running all of our code. The way it works is to open a terminal in Mac OS X or *nix, type `lua`, and press Enter. After doing this, you should see the screen shown in Figure 1-2. Under Windows, you can start the Lua console from the Start menu.

> **Note** In this book, most of the screenshots and references will be for the Mac OS X version.

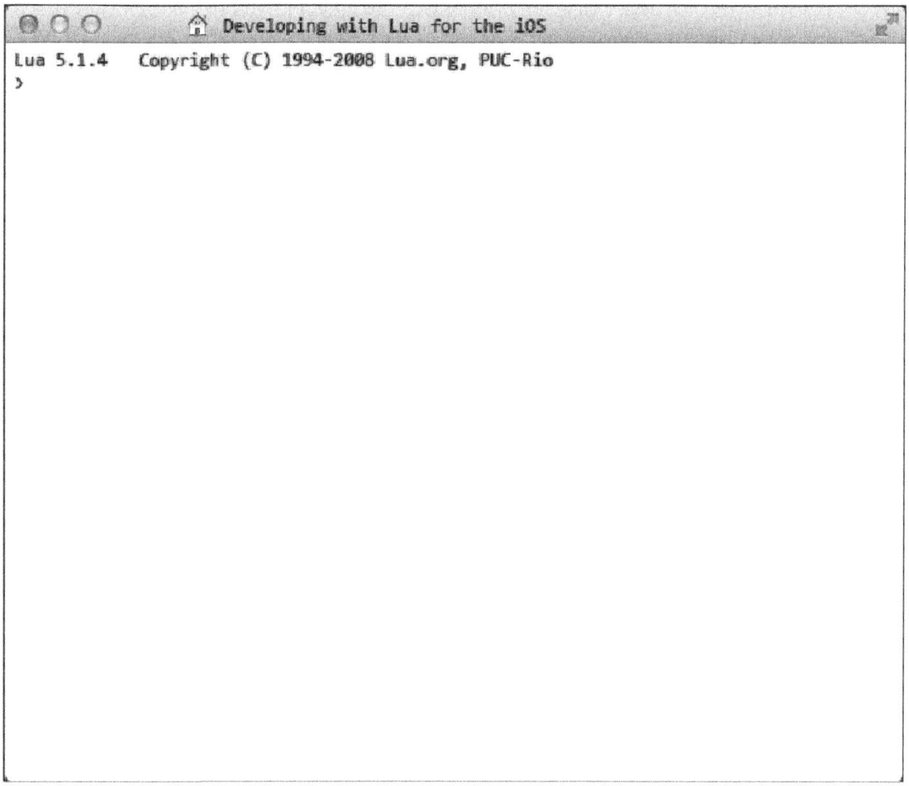
Developing with Lua for the iOS
Lua 5.1.4 Copyright (C) 1994-2008 Lua.org, PUC-Rio
>

Figure 1-2. *The Lua interactive shell running in the terminal on a Mac*

The > on the line is the prompt where you can type the Lua code you want to run. We shall start with writing a simple Hello World example. Type the following at the prompt:

```
print ("Hello World")
```

You should see the text "Hello World" printed on the next line. The `print` function is used to display the text in the terminal. Let's take this a step further:

```
message = "Hello World"
print(message)
```

What we have just done here is assign the string "Hello World" to the message variable; then we use the print function to display the value of message in the terminal.

Just like strings, we can also print numbers, and the simplest way to do so is

```
print(5)
age = 1
print(age)
print("Age :", age)
print(1,2,3,4,5,"One")
```

The aim of this is to demonstrate that using print, we can display variables, numbers, and strings to the terminal.

Strings

Strings in Lua can be enclosed in single or double quotes. So, for example, both 'Lua' and "Lua" are valid. Literal strings can be used in a manner similar to C by preceding them with a blackslash (\) and enclosing them in the single or double quotes. These can be used to include commonly used escape sequences such as \b, \t, \v, \r, \n, \\, \', and \". They can also be used to specify a numeric value with the format \ddd, where d is a digit.

```
print("\65")
```

There are times when you want to include chunks of text, and keeping track of the quotation marks can sometimes get a bit tricky, especially when trying to get them to match and line up. In such cases, you can use the long-bracket format, by which you enclose the text within [[and]]. Here's an example:

```
message = [[That's "Jack O'Neill", with two ll's]]
```

If you used single quotes for enclosure in a scenario like this, you would get an error:

```
message = 'That's "Jack O'Neill", with two ll's'
```

Likewise, you would also get an error using the following line, as the single and double quotes need to have a matching pair or be escaped.

```
message = "That's "Jack O'Neill", with two ll's"
```

The correct way to declare the same would be to place a backslash before the literal quotes, like this:

```
message = 'That\'s "Jack O\'Neill", with two ll\'s'
```

or like this:

```
message = "That's \"Jack O'Neill\", with two ll's"
```

You will notice that it is easy to miss that, in which case the interpreter will only spawn errors. In such cases, using the long brackets is very helpful.

Lua also has levels of nesting with long brackets; you can have various levels by inserting an equal sign between the two opening brackets and one between the two closing brackets, like so:

```
testmsg = [=[ One ]=]
print(testmsg)
```

You can use this for some very interesting-looking source code where you can use

```
testmsg = [======[ One ]======]
print(testmsg)   -- Prints One
```

Numerals

Numbers can be expressed in Lua as decimals, floats, hexadecimals, and scientific notations. Here's an example of each:

```
print(5)          -- 5        This is a decimal number
print(5.3)        -- 5.3      This is a floating point number
print(5.31e-2)    -- 0.0531   This is a scientific notation number
print(0xfeed)     -- 65261    This is a hexadecimal number
```

Values and Types

In languages like C, you have to define a variable with a particular type. For example, you might need define a variable i as an integer (int), like so:

```
int i;
```

With Lua, you do not have to define the type of variable; you can simply assign the value, and the value can change on the fly. In Visual Basic 6 (not to be confused with Visual Basic.NET), this type of variable was called a *variant* variable, and had to be explicitly defined as follows:

```
dim i as variant
```

In contrast, Lua stores variables in memory. Lua stores a variable's value and type together. All variables in Lua are first-class values. This simply means that these values can be stored in variables, passed to other functions as arguments, and returned from a function.

There are eight different types of variables in Lua, which I'll describe next.

nil

This is the same as null. If you have a variable that holds a reference to the last-held value and the garbage collector doesn't clean it up, you can set the variable to nil to indicate that the space referenced can be garbage collected.

boolean

boolean variables are our trusty `true` and `false`. These are used to check for conditions; however, it should be noted that both `nil` and `false` will result in the condition being `false` and any other value resulting in `true`.

```
trusted = false
if (trusted) then print("Yes") end        -- Nothing is printed
trusted = 1
if (trusted) then print("Yes") end        -- Yes is printed
trusted = nil
if (trusted) then print("Yes") end        -- Nothing is printed
```

number

number variables are numbers that can be expressed as decimals, longs, integers, hexadecimals, and floats. Lua saves the numbers as double-precision floating-point numbers.

string

Lua strings are generally 8-bit clean strings (i.e., they can hold any 8-bit character, including embedded zeros). Unicode variables are a slightly different matter, but are handled by Lua if the platform supports Unicode.

function

In Lua, functions can also be stored and passed as variables. This functionality of being able to store and pass functions as parameters makes the functions in Lua *"first-class functions."*

userdata

This is a memory block that is allocated from C, allowing C functions to store and access data. userdata variables cannot be created or manipulated in Lua, but only through the C API.

thread

This is a special type of variable; this specifies an independent thread of execution. This is not the same as the operating system thread.

table

table variables are what we would call arrays, associative arrays, hash tables, sets, records, lists, trees, and even objects in Lua.

> **Note**   Tables, functions, and threads do not really hold any values—only references to them.

Code Blocks and Scopes

In Lua, every variable has a scope, which means that it is accessible to the code depending on its life cycle as determined by the scope. Variables are either *global* or *local*. By default, variables are defined as global unless explicitly defined as local.

In code, variables set between a do and an end block are not accessible outside of the block, and any local variables that are set outside of the block are accessible inside the block.

Let us look at this with an example:

```
i = 1
print("i = ", i)
do
  local i = 2
  print("i = ", i)
end
print("i = ", i)
```

Coercion is a simple term given to the process of converting a string into a number following the conversion rules (if possible) to provide arithmetic operations between a string and a number.

```
one = "1"
two = 2
print(one + two)        -- 3 is printed
```

In many languages, attempting such an arithmetic operation between two different data types (in this case a string and a number) would fail. In some other scripting languages, this code would instead add the value to the string, resulting in the string "12". However, in Lua, this outputs the value 3, where one is converted into numeric 1 and then added to the value of two to output 3.

However, if we wanted to add the two strings "1" and "2" to get "12", then we would need to use what is called *concatenation*. In Lua the concatenation operator is the double-dot (..). This combines the two strings and returns a new string that contains the two strings passed.

Lua Operators

The operators in Lua can be grouped into different types of operators, which include arithmetic, relational, and logical operators, among others.

Arithmetic Operators

These do not need much of an introduction; they are simple and straightforward. Table 1-1 lists them.

Table 1-1. Arithmetic Operators

Operator	Description
+	Addition
-	Subtraction
*	Multiplication
/	Division
%	Modulo
^	Exponent
-	Unary negation

Relational Operators

These are the operators used for comparing or conditions. They're listed in Table 1-2.

Table 1-2. Relational Operators

Operator	Description
==	Equality (to check for equality between two values)
~=	Not equal to (the opposite of equality)
<	Less than
>	Greater than
<=	Less than or equal to
>=	Greater than or equal to

These operators will always result in a true or a false return value. It should be noted that when comparing two numbers or values, use the == where as a single = in Lua signifies assignment.

Logical Operators

The logical operators in Lua are

```
and
or
not
```

The way the and and or work in Lua is by what's called the *shortcut evaluation*. It checks for a value, and checks further only if it is required. and returns the first arguments if the value is false or nil; if it isn't, then it returns the second argument. or, on the other hand, returns the first value if the result is not false or nil, and returns the second argument if the first argument is false or nil.

The best use of or is in functions for assigning default values:

```
a = a or 5 -- Can be used to assign the value of 5 if the value of a is nil or false
```

We can test how these work as follows:

```
testing = nil
print(testing)
print(testing and 5)
print(testing or 5)
print(not testing)
testing = 15
print(testing)
print(testing and 5)
print(testing or 5)
print(not testing)
```

Other Operators

Apart from the standard operators that we have discussed, there are a couple of other operators offered to us by Lua. They are used for operations like concatenation and obtaining the length of something; these two work with strings, though the # operator can also be used with arrays.

- Concatenation operator: ..
- Length operator: #

As mentioned previously, the concatenation operator in Lua is the double-dot (..). It is used to add two strings together, like so:

```
print("one, two, " .. " buckle my shoe")
```

The length operator returns the length of the string.

```
print(#"this is a long string") -- prints 21 as the length of the string
```

Summary

The portability of Lua means that we can run our code on various devices and desktops. The small footprint of Lua and a very flexible and forgiving syntax allows for rapid prototyping and code testing. We have seen that Lua is increasing in popularity with game developers. In the next chapter, we shall take a closer look at the standard Lua libraries that provide all the commands that make up standard Lua.

Chapter 2

Lua Libraries

In the previous chapter, you learned the reasons behind Lua and that Lua is, after all, made up of C code libraries. One of the advantages that the developers of Lua got from this architecture for Lua was that they could add functionality as required. Adding functionality involved writing new functions and making them available in Lua. It is quite a surprise that Lua does not have multiple distributions and remains as intended by the developers; there are not many modified versions. However, many developmental studios do modify, or rather adapt and customize, Lua for their own editors and tools.

In this chapter, we shall look at the standard Lua libraries and namespaces that provide us with their functions. Then we'll have a detailed look at the system- and table-related functions.

Basic Functions

Lua has some basic functions that are part of the Lua system, we'll have a look at the following subsections. These form part of the core library and are generally available to most of the distributions.

assert (v [, message])

This function is similar to the assert function used with C; it returns an error if the value of the argument v is `false` (either `nil` or `false`);. The message, if present, is displayed as an error; if absent, the default text "assertion failed!" is displayed.

```
assert(money>0,"you need to have some money to buy something")
```

collectgarbage ([opt [,arg]])

This function is a generic interface to the `garbagecollector`. The function acts differently depending on the parameter opt. The options that you can pass to this function as opt are

- collect: Performs a full garbage-collection cycle. This is the default option.

- stop: Stops the garbage collector.

- restart: Restarts the garbage collector.

- count: Returns the total memory in use by Lua.

- step: Performs a garbage-collection step. The step size is governed by arg.

- setpause: Sets arg as the new value for pause and returns the previous value of pause.

- setstepmul: Sets arg as the new value for the step multiplier and returns the previous value for step.

> **Tip**   If you want to know the memory usage of your app and clear up the memory and objects, you can force the garbagecollector to free up and reclaim the memory allocated and then print the amount of memory used after a cleanup by using the print(collectgarbage("count")) command.

dofile ([filename])

You saw in Chapter 1 that Lua executes the code in chunks. This function opens the named file and executes its contents as a Lua chunk. When called with no arguments, it executes the contents from the standard input (stdin). It returns all values returned by the chunk. stdin is not available on iOS devices, and with CoronaSDK the function is sandboxed (i.e., disallowed).

```
dofile("somefile.lua")
```

error (message [,level])

This function terminates the last protected function and returns the message as the error message.

```
error("This operations is invalid")
```

_G

This is not exactly a function, but a global variable. Lua does not use this variable, but it holds all the global variables and function.

getfenv ([f])

This function returns the current environment in use by the function. The function f can be a Lua function or number.

getmetatable (object)

This function retrieves the metatable associated with the object. It returns `nil` if there is no metatable present. This is mostly used to add functionality to an object table. In some cases, this is also used as a signature of the object. So while the type function does not tell you much, the metatables can be compared with a list of known metatable signatures to get more information.

ipairs (t)

This function returns a function that returns three values, an iterator function, the table t and 0. It works with the array tables only. The following code will iterate over the pairs up to the first integer key missing from the table:

```
t = {1,2,3,4,test = "test",5,6}
t[3] = nil
for i,v in ipairs(t) do
 -- body
  print(i,v)
end
```

load (func [,chunkname])

This function is similar to the `dofile` command; it loads a chunk using the function `func`. Each time the function is called, the function must return a string that concatenates with the previous result. When the chunk is complete, it returns `nil` and an error message. The `chunkname` is used for debugging. When the function is called and an error occurs, Lua displays debugging information, including the line number where the error occurred and the name of the Lua file in which the error occurred. When we have compiled chunks, there is no filename and hence, for debugging purposes, it is up to you, the developer, to provide that information in the form of the `chunkname` parameter.

loadstring (string [,chunkname])

This function is similar to `load`, but instead of loading the compiled bytecode from a file, it takes the compiled code (chunk) from a string.

```
loadstring(compiledChunk, "OurChunk")
```

next (table [,index])

This function allows the program to iterate through all the fields of a table. The function returns multiple values. Internally, the function takes on system commands.

```
t = {"One", "Deux", "Drei", "Quarto"}
print(next(t, 3))
```

pairs (t)

This function is used to iterate through the keys and values in a table.

```
t = {one="Eins",two="Zwei", three="Drei"}
for k,v in pairs(t) do
 -- body
  print(k,v)
end
```

pcall (f, arg1, ...)

This function calls the function f with the arguments in protected mode. This means that any errors inside of the function f are not propagated outside of the function.

print(...)

This function is the one that you will use most during development. It can receive any number of arguments, and it prints all of their values to stdout. It uses tostring and tonumber for conversion, and it provides an easy way to show a value quickly. However, it is not intended for formatted output.

rawequal (v1, v2)

This function is used to check if the value v1 is equal to v2. It returns a Boolean indicating the outcome of the comparison.

rawget (table, index)

This function returns the value of table[index] without invoking any metamethod. The table must be a valid table and the index a non-nil value. This is equivalent to

```
table[index]
```

rawest (table, index, value)

This function sets the value of table[index] without invoking any metamethods. The table must be a valid table and the index a non-nil value. This is equivalent to

```
table[index] = value
```

select (index, ...)

This function returns all of the arguments passed to the function starting with the argument after the index specified.

setfenv (f, table)

This function sets the environment to be given to the function f. f can be a Lua function or a number that specifies the value of the platform.

setmetatable (table, metatable)

This function is used to set the metatable for any table.

tonumber(e [,base])

This function is used for converting between the numbers from string to numerical values. If the argument e is in a form that can be converted, it is converted and returned; otherwise, nil is returned.

```
print( tonumber("42") )
print( tonumber("2A",16))
```

tostring (e)

This function tries to convert the given argument to string format. If the passed parameter is a number, it is converted into a string. If it is an object and its metatable has a __tostring function, the __tostring function is called to convert the passed parameter.

> **Note**   Lua converts between numbers and strings as required (and if possible). However, calling the tostring function is a way to tell Lua to convert the value into a string. Objects and tables are not automatically converted into strings; instead, the function tostring (if present) is called, which returns the string representation of the object/table.

type (v)

This function returns the type of the arguments, coded as a string. The possible results are "nil", "number", "string", "boolean", "table", "thread", and "userdata".

```
print(type("Hello World"))
print(type(4))
print(type({}))
```

unpack (list [, i [, j]])

This function returns the elements from an array table. This function is equivalent to

```
return list[i], list[i+1], ... , list[j]
```

Manually, this code can only be written for a fixed number of elements, and we cannot use a loop, as we have values to return. The parameter i specifies the start element and j specifies the last element, by default. (When these values are not provided, i is 1 and j is the length of the list as defined by the # operator.)

```
local color = {255,255,255}
function tableToParams(theTable)
    return unpack( theTable)
end
print( tableToParams(color))
```

_VERSION

This is not a function, but a global variable. This holds the current interpreter version.

```
print ( _VERSION ) -- This will return the version of Lua in use
```

xpcall (f, err)

This function is similar to the pcall function, except that with this call, you can specify a new error handler. If there is an error inside of the function f, it is not propagated, and xpcall catches the error and in turn calls the err function with the original error object

```
function spawnError()
    -- this function shall spawn an error
    local  this = someFunctionNotDeclared()
end
print(xpcall(spawnError, function(err) print("Error:", err) return 1 end))
```

System Libraries

The commonly bundled system libraries that you will end up using while working with Lua are

- table
- string
- math
- file
- os

The table namespace provides us with the functions related to array manipulation, as these functions are not applicable to hash arrays or associative arrays. This is explained in detail in the following section.

The string namespace provides us with functions to deal with string manipulation. These allow for searching, splitting, and replacing strings, and are quite helpful for parsing and displaying information. We shall have a close look at the string namespace in Chapter 5.

The math namespace provides all the math-related functions; these are the basis for all the logic in most games. The math namespace provides all math-related functions that can help calculate things like where the player is, where the objects are, whether the player won or lost, and much more. We shall look at this namespace in detail in Chapter 4.

The file namespace, covered in Chapter 3, provides file-related functions, including those that allow the user to read, write, and delete files. Note that file operations do not include much file system–related functionality, and there is a third-party library called *Lua File System (LFS)* that offers the missing functionality.

The os namespace provides functions that are related to OS-specific functions, including functions that deal with things like time, date, and locale. We shall look into this further ahead in the "OS Functions" section of this chapter.

The way to use these libraries is to prefix the library name followed by a dot and the function. This is a good way of separating the functionality available in the library from the common or global area. With libraries, variables and functions can be part of the namespace. For example, if we had a function a1, and the namespace myFunc had a function defined as a1, these two would be completely different functions. To access these functions, simply add the namespace as a prefix in front of the function name, as follows:

```
-- call the global a1 function
a1()
-- calling the a1 function available in the namespace myFunc
myFunc.a1()
```

> **Note**   There is no function called a1, so these commands will not work; these are just for illustration purposes.

Table Functions

You may have already noticed that in Lua, if anything is not a string or a number, then it is an object (i.e., a table). Tables are the most important data type in Lua. There are a handful of functions to manipulate end work with the tables. These are useful functions for working with array-type tables. The functions available are described in the following subsections.

table.concat (aTable [,sep [,i [,j]]])

This function returns the elements of an array (if they are either strings or numbers) concatenated as a string. These are separated by a separator, as indicated by sep, which is a blank string by default. If no parameters are passed for i and j, then i is the first element and j is the length of the table. If i is larger than j, then an empty string is returned.

If you were to write this function yourself, it would look like
return aTable[i]..sep..aTable[i+1] ... sep..aTable[j].

```
local aryTable = {1, "deux", 3, "vier", 5}
print( table.concat( aryTable, ",", 1,3))
print(table.concat(aryTable))
```

table.insert (aTable, [pos,] value)

This function is used to insert a value into the array table, as indicated by aTable. The value is inserted at the position indicated by pos; if no value is indicated for pos, then it is assigned the default value of the length of the table plus 1 (i.e., at the end of the table).

```
local aryTable = {1, 3, 4, 5}
table.insert(aryTable, 2, 2)
print(table.concat(aryTable, ","))
table.insert(aryTable, 6)
print(table.concat(aryTable, ","))
```

table.maxn (aTable)

This function returns the largest positive numerical index of the given array table. Remember from Chapter 1 that the # operator returns the length of an array, but only of a contiguous section. So, if in a program you added values to the indices in a nonserial manner (i.e., not continuous), then the # operator would return the length as the block that was continuous. table.maxn, on the other hand, iterates through all the elements and returns the largest numerical index.

```
local aryTable = {1,2,3,4,5}
print(#aryTable, table.maxn(aryTable))
aryTable[10]=10
print(#aryTable, table.maxn(aryTable))
aryTable[25]=25
print(#aryTable, table.maxn(aryTable))
```

table.remove (aTable [, pos])

This function is like insert, but with the difference that it removes an element from the array table and returns the element being removed. In both insert and remove, the elements are shifted to accommodate the new index as required. The default position for pos is the length of the table (i.e., the last element).

```
local aryTable = {1, 2, 3, 4, 5}
table.remove(aryTable, 2, 2)
print(table.concat(aryTable, ","))
table.remove(aryTable)
print(table.concat(aryTable, ","))
print(aryTable[3])
```

table.sort (aTable [, comp])

This function is very useful when working with a series of values that need to be sorted. When no comp is specified, it uses the standard > Lua operator to compare two values, which works fine with numeric values. However, there could be situations where you might need to sort multidimensional arrays or arrays that contain non-numeric data. For such cases, the comp function is used. comp receives two table elements and returns true when the first is less than the second.

```
local aryTable = {4,7,1,3,8,6,5,2}
print(table.concat(aryTable, ","))
table.sort(aryTable)
print(table.concat(aryTable, ","))
```

> **Note** These functions can be used only with array-type tables and are available in the `table` namespace. In order to use these functions, you need to prefix them with `table`.

OS Functions

There are a few functions that are available to interact with the OS; these can be found in the os namespace and hence are prefixed with os. The following subsections describe how they're used.

os.clock ( )

This function returns the approximate CPU time used by the program, in seconds. Every time some code is executed, this is incremented with the amount of CPU time used by the code.

```
print(os.clock())       -->0.030148 (could be different on your system)
print(os.clock())       -->0.030250 (could be different on your system)
```

> **Note** This does not return the time from the system clock; this is just the total CPU time used.

os.date ([format [,time]])

This function returns a string or a table containing the date and time, formatted as specified by the given string format. If no parameters are passed, it returns the string containing the current date and time based on the host system and the current locale. If the format is "*t", then the function returns a table with the following fields:

- year (four digits)
- month (1–12)
- day (1–31)
- hour (0–23)
- min (0–60)
- sec (0–60)
- wday (1–7, beginning with Sunday)
- yday (day of the year; 1–366)
- isdst (Boolean indicating if daylight saving time is in effect)

os.difftime (t2, t1)

This function returns the difference in the number of seconds between t2 and t1.

os.execute ([command])

This function is the equivalent of the C system command. It executes the command passed in the OS shell. It also returns the status code, which is very much system dependent. This is not applicable on iOS, as it would be sandboxed and not execute.

os.exit ( )

This function calls the C function exit, which terminates the application. Though this works on iOS devices, it should not be used. Any app that exits in this manner is considered to be an app that has crashed. The only way to exit an app should be when the user explicitly presses the Home button to exit the app. You can run the risk of Apple rejecting your application if it uses this function. Having said that, there are a couple of apps that have managed to slip under the Apple radar and exit an app in this manner (and the experience is indeed that of when an app crashes).

os.getenv (varname)

This is not applicable on iOS devices.

os.remove (filename)

This function deletes a filename or directory with the given name. The directories are removed if they are empty. If the function fails, it returns nil and a string describing the error. This will work only on the directories and files that you can work with (i.e., the ones in the Documents directory on an iOS device). The other directories are sandboxed and unavailable.

os.rename (oldname, newname)

This function renames a file or directory with the given *oldname* to the *newname*. If the function fails, it returns nil and a string describing the error. This works only with files in the Documents directory.

> **Note**   The reason this works with files in the Documents directory is that most of the other directories are sandboxed or restricted from use. Any command that tries accessing the restricted directories will fail and do nothing.

os.setlocale (locale [,category])

This function is not available in the context of iOS devices.

os.time ([table])

This function returns the current time when called without arguments. The `table` passed as parameters should have the fields set to at least `year`, `month`, and `day`. Other fields, such as `hour`, `min`, `sec`, and `idist`, are optional.

os.tmpname ( )

This function returns a string with a filename that can be used for a temporary file. This file needs to be explicitly opened and explicitly removed when not required. This is different from an `io.tmpfile` function (discussed in the next chapter), which automatically removes the file when the program ends.

Tables: A Quick Overview

I have noted that tables are one of the many types of variables available in Lua. Though it might sound trivial, tables are the backbone of Lua, and they're used in many ways: as arrays, hash tables (associative arrays), and objects, and in plenty more. The following subsections will discuss tables as arrays and hash tables.

Tables As Arrays

The Lua equivalent of an array is a table. All arrays in Lua have an index base of 1, which means that the first entry starts at 1 (not 0, as in many other languages). Arrays need to have a numeric index. These can be multidimensional and do not need to be dimensioned at declaration. These can grow and be redimensioned at runtime.

```
local theArray = {}
for i = 1, 10 do
  theArray[i] = "item ". . i
end
```

Tables As Associative Arrays

Tables are the Lua equivalent of associative arrays, hash tables, and even `NSDictionary` objects. The difference between an array and an associative array is that, instead of having a numeric index to access an element of the array table, an associative array can use a string to access the elements.

```
local theTable = {}
for i = 1, 10 do
  theTable["item"..i] = i
end
```

> **Note**   Lua is very flexible and hence is very forgiving, even if you mix the two types of arrays.

```lua
local theMixedTable = {}
for i = 1, 5 do
  theMixedTable[i] = "item ".. i
end
theMixedTable["name"] = "mixedTable"
theMixedTable["subject"] = "coding"
print(theMixedTable.name, theMixedTable[3])
```

Functions: An Advanced Look

In the previous chapter we had a look at functions and how Lua sees them. Lua objects and structures are Lua tables, and the good part is that tables can hold functions and other tables, string, and numbers. In effect each object with a function is like a namespace that has its own set of functions. To access the function of a particular object, you need to access the function with the namespace prefixed.

```lua
myObj = {
    type = "furry",
  name = "Furry_1",
  description = "Fluffy furry teddybear",
  display = function ()
    print(description)
 end
}
myObj.show = function()
 print("Now Showing...")
end
```

To call the function, you use the following:

```lua
myObj.display()
myObj.show()
```

Tables As Objects

As you've seen, tables can be used as objects. In this next example, we'll create an object called myObj that has properties of type, name, description, and so on. In this example, you'll create a game that spawns a series of animals, each with different strengths and different functions for movement.

Since some of the functions might overlap, in order to avoid writing the same code over and over again, you'll create a new object based on the parent object, such that all of the functions are available to this object. (We shall create such objects later in the book.) So, when this object is passed, you can simply invoke the move function that is common to the animals, but might be specific to each of the animals depending on its type.

One way to manage this is as follows:

```
local cat_01 = animal.new("cat")
local mouse_01 = animal.new("mouse")
animal.move(cat_01)
animal.move(mouse_01)
```

This might work for some; however, an alternative method to manage this would be the following:

```
local cat_01 = animal.new("cat")
local mouse_01 = animal.new("mouse")
cat_01:move()
mouse_01:move()
```

Further, if you had this in an array of animals, you could just about as easily have something like this:

```
local i
for i=1,#aryAnimals do
  aryAnimals[i]:move()
end
```

Or you could very well also use something like

```
aryAnimals[i].move(aryAnimals[i])
```

Notice here how the function is invoked using the dot (.) or the colon (:). This is something a lot of beginning Lua developers come across, and they often have questions about the difference between, say, cat_01:move() and cat_01.move(). The following section will describe the differences.

The Difference Between . and :

In the preceding example, there's no difference between calling cat_01.move() and cat_01:move(). But let's consider that in the same function we also need to pass a parameter speed, which indicates how fast the animal should move. So we simply pass the speed as a parameter as

```
cat_01:move(10)
```

or

```
cat_01.move(10)
```

This on the face of things seems right, but will produce two very different results. The reason is that when we use the ., we are telling Lua to invoke the function that is a member of the object (table), and when we use the :, we are telling Lua to do this and we're also passing the function an unseen parameter of itself. So when we call the function with :, we are passing it two parameters: the first being the object itself and the second being the speed. With the . method, on the other hand, we pass it only one, which is the speed. Let's look at how it is defined in code (see Figure 2-1).

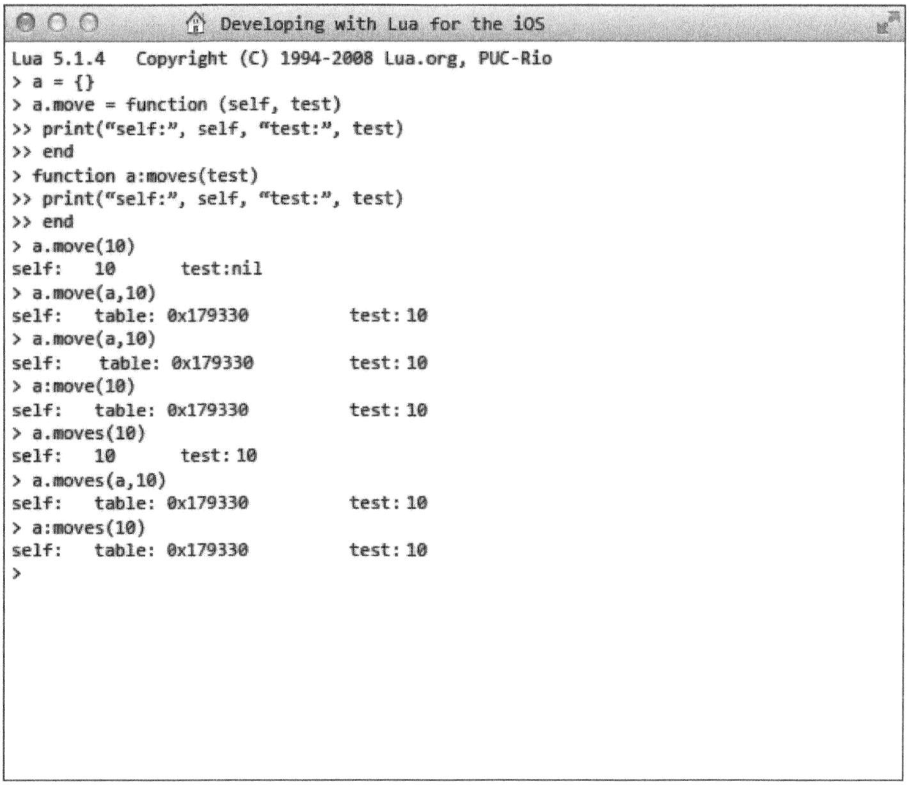

```
●○○                ⌂ Developing with Lua for the iOS                        ⬀
Lua 5.1.4   Copyright (C) 1994-2008 Lua.org, PUC-Rio
> a = {}
> a.move = function (self, test)
>> print("self:", self, "test:", test)
>> end
> function a:moves(test)
>> print("self:", self, "test:", test)
>> end
> a.move(10)
self:   10        test:nil
> a.move(a,10)
self:    table: 0x179330          test: 10
> a.move(a,10)
self:    table: 0x179330          test: 10
> a:move(10)
self:    table: 0x179330          test: 10
> a.moves(10)
self:   10        test: 10
> a.moves(a,10)
self:    table: 0x179330          test: 10
> a:moves(10)
self:    table: 0x179330          test: 10
>
```

Figure 2-1. *The output of the function in Lua running in the terminal*

Notice that the functions are declared differently, but the output of both is the same. In short, you can say that obj:func() is the same as calling obj.func(obj).

> **Note**   It is very easy to forget about the way you might have declared the function and hence end up calling it a different way, which can cause some hiccups in your code where a parameter passed would get shifted and give you strange results. To avoid that, keep a consistent method of declaring and calling functions.

From that last example, one question that might come to mind is, When do you use a single dot (.) and when do you use a colon (:) if Lua is not an object-oriented language? Why would you ever need that? In order to answer these questions, let's work on an object and give it some functionality. This sample doesn't use objects or external files, so it can be run in the Lua interactive console without any problems.

```
function newAnimal(name)
    local animal = {
    name = "unknown",
    says = "pffft",
    position = {x = 0,y = 0},
    }
    animal.name = name
    if name=="cat" then
        animal.says = "meow"
    elseif name=="dog" then
        animal.says = "bow wow"
    elseif name=="mouse" then
        animal.says = "squeak"
    end
    function animal:speak()
        print(animal.says)
    end
    function animal:move(speed)
        animal.position.x = animal.position.x+speed
    end
    return animal
end
```

Now we can create a new instance of an animal by simply calling

```
cat_01 = animal.new("cat")
cat_01:speak()
```

This is perfectly fine as an example that creates a new object every time it is invoked. However, this is also how many beginners would code—note that in the functions, while we are passing the object via self, we are not using it, and we are still referencing it by the fixed animal table that we created. This can cause a bit of grief later on if it's not checked right at the start. The way to avoid this being a problem in the future is to replace the namespace with the object referenced as self instead.

The modified code would look like the following:

```
function newAnimal(name)
    local animal = {
    name = "unknown",
    says = "pffft",
    position = {x = 0,y = 0},
    }
    animal.name = name
    if name=="cat" then
        animal.says = "meow"
    elseif name=="dog" then
        animal.says = "bow wow"
    elseif name=="mouse" then
        animal.says = "squeak"
    end
```

```
        function animal:speak()
            print(self.says)
        end
        function animal:move(speed)
            self.position.x = self.position.x+speed
        end
        return animal
end
```

This would work fine and not cause issues.

```
cat_01 = animal.new("cat")
cat_01:speak()
cat_02 = animal.new("dog")
cat_02:speak()
```

When we run the code, the functions get the object passed rather than the Animal namespace. This also ensures that the variables that are modified are specific to the object rather than the ones in the Animal namespace. That will thereby eliminate the issues mentioned earlier.

Summary

This chapter focused on functions and tables, the building blocks of Lua programming. It's important to remember that everything that is not a string, a number of boolean is a Table. Tables are very powerful and important in Lua. You'll be reading a lot about them (in some form or other) in most of the chapters.

Another important concept that we touched upon is the namespace. Namespaces help to distinguish between the functions available in the main namespace (the global functions) and the functions in a custom library.

Chapter 3

File Operations

When creating an app or a game, you need file I/O (input/output). You may not be working with a database, but there will always be the need to save something back to the disk; it could be the levels, the high score, a character the player might have unlocked, or some information regarding in-app purchases.

So, let's first look at what we have available in terms of functions that offer file operation functionality. Lua has two sets of functions for file operations, one called *implicit* and the other *explicit*. The difference between the two is that implicit functions work on the default file as provided by the io namespace, whereas explicit functions work with a file handle provided from a previous operation, such as io.open.

Implicit Functions

This section lists and describes the implicit functions you'll be using in your Lua programming work, accompanied by a short example of how each is used in code.

io.close ([file])

This function closes the output file; it is similar to file:close(), but when no file is passed, it closes the default output file. You can see how io.close is used to close a fileHandle. To confirm, we print the type of fileHandle to check if the file is open or closed.

```
fileHandle = io.open("file.txt", "w")
print(io.type(fileHandle))
fileHandle:write("Hello world")
io.close(fileHandle)
print(io.type(fileHandle))
```

io.flush ( )

This function runs `file:flush()` on the default file. When a file is in buffered mode, the data is not written to the file immediately; it remains in the buffers and is written when the buffer nears getting full. This function forces the buffers to write to file and clear up.

io.input ([file])

This function returns the current default input file when called without any parameters. The parameter passed can be either a filename or a file handle. When the function is called with a filename, it sets the handle to this named file as the default input file. If it is called with a file handle, it just sets the default input file handle to this passed file handle.

io.lines ([filename])

This function opens a given filename in read mode and returns an iterator function that returns a new line from the file every time it is called. When the iterator function detects that the end of the file has been reached, it closes the file and returns `nil`.

When `io.lines` is called without a filename, it is equivalent to `io.input():lines()`, and it reads from the default input file and does not close the file when the end is reached.

Here's a way to access this function:

```
for line in io.lines(filename) do
    print(line)
end
```

io.open (filename [,mode])

This function is the main function that you use in reading and writing files with Lua. The mode is a string value that can be one of the following:

- "r": Read mode (default).
- "w": Write mode.
- "a": Append mode.
- "r+": Update mode. All previous data is preserved.
- "w+": Update mode. All previous data is erased.
- "a+": Append update mode. All previous data is preserved and writing is only allowed at the end of the file.

The mode can also have a "b" at the end to indicate that the file is to be opened in binary mode rather than in text mode. This function returns a file handle that can be used in explicit file operations.

```
file = io.open("myfilename.txt", "r")
```

io.output ([file])

This function is similar to io.input but operates on the default output file instead. Using this function, you can redirect the output to the file you want. Here's an example of how it's used:

```
oldIOFile = io.output()
io.output("mynewfile.txt")
io.write("Hello world")
io:output():close()
io.output(oldIOFile)
```

io.read (...)

This function is equivalent to io.input():read().

```
print(io.read())
```

io.tmpfile ( )

This function returns a handle for a temporary file; the file is opened in update mode and removed automatically when the program ends.

```
fh = io.tmpfile()
fh:write("Some sample data")
fh:flush()
-- Now let's read the data we just wrote
fh:seek("set", 0)
content = fh:read("*a")
print("We got : ", content)
```

io.type (obj)

This function returns the result if the handle specified by obj is a valid file handle. It returns the string "file" if obj is an open file handle and the string "closed file" if obj is a closed file handle. It returns nil if obj is not a file handle.

```
print(io.type(fh)) - prints nil as fh is nil
fh = io.input()
print(io.type(fh))
```

io.write (...)

This function is equivalent to io.output():write().

```
io.write("Hello World")
```

Explicit Functions

This section lists and describes the explicit functions you'll be using in your Lua programming work.

file:close ( )

This function closes the file that is referenced by the file.

```lua
file = io.open("myFile.txt", "w")
file:write("Some Data")
file:close()
```

file:flush ( )

This function saves any data that is not as yet written (in the buffer) to the file.

```lua
fh = io.tmpfile()
fh:write("Some sample data")
fh:flush()
```

file:lines ( )

This function returns an iterator function that returns a new line from the file every time it is called. It is similar to io.lines, with the difference that this function does not close the file when the loop ends.

```lua
local file = io.open(filename)
for line in file:lines() do print(line) end
file:close()
```

file:read ([format])

This function reads data from the file according to the given format. By default, read reads the entire next line. The formats that are available for reading are

- '*n': Reads a number; returns a number instead of a string
- '*a': Reads the whole file starting from the current position
- '*l': Reads the next line; returns nil when the current position is at the end of the file (default format)
- number: Reads a string of characters as specified by the number, returning nil at the end of the file.

Following are some examples of using these:

```lua
local filename = "data_test.txt"
local file = io.open(filename)
```

```
local contents = file:read("*a")
file:close()
print("Contents of the file:", contents)
```

If this file were opened in binary mode and we needed to get only a particular number of characters, then we would use it as follows:

```
local filename = "test.zip"
local file = io.open(filename,"rb")
local contents = file:read(2)
file:close()
print("File Header:", contents) -- All ZIP files have the starting two characters as PK
```

file:seek ([whence] [, offset])

This functions sets and gets the current file position. whence is a string value that can be any of the following

- ▪ 'set': The base position 0 (beginning of the file)

- ▪ 'cur': The current position (default value)

- ▪ 'end': The end of the file

The offset value passed is measured in bytes from the base specified as per one of these three options.

file:seek is one of most important functions when working with binary files and fixed formats; it allows the developer to iterate back and forth to overwrite or update certain portions of the file.

```
fh = io.tmpfile()
fh:write("Some sample data")
fh:flush()
-- Now let's read the data we just wrote
fh:seek("set", 0)
content = fh:read("*a")
print("We got : ", content)
```

file:setvbuf (mode [, size])

This function sets the buffering mode for an output file. There are three buffering modes available in Lua, and their values are passed as strings:

- ▪ 'no': No buffering is set, so the output of any operation appears immediately.

- ▪ 'full': Full buffering is set, so the output operation is only performed when the buffer is full. You can force a flush to write the buffers.

- ▪ 'line': Line buffering is set, so the output is buffered until a newline character (Enter) is found.

  ```
  io.output():setvbuf("no")
  ```

file:write(...)

This function writes to the file each of the arguments passed to the function. The arguments must be either strings or numbers. To write other values, you might have to convert them to string format.

```
file = io.open("myfile.txt","w")
file:write("Writing to a file")
file:close()
```

> **Note**   The pure implementation of Lua lacks the functions and commands required for file system access. This is generally available as an external library that can be added. It is called *Lua File System (LFS)*. As of this writing, you can integrate it with all frameworks (the amount of effort this takes, however, depends on the framework.)

Uses of File I/O in Gaming

Though this is a no-brainer, there are so many reasons why you might want to read or write data from the storage. It can be for little things like level-related data and high scores, or for complex things like saving the state of the game with the entire inventory, units, and so on. In the game, the onus is on you to save and load the data to help provide continuity and seamless game play to the player.

Let's look at how we would do that when dealing with stuff like life, health, score, level, and so forth.

Saving a Variable

In many games, you generally get only about three lives. So, consider the following code:

```
local lives = 3
print("You have " .. lives .. " lives left")
```

There are many ways of dealing with this. One good way would be to save the data as soon as you change it—something like an autosave option. So, let's write out lives variable to the storage so that it persists.

```
function writeToFileSingle(value, filename)
    local hfile = io.open(filename,"w")
    if hfile==nil then return end -- Did not get a handle on the file
    hfile:write(value)
    hfile:close()
end
```

In the preceding code, we declare a function called writeToFileSingle that takes two parameters: value and filename. The function opens a file, writes the data to the file, and then closes the file.

If we open a file, we are responsible for closing it too. When we try to open a file using the io.open function, it returns the file handle and a string that contains the reason for the failure (if it fails to open the file).

To save our value using this function, we simply call

```
writeToFileSingle(score, "score")
writeToFileSingle(health, "health")
```

and so on.

Congratulations, you have now written code to save a variable, and it can be run in the interactive Lua shell, as expected.

> **Note**   Irrespective of which platform you choose as a developer, the preceding Lua code should work across most of the platforms and Lua frameworks.

Grabbing the Data

In addition to saving data, we also need to retrieve it. In a game, dumping data that we cannot retrieve is as good as not saving any data at all. We have, with the earlier function writeToFileSingle, saved our data to a variable. Now comes the tricky part: reading the values from the file.

In theory, reading the data from a file should be the reverse process of writing to the file. So, we open the file that we have saved our data into and then we read all of the data from the file.

```
function readFromFileSingle(filename)
    local hfile = io.open(filename, "r")
    if hfile==nil then return end
    local value = hfile:read("*a")
    hfile:close()
    return value
end
```

Since we've saved our data using the writeToFileSingle function, we can retrieve our data easily, like so:

```
print(readFromFileSingle("score"))
print(readFromFileSingle("health"))
```

> **Note**   Since the data is one piece of information per file, the order in which you save it and the order in which you load it shouldn't matter.

If the file does not have any data, it just returns nil, which pretty much means the same and can be managed if required.

How the Code Works

It is rather easy. Most of the code is similar to what we used in `writeToFileSingle`, which involves opening a file, but in read mode instead. (If you do not specify a mode while opening a file to read, the default mode is read mode). Then we use the read function with the "*a" parameter to read the entire contents of the file. This is fine for this scenario, as we only have a small amount of data to read. Then we close the file and return the data read from the file.

Potential Issues

These two functions work well for loading and saving data. But, as mentioned, it's not good to have a file for each piece of data that we want to save; it would be better to have a single file than multiple files with scraps of data in them. So, the next possible option is to save all of the data in a single file. Doing so isn't much different than what we did in the preceding code. The difference is that we save multiple values to the file, like so:

```
function readFromFile(filename)
    local results = {}
    local hfile  =io.open(filename)
    if hfile==nil then return end
    for line in hfile:lines() do
        table.insert(results, line)
    end
    return results
end
```

There are a couple of differences in this code as compared to the earlier code. The first is that we use an array table called `results` to store everything we read from the file. The next is that instead of using `hfile:read("*a")` to read the content, we use `hfile:lines()` to get one line at a time from the file. The newline character (Enter) separates the data and is the delimiter between the two lines. Once we get this data, we store it into the array results by using the `table.insert` function to add the data to the end of the table.

Once we get the array returned to us, the positioning of the data is important. The positions of the data shall be fixed, so we need to know in advance what position coincides with what data.

Saving Data to a Variable

Here's a quick tip on how to manipulate global variables. In Chapter 2, you read about a variable _G, which is actually a table object and holds all the global variables, functions, and so on. When we declare a variable (without local scope), it is assigned to this table as a global variable. What we are going to do in this quick exercise is declare a global variable, read the value of the variable, and then manipulate it using the _G table.

```
myVar = 1
print(myVar)
myVar = myVar + 1
print(_G["myVar"])
```

```
_G["myVar"] = _G["myVar"] + 1
print(myVar)
_G.myVar = _G.myVar + 1
print(myVar)
```

How the Code Works

We start our code with declaring a global variable called myVar and assigning it a value of 1, and then we print it to the screen. Next we increment it by 1 using myVar = myVar + 1. This time we print the value again, but instead of using print(myVar), we access it directly from the global table _G via print(_G["myVar"]). Then we increment the variable by 1 again but using _G["myVar"] and print the value using print(myVar).

Lastly, we increment the value again by 1, but this time we access it using the _G.myVar method to access the value and print the results. The idea of this exercise is to demonstrate how Lua uses global variables and how they can be accessed using _G.

> **Note**   Though global variables can be accessed in this manner, it is suggested that local variables be used instead; this reduces the number of variables used, saves on stack memory, and also had a speed advantage over global variables.

Back to our saving and loading of data, we want to consolidate our data into one file so that we can read our data in one go. In our modified version, we are reading the data into an array called results. The only issue is that to access the values, we need to access the data by the numbered index—but how would we know what each numeric index corresponds to?

Let's try to read the data and also set the global variables with the values.

```
function readFromFile(filename)
    local results = {}
    local hfile = io.open("filename")
    if hfile==nil then return end
    local lineNo = 0
    for line in hFile:lines() do
        table.insert(results, line)
        lineNo = lineNo + 1
        if lineNo == 1 then
            _G["score"] = line
        elseif lineNo == 2 then
            _G["lives"] = line
        elseif lineNo == 3 then
            _G["health"] = line
        elseif lineNo == 4 then
            _G["level"] = line
        end
    end
    return results
end
```

This is more or less what our code looked like earlier, only we have added a variable called lineNo and we keep incrementing it based on the lines read. When lineNo is 1, we save the value we have read into the variable score. Then we save lineNo 2 into lives, and so on, till lineNo is 4, after which (if there are more lines) we just don't read them.

Potential Issues

In your app, the number of variables that you might store could be different for each application. You would never know the order in which your data is saved, and if the order of saving the data or reading the data is changed, you might have values that end up in the wrong variables. Most importantly, it would be near impossible to set up multiple if .. then statements to load the variables, not to mention the names for those variables.

So what we are going to do to fix this issue is have a table with the data and field names in it. This will provide us with the flexibility to expand this further in the future.

```
function readFromFile(filename,resTable)
    local hfile = io.open(filename)
    if hfile == nil then return
    local results = {}
    local a = 1
    for line in hfile:lines() do
        _G[resTable[a]] = line
        a = a + 1
    end
end
```

We read through the data one line at a time, and with each loop, we increment the index variable a. We store the value that we have read into a global variable with a name specified in the array. For example, if we had specified in our array that we wanted the values to be Line1 = Score, Line2 = Lives, and Line3 = health, then the function will automatically create global variables with these names and assign the value to them.

This function will now read the data, save it into the array table, and access it via the global variable. However, we need to pass it the table that is modified for this.

```
local aryTable = {
    "Score",
    "Lives",
    "Health,
}
```

We call the function simply as follows:

```
readFromFile("datafile", aryTable)
```

This method has its own set of problems. What if we were to add some data in aryTable not at the end, but in the middle? This would make the variables all mixed up and in the wrong places. So how do we fix that? There are many easy ways to approach this issue, and each has its own set of pros and cons. However, the best method would be to get the name of the variable and the value of the variable from the file.

Writing Data to the File

We have written some code to read our data from the file. Now we'll write some code to write the data, which could be read using the preceding function.

```
function writeToFile(filename, resTable)
    local  hfile = io.open(filename, "w")
    if hfile == nil then return end
    local  i
    for i=1, #resTable do
        hfile:write(_G[resTable[i]])
    end
end
```

The code for writing the data to the file is not very different. We open the file in write mode, and then we iterate through the list of variables that we want to save to the file. These are found from the resTable parameter passed. So, whatever we have in this table, the function shall attempt to save those variables to the file.

Saving a Table

We just saved data that is in the form of either strings or numbers. If the data to be saved is anything else, the functions will start to fail, and more so if the variable is a table. The biggest issue with tables is iterating through the depths of the table.

If you were to use any other programming language, you would hear, "Why not serialize the data?" I'll explain why this isn't a good idea in Lua.

The mark of good developers is their ability to avoid reinventing the wheel, instead spending their time with things that warrant their focus. Lua has a third-party Lua library that allows you to use JSON in your Lua projects; this library can help encode or decode the information between the table object and a JSON-encoded string, like so:

```
local json = require("json")
local theTable = {
    title = "Learn Lua for iOS game development",
    author = "Jayant Varma",
    publisher = "Apress",
    eBook = true,
    year = 2012,
}
local resString = json.encode(theTable)
writeToFileSingle(restring,"mytable")
local readString = readFromFileSingle("mytable")
local resTable = json.decode(readString)

for k,v in pairs(resTable) do
    print(k,v)
end
```

When you run this code, you will see that we save the data we create as a string to a file called `mytable`. In the example, we read the data back and decode the JSON-encoded string to an expanded Lua form table. Then we list the fields available in that table to prove that the code works.

> **Note** Though this code is completely valid, if you run the code in the Lua interactive shell, you might face issues such as error messages, as there is no `json.lua` file in the path.

Dynamic Variables

How do I create dynamic variables? is one of the most commonly asked question by many developers, especially ones that are beginning their journey with development. Some beginner developers use variables as follows:

```
Object1 = "Apple"
Object2 = "Ball"
Object3 = "Cat"
Object4 = "Dog"
```

In this code, the developer wants to create a series of such variables dynamically and be able to access them by specifying the last digit, so the access expected would be

```
number = 3
print("Object" .. number)
```

and the expectation is that it should output `Cat`. However, what it outputs is `Object3`. Most beginning developers assume that it should have worked as expected. If you need to access the variable in this manner, it is not by creating multiple variables. The proper way to do so is to create an array. The array can be accessed by passing it the number as we expected to do.

```
Objects = {"Apple", "Ball", "Cat", "Dog"}
number = 3
print(Objects[number])
```

This works perfectly fine for what we need. This time around we see the output `Cat`.

Summary

In this chapter you learned about the implicit and explicit functions relating to file I/O. You also saw how to read and write data as singular values, and how to write an entire table of data onto the storage space on the device. Files are good for saving scraps of data; however, when you need to access larger amounts of data, it would be better to use a database.

In the next chapter we shall look at the `math` namespace, which offers functions that we can use to do all of the calculations required for our apps.

Chapter 4

Math with Lua

Love it or hate it, if you have decided to be a developer, you will have to come face to face with math. It is indeed surprising to see how many students dislike or shy away from math, but it just comes back to us in some form or the other, irrespective of our profession. An accountant needs to look at the accounts and add them up (requiring math), a surveyor needs to apply trigonometric principles to get elevation and terrain information, a banker needs to calculate interest and yield for investments, and so on. It reminds me of Homer Simpson, who once said, "English? Who needs that? I'm never going to England!" However, you have decided to be a developer, and you will come back to this time and time again, as many of the things that you need to do are based on simple math principles. These can be applied with any framework or language.

Introduction to Math in Lua

There is a system library included with Lua that offers a series of math functions. The following is a list of the functions available. Most of these functions are self-explanatory.

math.abs (x)

This returns the absolute value of x. If you pass this function a negative value, it returns the positive value of x.

```
print(math.abs(-10))   -- Will return 10
```

math.acos (x)

This returns the arc cosine of the value x in radians.

```
print (math.acos(1))   -- Prints zero '0'
```

math.asin (x)

This returns the arc sine of the value *x* in radians.

```
print(math.asin(1))   -- Prints 1.5707963267949
```

math.atan (x)

This returns the arctangent of the value *x* in radians. This is in the range of –pi/2 to pi/2.

```
print(math.atan(1))   -- Prints 0.78539816339745
```

math.atan2 (y,x)

This returns the principal value of the arctangent of the quotient of the two numbers passed.

```
print(math.atan2(1, 0))     -- pi/2
print(math.atan2(-1, 0))    -- -pi/2
print(math.atan2(0, 1))     -- 0
print(math.atan2(0, -1))    -- pi
```

> **Note**   The parameters passed are *y* and then *x*, not *x,y*, as are generally passed.

math.ceil (x)

This returns the integer value of the passed value of *x* closest to the next integer.

```
print (math.ceil(0.1))   -- Returns 1
print (math.ceil(0.5))   -- Returns 1
print (math.ceil(0.6))   -- Returns 1
```

math.cos (x)

This returns the cosine value of *x* passed in radians.

```
print(math.cos(1))   -- 0.54030230586814
```

math.cosh (x)

This returns the hyperbolic cosine of a value.

```
print(math.cosh(1)) -- 1.5430806348152
```

math.deg (x)

This function converts a value from degree to radians.

```
print(math.deg(math.pi))  -- 180
```

math.exp (x)

This returns e, the base of natural logarithms raised to a given power.

```
print (math.exp(2)) -- 7.3890560989307
```

math.floor (x)

This returns the lower integer value from the passed value of *x*.

```
print (math.floor(0.1))  -- 0
print (math.floor(0.5))  -- 0
print (math.floor(0.9))  -- 0
```

math.fmod (x)

This returns the remainder of the division of the arguments that rounds the quotient toward zero, according to the following equation:

$$remainder = numerator - quotient * denominator$$

The function itself is used like this:

```
print(math.fmod(7.5,3))  -- 1.5
```

math.frexp (x)

This function splits the value into a normalized fraction and an exponent. The results are two numbers. The number *x* can be represented as follows:

$$fraction * 2^{exponent}$$

Here are some examples of the function in code:

```
print(math.frexp(2))  -- 0.5   2
print(math.frexp(3))  -- 0.75  1
print(math.frexp(1))  -- 0.5   1
```

math.huge

This is a constant than a function; it returns `inf`, which is a very large number.

```
print(math.inf)
```

math.ldexp (m, e)

This returns a number generated from the combination of the mantissa *m* and the exponent *e*. The formula used is

$$number = m * 2^e$$

Here's the function in use:

```
print(math.ldexp(0.5, 8)) -- 128
```

math.log (x)

This returns the natural logarithm value of *x*.

```
print(math.log(0.5))  -- (-0.69314718055995)
```

math.log10 (x)

This returns the base 10 logarithm value of *x*.

```
print (math.log10(0.5))  -- (-0.30102999566398)
```

math.max (x, ...)

This returns the maximum value among the passed values.

```
print(math.max(2,5,3,8,3,4,5))  -- 8
```

math.min (x, ...)

This returns the minimum value among the passed values.

```
print(math.min(2,5,3,8,3,4,5))  -- 2
```

math.modf (x)

This returns the integer and the fractional part of the number passed. So, if we passed it *x.y*, it would return *x* and *y*.

```
print(math.modf(3.75))  -- 3    0.75
```

math.pi

This returns the math constant of pi.

```
print(math.pi)  -- 3.1415926535898
```

math.pow (x,y)

This returns the number that is the result of raising the number *x* to *y* (i.e., x^y).

```
print(math.pow(3,3))  -- 27 => 3^3
print(math.pow(5,2))  -- 25 => 5^5
```

math.rad (x)

This returns the angle *x* converted into radians.

```
print(math.rad(math.pi))  -- 3.1415296535898
```

math.random ([m [,n]])

This returns a random value in the range between *m* and *n*. If the values of *m* and *n* are not passed, then the function returns a value between 0 and 1. If a single value is passed to this function, then an integer value between 1 and this number is returned.

```
print(math.random())  -- A decimal value between 0 and 1
print(math.random(10))  -- An integer value between 1 and 10
print(math.random(5,25))  -- An integer value between 5 and 25
```

math.randomseed (x)

This sets the seed for the random number generator. If you seed the value, you can get the same random values.

math.sin (x)

This returns the sine of an angle passed in radians.

```
print(math.sin(30))  -- (-0.98803162409286)
```

math.sinh (x)

This returns the hyperbolic sine of a value.

```
print(math.sinh(1))  -- 1.1752011936438
```

math.sqrt (x)

This returns the square root of the number specified by *x*.

```
print(math.sqrt(144)) -- 12
print(math.sqrt(9))   -- 3
```

math.tan (x)

This returns the tangent of the angle passed in radians.

```
print (math.tan(45))   -- 1.6197751905439
```

math.tanh (x)

This returns the hyperbolic tangent of a value.

```
print(math.tanh(1))   -- 0.76159415595576
```

Practical Uses of Math in Gaming

If you develop games, you will be surrounded with math. The simplest scenario that any game will involve is moving a character, and that involves moving the character on the x- or y-axis, or in plain terms, moving it left and right or up and down. This movement of the character left and right is said to be on the *x-axis*, and the up-and-down movement is on the *y-axis*.

Another example where you would use math is simple scorekeeping, in which you increment the score by a value based on what object you might collect in the game. You would also use math to handle players with multiple lives, whereby a value is decreased every turn until it reaches zero, after which the game is over.

But first, let's brush up on a few basics about math (even though we all learned it in school).

Assignment

The first thing that we shall look at is assignment. Remember the school days when we had

$$\text{let } x \text{ equal } 5$$
$$\text{let } y \text{ equal } 3$$
$$x + y = 5 + 3$$
$$= 8$$

This concept remains even today. With Lua, when we assign a variable a value, this value can be one of the eight basic types discussed in the Chapter 1. The most commonly used ones are numbers, strings, and tables.

The preceding algebraic equation would translate to the following:

```
x = 5
y = 3
print( "x+y=" .. x+y)
```

Increasing and Decreasing

If you are coming to Lua from a C/C++ background, you may be used to operator overloading. This is why a lot of developers ask why Lua doesn't have the var++ or var-- operator to increment or decrease values. While there are many reasons Lua doesn't have that functionality, a simple one is that Lua was written to be easy to use. However, this type of functionality is not very difficult to achieve in Lua; it is as simple as this:

```
var = var + 1
```

or

```
var = var - 1
```

If this is critical, the best part about Lua is that you can create your own functions that provide you that secure feeling of working with the languages of your choice by integrating their syntax.

There are quite a few limitations on how much you can modify Lua via code. We shall attempt to create inc and dec functions that will increment or decrease the value as per the value passed to the functions. We shall create two functions, inc and dec. These functions will take the variable and the value that we want to increase or decrease the variable value by. The function shall return the increased or decreased value.

```
function inc(theVar, byVal)
    local byVal = byVal or 1
    return theVar + byVal
end

function dec(theVar, byVal)
    local byVal = byVal or 1
    return theVar - byVal
end
```

Now you can just call the inc or dec as follows:

```
local theValue = 20
print("The Value = ", theValue)
theValue = inc(theValue, 5)       -- Equivalent of theValue = theValue + 5
print("The Value = ", theValue)
theValue = dec(theValue)          -- Equivalent of theValue = theValue + 5
print("The Value = ", theValue)
```

The function dec does not get a value for byVal and therefore the value of byVal is nil. In the function we first declare a local variable and assign it the value of byVal, and since it is nil, we assign it the value of 1. Then we return the value of theVar less byVal.

Introducing the Point

We need to hold two-dimensional coordinates; namely, the x- and y-coordinates. In most languages, we use two variables: *x* and *y*. In C and other such languages, we use a structure that has the members x and y. With Lua we can use a table to hold this structure. Let us call this structure a *point*.

```
local myPoint = {x = 0, y = 0}
myPoint.x = 160
```

```
myPoint.y = 240
print(myPoint.x, myPoint.y)
```

A point is a better way to store your coordinates than to have pairs of variables such as `playerX`, `playerY`; `monster1X`, `monster1Y`; `monster2X`, `monster2Y`; and so on. By having a point table structure, you can just have `playerCoords`, `monsterCoords`, and so on. This will also be useful when we look into vectors, which are slightly more complicated than simple tables. The best part is that our two functions `inc` and `dec` shall work without any changes. It is as simple as coding

```
myPoint.x = inc(myPoint.x,8)
myPoint.y = inc(myPoint.y,4)
```

Conditional Branching

We might want to run some code depending upon a particular condition; for example, if a level is completed, then display the Level Complete banner. Or if the level is completed and the score is greater than a particular score, then display the "You have a new high score" message. Otherwise, just display the score.

```
local score = math.random(1,10)*1000
if score >= 5000 then
    print("Well done")
elseif score >= 2000 then
    print("There is always a second chance")
else
    print("you have missed even the second chance")
end
```

What we have done here is use `math.random`, a function that helps generate a random number. We request a whole number (integer) in the range of 1 to 10, and then we multiply that by 1,000 to get a score in the range of 1,000 to 10,000. This score is then used to determine the message that will be printed. For that conditional evaluation, we use `if .. elseif .. end` blocks to check for our conditions.

Flipping a Coin

You just learned about the random number generator used in many games and languages. In this exercise, we'll try to use the random number generator to emulate a coin flip. The good thing about a coin flip is that it is either heads or tails. There are many ways of handling this, but we shall try the simplest one: getting a random number that is either 1 or 2. So, if we get 1, we call it "heads," and if we get 2, we call it "tails."

```
local theFlip = math.random(1,2)
if theFlip ==1 then
    print("Got heads")
else
    print("Got tails")
end
```

Throwing a Die

In some RPG-style games, a coin flip might not be enough. You might want to have more possible values than either 1 or 2—something that would emulate the roll of a die. The most common die has six sides, and the numbers that one can get are in the range of 1 to 6.

```
local theDice = math.random(1,6)
print("we got ", theDice)
```

In RPG-type games or board games of a similar genre, the dice are often nonstandard and could have more than six sides. It is just as easy to simulate that as the previous example. The only change that we need to make is the maximum value that we can get on the die. For example, for a 20-sided die, we'd use this:

```
local maxValue = 20
local theDice = math.random(1,maxValue)
print("we got ", theDice)
```

In case you want multiple rolls, you can simply change this into a function and get the dice-roll values:

```
function diceRoll(maxSides)
  local maxSides = maxSides or 6
 return math.random(1,maxSides)
end
```

In the preceding example with inc and dec, you might have noted that we used a nifty feature of Lua that allows for assigning a default value to a variable. In the diceRoll function just shown, if the function is called without any value (i.e., the maxSides parameter is nil), then the second line creates a local variable called maxSides and assigns it the value of the parameter maxSides (or 6 if the parameter is nil or missing).

Using Flags

This doesn't refer to the flag that we all recognize flying from the flagpole. The flag in reference here is instead a variable that holds the value true or false. For example, in a game, one flag could indicate whether you have a treasure chest's key or not; if you have the key, then you can open the treasure box, but if you don't, then you can't. So the code would check if you have the key or not and allow you to open the treasure chest accordingly.

```
function openTreasureChest(withKey)
    if withKey == true then
        print("The treasure chest opens")
    else
        print("Nothing happens, you are unable to open the chest")
    end
end
local hasKey = false
openTreasureChest(hasKey)
hasKey = true
openTreasureChest(hasKey)
```

Notice that we have a variable called hasKey, and at first, the value is set to false. With that, we call the function openTreasureChest, and the functions prints Nothing happens. But when we call it again after setting hasKey to true, it prints The treasure chest opens. This is the simplest example of a flag. In a game, you could have many flags that might be used together to determine certain actions.

In some cases, you can also use a flag to prevent certain things from happening. For example, you can have a flag that would prevent a function from running.

Using a flag to manage if some actions can be run or not, it is very simple:

```
onHold = false
function giveBlessings()
    if onHold == true then return end
    print("Bless you")
end
giveBlessings()
onHold = true
giveBlessings()
```

When we start, onHold is false, so when the giveBlessings function is called, it prints Bless you. The next time around, we call it with onHold set to true, and the function simply returns and nothing is printed.

Swimming Between the Flags: Multiple Flags

Let's consider a scenario where we need to get multiple items before we can go and slay a dragon. These would include having armor, a sword, a steed, a shield, and some spells. These are five items. To check for multiple items, we use the Boolean and and or operators. In Lua, they work in a short-circuiting manner—in plain terms, this just means that they evaluate a condition only when required.

Assuming that the flags for our items are called item1 through to item5, we can do the following:

```
if item1 and item2 and item3 and item4 and item5 then
    print("The king blesses you on your journey to battle the dragon")
else
    print("You are still not ready for battling the dragon")
end
```

This code works perfectly fine, but it can be made better. If the game had to report back to the player on the number of items collected vs. the total number of items that were to be collected, we would be left wondering how to achieve that. Here's one way to accomplish it:

```
local items = {} -- Better to have an array for multiple items
local maxItems = 5        -- Number of items required to be ready

function isPlayerReady(theItemsArray)
    local count = 0
    local i
    for i = 1,maxItems do
```

```
        if theItemsArray[i] then count = count + 1 end
    end
    return count
end
```

Now we can call this function to check if the player is ready or not, as follows:

```
if isPlayerReady(items)==5 then
    print("The king blesses you on your journey to battle the dragon")
else
    print("You are still not ready for battling the dragon")
end
```

By having an array, we not only reduce the number of variables required, but also make it easier to work with while saving a list of items; in other words, if the number of items that you could collect were 100, it would be silly to have item1 through item100. Creating arrays to hold those values is easier.

Another common question that a lot of new developers ask is, How can I create dynamic variables? The answer is to use arrays instead; they are the equivalent to the dynamic variables in the context that they were to be used.

Using Math to Loop

The safest loops to use in Lua are for loops. There are other ways to use loops, but some of them can cause Lua to hang if not used properly.

```
local result = false
local  value = 0
while result == false do
  print("The value is ", value)
  value = value + 1
  if value>=5 then
    result = true
  end
end
```

When we reach a value of 5 or greater, we simply set the result to true, which does not evaluate the condition result==false as being true, and hence breaks the loop. It is a good practice to have a flag to exit a while loop, but if you ever face a situation where you need to have a while true do loop, you can use the break statement to exit the loop.

```
local  value = 0
while true do
 print("The value is ", value)
value = value + 1
if value>= 5 then break end
end
```

Using a Grid in a Game

If you ever end up creating a simple board game, you will realize that the game is basically a grid made up of squares that hold items. This example will look at this type of organization. For simplicity's sake, each square on the board shall hold only one piece per slot on the board.

```lua
local board={} -- Note that this is a single-dimension array only
local i,j
local boardW, boardH=5,5..   -- A 5x5 board
for i=1,boardH do
    board[i]={}
    for j=1,boardW do
        board[i][j]=0  -- Initialize it to nothing; i.e., 0
    end
end
```

So, we have just created a 5×5 board that can hold the tiles. Let's fill the board with some item (i.e., a nonzero number).

```lua
local board={} -- Note that this is a single-dimension array only
local i,j
local boardW, boardH=5,5     -- A 5x5 board
for i=1,boardH do
    board[i]={}          -- Now we create the second dimension for the array
    for j=1,boardW do
        board[i][j]=0  -- Initialize it to nothing; i.e., 0
    end
end
for i=1,7 do -- Let's place 7 items randomly in some of the 25 slots
    local xCo, yCo=math.random(1,boardW), math.random(1,boardH)
    board[yCo][xCo]=1
end
for i=1,boardH do
    for j=1,boardW do
        print(i, j, board[i][j])
    end
end
```

We can see which of the squares are randomly filled.

Snakes and Ladders

You very likely played this game as a child. It consists of a 10×10-square board with some ladders and some snakes drawn on the board. You roll the dice and move the number of squares you rolled. If you land on a square that has the top of a ladder, you move to the square that has the bottom of the ladder, and if you land on a snake, you move to the tail of the snake (see Figures 4-1 and 4-2).

Figure 4-1. Snakes and Ladders

Figure 4-2. The Snakes and Ladders board

Next, we'll try coding a version of Snakes and Ladders ourselves. Note that we have not as yet gotten to using a framework, so we won't have much to display on the screen. Later on, when frameworks are introduced, we shall integrate this idea with them. For now, we'll concentrate on the logic behind the game and work out how to write the logic using Lua first.

Where Are the Snakes and Where Are the Ladders?

Let's take the board shown in Figure 4-3 as the starting point for our game.

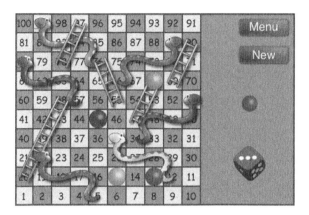

Figure 4-3. The board of Snakes and Ladders game

There are six snakes and five ladders on the board. The ladders are at the following positions, from bottom to top:

- Starting at 58 and ending at 20
- Starting at 68 and ending at 47
- Starting at 76 and ending at 55
- Starting at 90 and ending at 69
- Starting at 97 and ending at 78

And the snakes are at the following positions, from front to back:

- The head starts at 22 and the tail ends on 5.
- The head starts at 35 and the tail ends on 12.
- The head starts at 51 and the tail ends on 34.
- The head starts at 80 and the tail ends on 57.
- The head starts at 89 and the tail ends on 66.
- The head starts at 99 and the tail ends on 76.

Some Board Facts

The board is numbered from 1 to 100, in a zigzag where the first ten numbers go from left to right, the next ten right to left, the next from left to right, and so on.

The player can be at any square, and when they reach 100, they win the game. This game can be played with multiple players, and there can be multiple players on the same square.

Converting This to Code

We can have the board set up like a class that would hold information about the snakes and ladders, as in the preceding code where we randomly stored a value to the board. However, for now, we shall store this code in an array. Each record in this table shall have two fields: a start and an end square.

```lua
local tableSquares = {
{startPos = 20,  endPos = 58},
{startPos = 47,  endPos = 68},
{startPos = 55,  endPos = 76},
{startPos = 69,  endPos = 90},
{startPos = 78,  endPos = 97},
{startPos = 22,  endPos = 5},
{startPos = 35,  endPos = 12},
{startPos = 51,  endPos = 34},
{startPos = 80,  endPos = 57},
{startPos = 89,  endPos = 66},
{startPos = 99,  endPos = 76},
}
```

We also need to have an array to hold the player's locations, so we create an array:

```lua
local players = {}
local playersInGame = 0
local playersTurn = 1
```

Because this is an array, we can add as many players are we want by simply inserting their record into the table. Let's create a function to add a new player:

```lua
function addPlayer(playerName)
    playersInGame = playersInGame+ 1
    table.insert(players, {name=playerName, square=0, isPlaying=true})
end
```

What this function does is first increase the number of players represented by the `playersInGame` variable by 1, and then add a record for the player that includes fields called `name`, `square`, and `isPlaying`. The name is taken from what we pass to the function, and we set the player to be on square 0 and also set `isPlaying` to `true`. So, we can track the players and check if they are still playing or if they have already finished the game.

We can always get the number of players from the array using the # operator, but when players finish the game, we reduce `playersInGame` to reflect how many are still in the game instead of looping through all of the players and checking if they are in the game or not.

We will need another function that returns a dice roll for us, similar to the one we wrote earlier:

```lua
function rollDice(maxSides)
    local maxSides = maxSides or 6
    return math.random(1,maxSides)
end
```

We can get the number from a dice roll, and now we need to move the player based on that dice roll. Let's create the function that moves the player based on the dice roll:

```
function movePlayer(playerNo, paces)
    if paces<1 or paces>6 then return end
    -- Just to make sure that we do not get an invalid number of paces
    if playerNo>#players or playerNo <1 then return end
    -- Just to make sure that we do not get an invalid player number
    if players[playerNo].isPlaying == false then return end
    -- Make sure that the player is still playing

    local square=players[playerNo].square+paces
    if square>100 then return end
    -- You need to have the exact paces to reach the 100th square
    if square == 100 then
        -- Reached the 100th square, won or finished the game
        player[playerNo].isPlaying=false
        print("Player " .. players[playerNo].name  .. " has completed the game.")
        playersInGame=playersInGame - 1
    end

    -- Check if we have reached a snake or a ladder
    local square1=specialSquare(square)
    if square1 then
        print("Got a special square on " .. square .. ", leading to " .. square1)
    end

    players[playerNo].square=square
    -- The player is now at the new square

    print("The player " .. players[playerNo].name .. "is now on sqaure " .. square)
end
```

In the preceding function, movePlayer takes two variables, a playerNo and paces. First, we do a few checks to make sure that we do not get any invalid parameters. First we check the paces, which have to be in the range 1 to 6, as this is what we get from the dice roll. If the paces are invalid, then we return from the function. Next, we check if the playerNo is valid, which should be between 1 and the number of elements in the players array. We also check if the player is still in play and has not completed the game. We check that using the player[playerNo].isPlaying flag, which tells us if the player is still playing or not. After all these checks, we are sure that the player is valid and in play, and that the number of paces is valid too. We then store the value of the square the player is at with the paces into a variable called square. According to the game rules, the player can only win by arriving at the 100th square, so if the player is on 99 and rolls a 2, they cannot move; they *must* roll a 1 to win. The first thing we do is check if the total is greater than 100; if it is, then we return from the function (i.e., do nothing). If the total is 100, then we flag the player as having finished and set the isPlaying flag to false. We also display the message that the player has completed the game.

Since this is Snakes and Ladders, we also need to check if the player has reached the head of a snake or is at the bottom of a ladder. When you arrive at the head of the snake the player moves to the tail and if the player arrives at the bottom of the ladder, the player moves to the top of the ladder.

We check that via a specialSquare function, which takes a parameter of square and returns the corresponding square for a snake's tail or the top of the ladder; otherwise, it simply returns the same square. This way we can simply set the value without a lot of code.

```
function specialSquare(theSquare)
    local theSquare = theSquare
    local  i
    for i = 1,#tableSquares do
        local currSquare = tableSquares[i]
        if currSquare.startPos == theSquare then
            -- We have reached a special square
            return currSquare.endPos
        end
    end
    -- There was no special square, so simply return the same square value back
    return theSquare
end
```

With these functions, we have covered the major logical bulk of the game. The rest of the functions are mostly cosmetic and deal with UI interactions and updating the display.

We also need an init function that sets or resets the game defaults before we start:

```
function init()
    -- Blank out the players table
    players = {}
    playersInGame = 0
end
```

First, to test, we shall try the game with two players. The easiest way to do so is as follows:

```
function reset()
  init()
  addPlayer("Jayant")
  addPlayer ("Douglas")
end
```

We have almost everything in place for it to conceptually work, but we need to stitch it all together to make it work. When we start the game, what we need is a function that shall roll the die, move the player to a new square, change to the next player, and repeat, till there is one player left. Therefore, the game cannot start unless there are at least two players.

Because we are going to run this game in the Lua terminal rather than with a graphical framework, we shall not be able to avail ourselves of the various graphical and touch functionalities. This shall limit the interactivity of our sample for now. Though many games give the players a great deal of interactivity, this particular game doesn't need that much. In this game, the die is simply thrown (a random number is generated) and the player token is moved (by the program), so the only interactivity we would need is to have the players tap the screen at every stage to proceed to the next, and tap to roll dice. While we are in text mode, we are not able to get any touch events, hence the game might look more like a self-running simulation, which announces to the terminal whose turn it is and then what they rolled and where the player is currently, till one player is left.

```
function startGame()
    if #players<2 then return end
    -- Need to have at least 2 players
-- This is our check that if one player is left, then the game is over
    while playersInGame>1 do
        local thePlayer=players[playersTurn]
        if thePlayer.isPlaying == true then
            print("it is " .. thePlayer.name .. " turn")
            local diceRoll=rollDice()
            print("and rolled a " .. diceRoll)
            movePlayer(playersTurn, diceRoll)
        end
        -- It's the next player's turn
        nextPlayer()
    end
    print("Game over")
end
```

We can increment playersTurn in the preceding function block, but we need to make sure that playersTurn is in the range of 1 and the maximum number players. We also need to ensure that the player is still playing.

```
function nextPlayer()
    playersTurn=playersTurn+1
    -- Loop back to the first if the current player was the last player
    if playersTurn>#players then playersTurn=1 end
    if players[playersTurn].isPlaying == false then
        nextPlayer()
    end
    -- All done, nothing more to do really...
end
```

Put all of the code together, and we have an automatic-running game of Snakes and Ladders. The idea behind this code is to teach you how to create functions that are modular, and that it is mostly Lua code that runs the app; the framework is more of glue that allows the glitter to stick.

In case you are wondering why we do not see any output to the terminal window, it is because we need to start the game. We can quickly create a function called restart, which will set all the variables to the initial values and then start the game for us:

```
function restart()
  init()
  startGame()
end
```

To run the game, we simply call restart(), and the game runs in the console (see Figure 4-4).

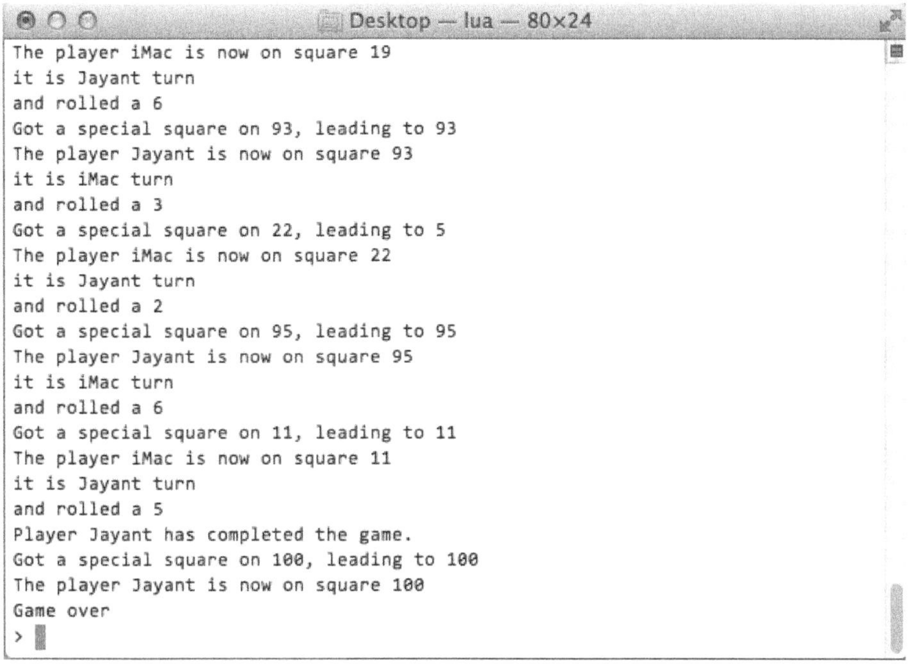

```
● ○ ○                          Desktop — lua — 80×24
The player iMac is now on square 19
it is Jayant turn
and rolled a 6
Got a special square on 93, leading to 93
The player Jayant is now on square 93
it is iMac turn
and rolled a 3
Got a special square on 22, leading to 5
The player iMac is now on square 22
it is Jayant turn
and rolled a 2
Got a special square on 95, leading to 95
The player Jayant is now on square 95
it is iMac turn
and rolled a 6
Got a special square on 11, leading to 11
The player iMac is now on square 11
it is Jayant turn
and rolled a 5
Player Jayant has completed the game.
Got a special square on 100, leading to 100
The player Jayant is now on square 100
Game over
>
```

Figure 4-4. The game running in the console

Moving a Character

In any 2D game, you are in control of a character, and this character moves on the screen as you tap or swipe the screen of the mobile device. Let's examine the code that makes the character move. The screen is a grid that has two dimensions: height and width. Most screens start with (0,0) being the top-left corner of the screen, with a positive x value indicating that the character is to the right from the origin and a negative value indicating that the character is to the left of the origin. Similarly, a positive y indicates that the character is below the origin and a negative y indicates that the character is above it. Using this information, we can safely deduce that to move a character to the right, we need to add a positive increment to the x-coordinate, and to move the character to the left, we add a negative increment to the x-coordinate.

Let's create the structure for our character as a table structure like a point that will hold the x and y position of the character:

```
local point={x=0,y=0}
-- Initialize the point structure with x and y as 0
```

Now let's move the character 5 units to the right:

```
local i
for i=1,5 do
 point.x=point.x+1
end
```

This can also be used to increment the position one pixel a time. However, in the preceding example, we could have also used `point.x = point.x + 5`, like so:

```
print(point.x, point.y)
```

We do not see anything on the screen as yet, as we have not written any code to display anything. Some might feel this to be a rather boring method, but if you look at it in the larger scheme of things, you shall find that if you can get this code working perfectly fine, you can use it with any framework and language. This shall help you keep your code as modular and portable as possible.

Going Offscreen

One of the most common issues that many beginner developers face is that of how to limit a character to a confined space on the screen. The approach with this book is a bit different than you might expect. Rather than describing a graphical solution, we shall look at the problem in the debug window. Not only will this strengthen your debugging skills, but it will also help you look at the data for conceptual code, where you might not be able to have a visual representation.

Let's bounce a ball on the screen. The ball has x- and y-coordinates in the point table structure that we defined earlier. The ball keeps moving in a particular direction, and as soon as it reaches the edge of the confining dimensions, it bounces in the opposite direction.

```
local point = {x = 0, y = 0}
local speed = {x = 1, y = 1}
local dimensions = {0,0,320,480}

function positionBall(thePoint)
   print("ball is at" .. thePoint.x .. " , ".. thePoint.y)
end
function moveBall()
  local newX, newY = point.x + speed.x, point.y + speed.y
  if newX > dimensions[3] or newX < dimensions[0] then speed.x = - speed.x end
  if newY > dimensions[4] or newY < dimensions[1] then speed.y = - speed.y end
  point.x = point.x + speed.x
  point.y = point.y + speed.y
end

-- When run, this will get into an infinite loop
while true do
 positionBall(point)
 moveBall()
end
```

Here's how it works. The structure point and speed hold the values that tell which direction the ball should move. To start with, these are both 1, so the ball starting from the top left moves toward the bottom right diagonally; however, since the width of the screen is less than the height (in portrait mode), the ball reaches the side before it reaches the bottom of the screen.

newX and newY are the current position and the speed. If these values are greater than the confining box, then the speed value is negated, so the ball begins moving in the opposite direction. What was increasing in the x will now start to decrease. When the ball hits the bottom of the screen, speed.y is changed to a negative value, which will make the ball move upward till the ball reaches 0 on the x-axis, where the speed will once again be negated and the ball will start to move to the right again.

We also have a function called positionBall, which currently just prints the coordinates to the screen; later on we'll get the ball to display on the screen as well.

Determining the Distance of a Character from an Object

Often, you'll need to know the distance between the player character and a particular object on the screen. You may also need to know the angle at which the object is to the player.

Let's say we want the player character to turn and look at the object, so we need to know the distance and the angle between these. Once again, math will come to the rescue—trigonometry, to be precise. For this, we'll use the help of the Pythagorean theorem. To recap what it is, according to Wikipedia, it states, "In any right triangle, the area of the square whose side is the hypotenuse (the side opposite the right angle) is equal to the sum of the areas of the squares whose sides are the two legs (the two sides that meet at a right angle)" (see http://en.wikipedia.org/wiki/Pythagorean_theorem).

The theorem can be written as the equation $a^2 + b^2 = c^2$.

If the player character is at point a and the object that we want to calculate the distance for at point b, we can use the Pythagorean theorem for calculating. Point a provides us with x1,y1, and point b provides us with x2,y2.

If we draw a line extending on the x-axis from the player character and a line extending on the y-axis from the object, we can find that these two lines meet at a common point, forming a right angle. Now we can apply the Pythagorean theorem to find the hypotenuse, which incidentally is also the distance between the two points.

We could represent this in code as

```
local dx, dy = math.abs(object.x - player.x), math.abs(object.y - player.y)
local distance = math.sqrt(dx*dx + dy*dy)
```

To get the angle between these two points, we need to get atan2, as follows:

```
local angle = math.deg(math.atan2(player.y - object.y, player.x-object.x))
```

There might be a situation when you want to check if the player is in a special area, or if the player touched a specific area on the screen. The best way to determine that would be to check if the point is in that rectangle. In simpler words, each point on the screen is a combination of two values, the x and the y. A rectangle is made up of either two points—a start point and an endpoint—or a start point and attributes such as width and height (see Figure 4-5).

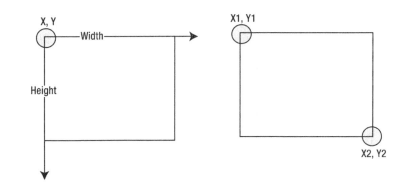

Figure 4-5. Two ways of defining a rectangle

If we have a starting point and an ending point, we can calculate the width and the height; or, if we have a starting point and the width and height of the rectangle, we can easily calculate the ending point.

```
function getPointsForRect(startX, starty, width, height)
   pointX = startX + width
   pointY = startY + height
return startX, startY, pointX, pointY
end

function getRectDimensions(startX, startY, endX, endY)
   local width = endX - startX
   local height = endY - startY
   return startX, startY, width, height
end
```

Now we need to find if a point or location either gotten from the position of an object or from the touch coordinates is within the rectangle or not. The logic behind this is simple: if the x-coordinate of the point is within the range of startX and endX and the y-coordinate of the point is within in the range of startY and endY, then we can conclude that the point is inside of the rectangle supplied as startX, startY, endX, and endY.

```
function isPointInRect(pointX pointY,  startX, startY, endX, endY)
   if (pointX > startX and pointX < endX) and
       (pointY > startY and pointY < endY) then
     return true
   else
     return false
   end
end
```

Generally, most developers use the 2D math and stop with the x,y-coordinates. If you extend this a bit further and make use of vector math, though, you can perform rotations and calculate distances much more easily. Some frameworks (e.g., Codea) actually integrate vector math as part of the framework.

Boolean Math

Boolean math is an important tool in the developer's arsenal. If you understand and harness the power of Boolean math, you can reduce the number of lines of code and also get results.

Let's have a look at the simplest example:

```
local function getTrueorFalse(thisCondition)
    if thisCondition == true then
        return true
    else
        return false
    end
end
```

Although most developers write their code like this, there are unnecessary if .. then statements that could be avoided. This function can be rewritten concisely as

```
local function getTrueOrFalse(thisCondition)
    return thisCondition==true
end
```

You can see that it is reduced and has just one line instead. This can also be used in functions where we might want to return true or false based on ranges. For example, say we want to write a function isNumberGreaterThanTen:

```
local function isNumberGreaterThanTen(theNumber)
    return theNumber > 10
end
```

We can just evaluate the results directly instead of using an if .. then statement to return true or false.

You might also want to know how to switch certain parts of code depending on a condition. The question is a bit too wide for this discussion, but let's try to narrow it down to fit the context of this section.

One way to allow or disallow certain portions of code to run is with a series of if statements:

```
local flag = false
function do Something()
    if flag == true then
        -- Execute this portion only if the flag is true
    end
    -- this portion is executed irrespective of the flag
end

doSomething()
```

Similarly, you can also use flags to disable certain functions. Let's say that we call a function every few seconds to update the player's location on an onscreen map. Before the map is fully loaded and displayed, there would be no reason to display the information onscreen. Or, in another scenario, there is a touch handler that handles touches or taps on the screen, but we might want to temporarily disable it to not handle them. In the code sample that follows, we check if the variable fDisable is true or not. If it is, we simply return from the code without executing the remainder of the code that follows.

```
function someFunction()
    if fDisable ==true then return end
    -- The code following is what you want to do if the code were to run
end
```

By just returning from the function, we do not in effect execute the code of the function, which is as good as disabling the function temporarily. In contrast to this, you might have to remove event handlers and then set them up again, which is more cumbersome than this simple flag method.

Another important feature of Lua is the way and and or work. Lua gives you the ability to not use them as bit operators (if you are coming from a C background).

The Boolean operator or is widely used in Lua is to assign default values to variables, like so:

```
local aVal = somevalue
if aVal == nil then
    aVal = defaultValue
end
```

In Lua, the preceding code can easily be converted into a single line, as follows:

```
local aVal = somevalue or defaultValue
```

Table 4-1 gives a quick overview of how and and or work.

Table 4-1. Boolean Operations

Boolean Operation	Value 1	Value 2	Operator	Result
print(5)	5	-	-	5
print(5 and 6)	5	6	and	6
print(5 or 6)	5	6	or	5
print(nil and 6)	nil	6	and	nil
print(nil or 6)	nil	6	or	6
print(5 and nil)	5	nil	and	nil
print(5 or nil)	5	nil	or	5

Summary

If you are serious about game development, you need to understand math. There are a lot of functions that can help you as a developer. You can check for collisions; check for intersections of lines, rectangles, and circles; and determine the angle and distance between two objects. Many Lua math functions are valid across frameworks, and there are some frameworks that have integrated math libraries. We have a lot of these generic functions in Chapter 7 and in Chapter 13, which discusses third-party libraries, we'll create a math vector library, which will be useful with frameworks that do not have vector functions.

Chapter 5

Strings

Hopefully you survived the previous chapter, on Lua math. The whole idea of these first few chapters is to introduce you to the fact that you can create your logic in Lua and then use any framework to add the graphics. So, many of the functions that we shall create in these chapters can be used universally across most of the frameworks without many changes. In this chapter we shall explore the topic of strings.

What Is a String?

A string is one of the many variable types available in Lua. It can hold alphanumeric characters of arbitrary lengths. It cannot have multiple dimensions like a table can. Lua automatically converts strings into numbers if the strings are used in any form of arithmetic operation. This process is called *coercion*, and it is automatic.

You have seen strings in many forms earlier, the simplest being

```
print("hello world!")
```

The string in this case is `"hello world!"`. It is mainly characterized by enclosing the alphanumeric characters within double or single quotes.

In this case, since the `"hello world"` is not assigned to a variable but used directly, it is called a *constant string*.

Most of the string functions are used to manipulate text. The functions available for use in Lua are described in the following sections.

> **Note** Many of the functions available are also provided within a namespace. So, you can also use the functions in an object-oriented style. For example `string.byte(s,i)` can be represented as `s:byte(i)`.

string.byte (s [,i [,j]])

For the devices, a character is an ASCII number from 0 to 255. While we recognize characters as an *A* or *a*, each character is represented with a number, such as 65, 97, and so on. The byte function returns the number or the ASCII code of the character at the position in question. There are three parameters that can be passed: the string itself (s) and the optional i and j; i marks the start position of the string (by default it is 1) and j marks the end of the string (its default is the same as i). Here's an example:

```
print(string.byte("One"))
print(string.byte("One",1,3))
```

string.char (…)

This function is similar to the previous function, except that instead of converting a character into a numeric value, this function converts a numeric value into a character. The function takes an integer and returns a string with a length equal to the number of integers passed.

```
print(string.char(72, 101, 108, 108, 111, 32, 87, 111, 114, 108, 100))
```

string.dump (function)

This function returns a string that contains the binary representation of the given function. This can later be used with the loadstring function on the string and returns a copy of the function. Though most of the frameworks allow loadstring, CoronaSDK has blocked this function, so there isn't much that one can do with this if using CoronaSDK.

string.find (s, pattern [,init [,plain]])

This function looks for the first match of the pattern in the string s. If found, it returns the indices of where the match starts and ends. If a match is not found, it returns nil. The parameter init (if passed) determines the starting position of the search. The default value for this is 1. The parameter for plain is a Boolean value that is either true or false. This determines if pattern is false; it is just plain text for substring matching. If this is true, then pattern can have placeholders and wildcards for matching. If pattern has captures, then the function returns the captured values after the two indices.

string.format (formatString, …)

This function returns a string that is formatted based on the format and the values passed. This is similar to the C function printf. The options/modifiers *, l, L, n, p, and h are not supported. This function has a new option, q, that formats the string in a form that is suitable and safe for use with the Lua interpreter. All the characters are correctly escaped to work. For example

```
string.format('%q', 'a string with "quotes" and \n new line')
```

will produce the string

```
"a string with \"quotes\" and \
new line"
```

While most of the options c, d, E, e, f, g, G, I, o, u, X, and x expect a number as an argument, s and q expect a string.

string.gmatch (s, pattern)

This function returns an iterator function that returns the next capture from `pattern` over string s each time it is called. If the patterns specified nothing to capture, the entire match is returned.

string.gsub (s, pattern, repl [,n])

This function replaces the string held in `pattern` with the string held in `repl`. n determines the number of substitutions to be made.

```
str="this is a red apple"
newstr=str:gsub( "red", "green" )
print(newstr)
```

Here's another example that explains the replacement strings using the n parameter. In this code, notice that the first `str:gsub` function replaces all of the instances of `"is"` with `"are"`. The second function replaces the first four instances of `"is"` with `"are"`, and the last time, the `str:gsub` replaces the first two instances of `"is"` with `"are"`.

```
str="The data is one, is two, is three, is four, is five"
print(str:gsub("is", "are"))
print(str:gsub("is", "are",4))
print(str:gsub("is", "are", 2))
```

string.len (s)

This function returns the length of the string s. This is similar to the # operator. The function also includes embedded zeros; so, for example, "a\000bc\000" has a length of 5.

string.lower (s)

This is a function that returns the string after converting all the characters in it to lowercase, while all other characters are left unchanged. Note that the definition of *uppercase* is dependent on the current locale. For instance, in the default English locale, accented characters are not converted to lowercase.

string.match (s, patterns [,init])

This function looks for and returns the first match of `pattern` in the string s. It will return `nil` if none is found. The `init` parameter specifies where to start the search and can be negative.

string.rep (s, n)

This function returns a string that contains n repetitions of the string s passed. This is equivalent to `replicate` in some other languages. For example

```
print(string.rep("*",10)
```

would print the following:

```
**********
```

string.reverse (s)

This function returns the string s in reverse.

```
print(string.reverse("madam"))
```

would not be the best example to test this function.

string.sub (s, i [,j]])

This function returns a substring, or a string that is part of the original string s, such that it starts at the position i and continues until j. While many other languages specify a length after the start position, Lua has an absolute position. The default value for i is 1, and it can also be set to negative. If j is absent, it is given the default value of –1 (i.e., the end of the string).

string.upper (s)

This function returns a copy of the string with all the lowercase characters changed to uppercase. All other characters are left unchanged. This again depends on the current locale for what letters are considered lowercase.

Patterns

If you are new to development or have not used languages that have built-in pattern matching or regex-like functions, then you might be wondering what patterns are. There are four fundamental concepts in Lua:

- Character class
- Pattern item
- Pattern
- Capture

Character Class

A character class is used to represent a set of characters and can be any of the following:

- x: Represents the character *x* itself, not one of the magic characters ^, $, (), %,., [,], *, +, -, or?

- .: Functions in same way as the wildcard that represents all characters

- %a: Represents all letters

- %c: Represents all control characters

- %d: Represents all digits

- %l: Represents all letters (lowercase)

- %p: Represents all punctuation characters

- %s: Represents all space characters

- %u: Represents all uppercase characters

- %w: Represents all alphanumeric characters

- %x: Represents all hexadecimal characters

- %z: Represents the character with the representation 0

- %x: Allows you to escape any magic character (note that *x* is not the literal character *x*, but any nonalphanumeric character)

- [set]: Represents a union of all characters in *set*. The range of characters can be specified with a hyphen (–), as in [0-9] or [a-z].

- [^set]: Represents the complement of *set*. So, [^0-9] would mean all characters that are not in the range 0 to 9.

For all classes that are represented by a single letter (e.g., %a, %c, %s, and so on), the corresponding uppercase letter represents the complement of the class. So, %S represents all non-space characters.

Pattern Item

A pattern item is a single character class that matches any single character in the class.

There are a few characters that help quantify the matches:

- *: This matches zero or more repetitions of characters in the class. This will always return the longest possible sequence.

- +: This matches one or more repetitions of characters in the class. This will return the longest possible sequence.

- –: This also matches zero or more repetitions of characters in the class, but unlike *, this will match the shortest possible sequence.

- ?: This will match zero or one occurrence of a character in the class.

Pattern

A pattern is a sequence of pattern items. A caret (^) indicates the beginning of a pattern and a $ symbol specifies the end of the pattern. At other positions, they have no special meaning, but only represent themselves.

Capture

A pattern can contain subpatterns enclosed in parentheses; these are described as *captures*. When a match succeeds, the substrings that the match captures are stored (captured) for further use. Captures are numbered according to their left parentheses. In the pattern "(a*(.)%w(%s*))", the part of the string matching "(a*(.)%w(%s*))" is stored as the first capture, the character matching the dot (.) is stored as the second, and the part matching the %s* is stored as the third.

Using the String Functions

While we can store text as strings and then print them to the screen, we also sometimes need to manipulate or transform them. Using some of the Lua functions described previously, we can do this.

Converting Strings to Uppercase

As described previously, the function that converts strings to uppercase is very simple. Here's a function that makes it even simpler to use:

```
function upper(theString)
    return string.upper(theString)
end
```

Converting Strings to Lowercase

This is similar to the previous function.

```
function lower(theString)
    return string.lower(theString)
end
```

Converting Strings to Title Case

This function converts a string to title case, in which the first character of all words is capitalized:

```
function title_case(theString)
  return (theString:gsub("^%a", string.upper):gsub("%s+%a", string.upper))
end
```

Alternatively, we can have the function work in an object-oriented manner, where we can directly invoke the function as part of the `string` namespace, like so:

```
tString="hello how are you?"
tString:title_case()
```

To achieve that, we need to declare the function as follows:

```
function string:title_case()
    return (self:gsub("^%a", string.upper):gsub("%s+%a", string.upper))
end
```

Padding a String

While working with text, sometimes text needs to be padded. This function helps to create strings of a particular length by padding them:

```
function pad(s, width, padder)
  padder=string.rep(padder or " ", math.abs(width))
  if width<0 then return string.sub(padder .. s, width) end
  return string.sub(s .. padder, 1, width)
end
```

This function caters for both left and right padding. For padding on the left, we just need to pass it a negative length, as in the second example in the following code:

```
print(pad("hello",20))
print(pad("hello",-10,"0"))
```

CSV Functionality

While creating a game, there might be a need to save data in *CSV (comma-separated value)* format, in which the data is stored as a long string of values separated by commas. CSV functions can help you convert tables to and from CSV format.

Converting a CSV String to a Table

This first example parses and converts a CSV-formatted string into a table:

```
-- Convert from CSV string to table (converts a single line of a CSV file)
function fromCSV (s)
    s=s .. ','          -- ending comma
    local t = {}        -- table to collect fields
    local fieldstart=1
    repeat
    -- next field is quoted? (start with `"'?)
    if string.find(s, '^"', fieldstart) then
        local a, c
        local i  = fieldstart
        repeat
        -- find closing quote
            a, i, c=string.find(s, '"("?)', i+1)
```

```
            until c ~= '"'      -- quote not followed by quote?
            if not i then error('unmatched "') end
                local f=string.sub(s, fieldstart+1, i-1)
                table.insert(t, (string.gsub(f, '""', '"')))
                fieldstart=string.find(s, ',', i)+1
            else                 -- unquoted; find next comma
                local nexti=string.find(s, ',', fieldstart)
                table.insert(t, string.sub(s, fieldstart, nexti-1))
                fieldstart=nexti+1
            end
        until fieldstart > string.len(s)
        return t
end
```

Converting from a Table to CSV

This next function converts a table into CSV format. This is useful for exporting the table data as a file that a spreadsheet program such as Excel can open and read.

```
-- Convert from table to CSV string
function toCSV (tt)
    local s=""
    for _,p in pairs(tt) do
        s=s .. "," .. escapeCSV(p)
    end
    return string.sub(s, 2)      -- Remove first comma
end
```

Escaping the CSV

Escaping in this context is not the same as *avoiding*, but instead means replacing the characters or altering them to be used as a string. Here's an example of escaping CSV-formatted data:

```
-- Used to escape "'s by toCSV
function escapeCSV (s)
    if string.find(s, '[,"]') then
        s='"' .. string.gsub(s, '"', '""') .. '"'
    end
    return s
end
```

Formatting a Number with the Thousand Separator

While displaying scores, you might want to display them in a readable format. You can use the *thousand separator* for this, like so:

```
function comma_value(amount)
    local formatted=amount
    while true do
```

```
        formatted, k = string.gsub(formatted, "^(-?%d+)(%d%d%d)", '%1,%2')
        if (k==0) then
            break
        end
    end
    return formatted
end
```

The comma_value function can be used to print formatted numbers, as in the following example.

```
print(comma_value(123456.78))    -- prints 123,456.78
```

Frequency of Letters

With the getFrequency function, we can determine the frequency of certain letters in a string. The gsub function calls the function passed for every match of the pattern. We can use this information to get the frequency of the characters. So, to get the frequency, we create a function called tally that will increase the character count of the character we pass to the function.

```
function string:getFrequency()
    local inst = {}
    function tally(char)
        char = string.upper(char)
        inst[char] = (inst[char] or 0)+1
    end
    self:gsub("%a", tally)
    return inst
end
```

We can test this function with the following code:

```
testString = "Hello, how are you?"
tbl = testString:getFrequency()
for i,j in pairs(tbl) do
    print(i,j)
end
```

Detecting Whether a String Is a Palindrome

We can use the reverse function to check if a string is a palindrome or not. The easiest way do this is to check whether the string is the same forward as it is when reversed.

```
function string:isPalindrome( )
    return self == self:reverse()
end
```

Splitting a String

Earlier, you learned how to split a string in a function and convert the string into a table. In this example, we shall use the function string.gsub to split a string based on patterns (as described earlier). Here's an easy way to do this:

```
function string:split(sep)
    local sep, fields = sep or ":", {}
    local pattern = string.format("([^%s]+)", sep)
    self:gsub(pattern, function(c) fields[#fields+1] = c end)
    return fields
end
```

This returns a table that has the strings split based on the separator. Here's an example of how we can use this:

```
str = "name = Jayant"
results = str:split(" = ")
print("The value of " .. results[1] .. " is " .. results[2])
```

Level Management

If you're creating a board game, you will be faced with creating levels for it. Though there are lots of ways to create levels, one of the easiest and best is to create a string that corresponds to each square on the board. For example, if the game has a board of 5 × 5 that contains a start position, an end position, and obstacles, then you could create it as shown in Figure 5-1.

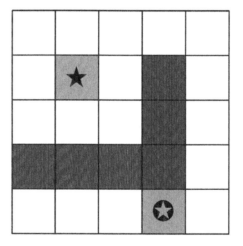

Figure 5-1. A graphic representation of the levels

In this example, the ' ★ ' marks the position where the player is when the game starts. The ' ✪ ' marks the spot the player needs to reach in order to complete the level. The gray squares are walls that obstruct the player's movements. So, we can now convert this to level data. We can store it in a 2D array, which would look like the following:

```
level1 = {
  {0,0,0,0,0},
  {0,0,0,1,0},
  {0,0,0,1,0},
  {0,1,1,1,0},
  {0,0,0,0,0},
}
```

```
start = {x = 2, y = 2}
endPos = {y = 5, x = 4}
currlevel = level1
```

In this arrangement, the start position is 2 and the end position is 3; the walls are represented by 1s. With this 2D array, we can access any element of the array as `level[y][x]`, where y is the row and x is the column.

We can set up the level information from a data file or from the code:

```
-- Setup
position = {x=start.x, y=start.y}   -- This indicates where the player currently is

-- Movement
function move(direction)
    local pX, pY = position.x, position.y
    if direction==1 and pX > 1 and level1[pY][pX-1] == 0 then
            position.x = position.x - 1
            return true
        end
    elseif direction==2 and pX < 4 and level1[pY][pX+1] == 0 then
        position.x = position.x+1
        return true
    elseif direction==3 and pY > 1 and level1[pY-1][pX] == 0 then
        position.y = position.y - 1
        return true
    elseif direction==4 and pY < 4 and level1[pY+1][pX] == 0 then
        position.y = position.y+1
        return true
    end
end
```

We can then use this function to update the GUI portion, as follows:

```
if move(direction) == true then
    local pX, pY = position.x, position.y
    if pX == endPos.x and pY == endPos.y then
        print("Congratulations, you have managed to reach the end.")
    else
        --updateGIU()
    end
end
```

Summary

String manipulation is an important part of any programming language. In this chapter we looked at the various functions available in Lua for string manipulation. We also created a few functions that you can use in your own apps. You can include these functions in your own utility library that you can use as a generic library for your app development.

Chapter 6

Threading

There was a time in the 1980s when a computer did one and only one task at a time. In the times of MS-DOS and CP/M, one could execute an application, exit from it back to the prompt, and then invoke another. Additionally, Unix-like systems used the concept of multiuser usage, where each user could run separate applications. While the OS can be multitasking—running several apps—each application can perform different tasks. For example, downloading a file asynchronously while playing music and updating the progress bar. To understand this concept better, we need to look into these three important topics: processes, multitasking, and threads.

- A *process* is an instance of a computer program—a list of code-based instructions—that is being executed, or run. Several processes can be associated with the same program, and several instances of the same program can be executed simultaneously; for example, each open window within a browser is a process of its own.

- *Multitasking* is a method that allows multiple processes to share processors and other system resources. With multitasking, a CPU can switch between tasks being executed without having to wait for one to finish. The way this works can differ from system to system.

- The smallest unit of processing that an operating system runs or executes is called a *thread*. A process can have multiple threads, and the CPU can switch between these threads to provide the perception of multiple threads running at the same time.

Coroutines

Programming languages use subroutine or functions to call a set of instructions. The function or subroutine is called and executed, and when it completes, it returns. A *coroutine* is a special type of subroutine; like a subroutine or a function, it has an entry point, but it can be *yielded* (paused in the middle) and then resumed from that point. A coroutine can be passed parameters at any time when it is called, not just at the point of entry.

Coroutine Functions

Several functions are associated with working with coroutines. This section provides brief descriptions of these functions.

coroutine.create (f)

This function creates a new coroutine with the function body f, which should be a Lua function. On successful creation, it returns the new coroutine an object with the type thread.

```
thread = coroutine.create(function() print("Started") end)
coroutine.resume(thread)
```

coroutine.resume (co [, val1, ...])

This function starts or resumes the execution of the coroutine co. The first time this function is called, it starts running its body. The values (val1, ...) are all passed as arguments to the main function. The function returns true plus any values passed to yield or any values returned by the body function. If the coroutine body is already finished or an error occurs while executing the coroutine body, resume returns false plus an error message.

```
thread = coroutine.create(function() print("Started") end)
coroutine.resume(thread)
```

coroutine.running ( )

This function returns the running coroutine, or nil when the running coroutine is the main one.

```
print( coroutine.running(thread))
thread = coroutine.create( function() print("Hello") end)
print( coroutine.running(thread))
```

coroutine.status (co)

This function returns the status of the coroutine co as a string. The possible return values are

- running: If the coroutine is running
- suspended: If the coroutine is suspended in a call to yield or hasn't started running
- normal: If the coroutine is active but not running
- dead: If the coroutine has finished its body function or has stopped with an error

```
print( coroutine.status(thread))
thread = coroutine.create( function() print("Hello") end)
print( coroutine.status(thread))
```

coroutine.wrap (f)

This function creates a new coroutine with the body f, similar to create. However, coroutine.wrap returns a function that can be used with the coroutines.

```
thread = coroutine.wrap( function() print("Hello") end)
thread()         -- to start the coroutine.
```

coroutine.yield (...)

This function suspends the execution of the calling routine. Any of the arguments to yield are passed as extra results to resume.

Creating a New Coroutine

You can use the following code to create a new coroutine:

```
co = coroutine.create(function() print("hello world") end)
print(co)
print(type(co))
coroutine.resume(co)
print(coroutine.status(co))
```

In this code, we create a new coroutine using the function coroutine.create and pass it a function. Notice that the function passed does not run. When we use print(co), we see that this is the coroutine object. type(co) reveals that co is an object of type thread. coroutine.resume(co) invokes the function, and "hello world" is printed to the screen. Lastly, coroutine.status(co) displays "dead" as the status.

Coroutines and Resuming

In this code, we shall look at how to work with coroutines, including how to create and resume them, and make them yield.

```
co = coroutine.create(function()
    for i=1, 10 do
        print("Loop:", i)
        coroutine.yield(i)
    end
end)
 coroutine.resume(co)
print(coroutine.status(co))
coroutine.resume(co)
...
coroutine.resume(co)
```

Progress Bars

Another practical example for using coroutines is with progress bars, as in the following example:

```
function doLongProcessing(a)
    -- Do something
    thread1 = coroutine.yield("25%")

    -- Do something
    thread1 = coroutine.yield("50%")

    -- Do something
    thread1 = coroutine.yield("75%")

    -- Do something
    return "100%"
end

thread = coroutine.create(doLongProcessing)
while coroutine.status(thread) ~= "dead" do
    local _, res = coroutine.resume(thread)
    print( "Progress is now " .. res )
end
```

In contrast, consider the following code:

```
tStep = 1000
for i=1,100000 do
  if i/tStep == math.floor(i/tStep) then print( i/tStep .. " % done")
end
```

When run in the Lua terminal, this code is responsive, but when run on some frameworks, this can be very unstable, as it can choke the CPU while running the loop (similar to the application freezing). This is a very good example of where coroutines can help.

We have a coroutine function that runs the code from 1 to 100,000. Every time this coroutine is called, it iterates to the next number and yields. We set up another loop that keeps calling this code till the coroutine status is dead, and when the iteration number is a multiple of 1,000, we print out the progress as the percentage done.

```
tStep = 1000
function showProgress()
    for i=1,100000 do
        coroutine.yield(i)
    end
end
```

We have the body of our function; now we need to have a loop that will work on this.

```lua
co = coroutine.create(showProgress)
while coroutine.status(co) ~= "dead" do
    _,res = coroutine.resume(co)
    if res/tStep == math.floor(res/tStep) then print(res/tStep .. " % done") end
end
```

The facility to resume midway and pass the function new parameters can be very useful when dealing with functions that rely on updated data. We shall not look at a complex example, but to illustrate the point, here's a simple one:

```lua
a = 100
co = coroutine.create(function()
    print( "we start at ", a)
    a = coroutine.yield(a)
    print("We restart this function with the value of ", a)
end)
_, res = coroutine.resume(co)
print("We stopped or yielded at", res)
_,res = coroutine.resume(co, 200)
```

Game Loops

A game in the simplest of terms is a repeating loop that takes inputs and updates the screen and characters. So in terms of pseudocode, a game might look like this:

```
while playing do
    getInput()
    updateCharacters()
    updateScreen()
end
```

In this case, *getInput()* is a function that would get some form of input from the player, either from the keyboard or via touch. *updateCharacters()* is the function that would update the game play elements, the characters on the screen, and the board. Lastly, *updateScreen()* would update the score, the lives, the messages, and so on. If this were written in C, C++, or similar, this would be fine, but in Lua, the while loops are not very stable. Coroutines come in handy to make these routines more responsive.

Another interesting thing is that although coroutines in Lua are not threads, they can be used like threads (i.e., you can define multiple coroutines). Here's an example:

```lua
c1 = coroutine.create(function()
    for i=1,20 do
        print( "function 1: ", i)
    end
end)
c2 = coroutine.create(function()
    for i=1,5 do
        print( "function 2: ", i)
    end
end)
```

```
c3 = coroutine.create(function()
    for i=10,1,-1 do
        print( "function 3: ", i)
    end
end)
while true do
    co1 = coroutine.resume(c1)
    co2 = coroutine.resume(c2)
    co3 = coroutine.resume(c3)
    if coroutine.status(c1)=="dead" and coroutine.status(c2)=="dead" and
coroutine.status(c3)=="dead" then break end
end
```

Working with Tables

Remember that in Lua, all variables other than numbers and strings are memory locations and are passed by reference, which means that if we declare table t and then assign b as t, we do not get a copy of t in b; instead, b would point to the same table as t.

```
t = {"One", "Two", "Three"}
b = t
print(b[2])
t[2]="Deux"
print(b[2])
```

In the case that we need to copy the table, not just provide a pointer to the same memory address, we need to do what is called a *deep copy*. Here's an example:

```
function deepcopy(t)
    if type(t) ~= "table" then return t end
    local res = {}
    local mt = getmetatable(t)
    for k,v in pairs(t) do
        if type(v)=="table" then
            v = deepcopy(v)
        end
        res[k] = v
    end
    setmetatable(res,mt)
    return res
end
```

This code first creates a new blank table object, res. Next, it saves the metatable signature, which is what identifies a table to be of a particular type. When this metatable is modified, the object may fail to be recognized as a particular type. Next, it copies all the data into the new table, and if the type of an element is another table, it recursively goes through every element and subtable present in that table, and when done, saves that data to corresponding new table data elements. Then it sets the metatable for this new table object and returns it a copy of the table object.

Customizing the Metatable

Remember that in Lua, one of the most important types of variables is the table. As mentioned, arrays, associative arrays, and objects are all basically tables. Arrays aren't very customizable, but objects are—they have some extra functionality and functions that arrays don't. All of this functionality forms a unique fingerprint for the object, and that helps identify the object type. Every table in Lua can have a metatable. A metatable is nothing more than an ordinary table that defines the behavior of the original table and the user data. If we set specific fields in the metatable, we can modify the behavior of the object. We can thereby create objects and allow them to have custom operations, similar to C++ operator overloading. However, there is a limited list of what can be altered in Lua.

The following subsections describe the keys that help Lua to alter or customize the behavior of tables.

__index

When we attempt to retrieve the value of an element in a Lua table, Lua attempts to locate that element; if the element does not exist, then Lua calls the __index metafunction. If there is no such method, then nil is returned.

For example, say we run the following code:

```
t = {}
print(t.name)
print(t.age)
```

This prints nil for both the name and the age, because we have not defined them yet. If we modify this code to include

```
default = { name ="Lua" }
t = setmetatable( {}, {__index=default} )
print(t.name)
print(t.age)
```

we see that the first print displays "Lua" and the second still prints nil.

The __index metafunction can be the data in a table, as in the preceding code, or it can be a function. When the __index function is called, it is passed two parameters: the Table and the Key.

We can see this behavior with the following code:

```
t = setmetatable({}, {__index=function(theTable, theKey) print(theTable, theKey)
return"." end})
print(t.name)
print(t.age)
print(t[1])
print(t[2][3])
print(t.whatever)
```

We are returning a . from the function, so we see it print the table address and the name of the element that we are trying to access, followed by a ..

> **Note**   Every time the table is accessed, the __index metafunction is invoked.

So, you have to be careful when accessing a table value from inside of the __index function. It can lead to a circular loop, causing a stack overflow, as shown in the definition following:

```
__index = function(tbl, key)
    local a = tbl[key]
    if a <=0 then a = 0 end
    if a > 5 then a = 0 end
    return a
end
```

Though the preceding code looks very innocent and tries to keep the value of the element in the table within a range, this code will cause problems and circular references. The first line in the function, a = tbl[key], will actually trigger another __index function call, and that in turn will invoke another, and so on.

Now that we've identified the issue, we still need to resolve it. To do this, we can use the Lua function rawget, which retrieves the value of the table without invoking the __index metamethod. So, we could write the same function as

```
__index = function(tbl, key)
    local a = rawget(tbl, key)
    if a<=0 then a = 0 end
    if a > 5 then a = 0 end
    return a
end
```

__newindex

This function is similar to the __index function, but is different in the way it's used to set a value; so, when we assign a value to a table, this function is called. This gets passed three parameters: the table, the key, and the value.

```
a = setmetatable({},{
    __newindex = function(t, key, value)
      print("Setting  [" .. key .. "]=" .. value)
      rawset(t, key, value )
    end})
a.year = 2012
a.apps = 15
```

In a way similar to the preceding example where table[key]=value would invoke the __newindex function and could get into an endless loop and cause errors, this example uses rawset to set the value of the key.

> **Note**   This function is called the very first time, when the value of the key is not set at all. If the value is set, the function is not invoked at all. The value is directly altered.

__mode

In programming languages like Lua that employ garbage collection, objects are said to be *weak* if they cannot prevent themselves from being collected. Lua can set the table as a weak table where the keys and the values are weak references. If the key or the value of such a table is collected, the entry of the table is collected.

The mode of these weak tables can be set using the __mode metafunction, and it can be used to set the keys or the values as weak using the k or v parameter, as follows:

```
local weaktable = setmetatable({}, {__mode="k"})
```

__call

This allows the table to be used like a function. If the table is followed by parentheses, the metatable tries to locate the __call function and invoke it; if it is not present, it returns an error. Otherwise, it is passed the table and the arguments passed.

```
t = setmetatable({},{
    __call = function(t, value)
            print("Calling the table with " .. value)
    end})

t("2012")
```

> **Note**   Every time the metatable is set, it overwrites the earlier metatable entries, which means that in the preceding example, we do not have an entry for __newindex. If we had that defined earlier, it would have been removed, and the only function set would have been __call. You need to define all the relevant keys in one go, or get the metatable and then add or alter the new metafunction.

__metatable

This hides the metatable. When the getmetatable function is used and the table has a __metatable string, then the value of that key is returned instead of the actual metatable.

__tostring

This function is called when a sting representation of a table or object is requested. This can be used to provide a description for custom objects.

```
t=setmetatable({},{__tostring=function() return "This is my custom table" end})
print(t)
print(tostring(t))
```

__gc

This function is called when the table is set to be garbage collected. If __gc is pointing to a function, this function is first invoked. This function is only available for user data (i.e., usable via the C APIs).

__unm

This function is the unary minus; it is equivalent to the - sign. To convert a number into a negative (e.g., 5 to –5), we add a – sign in front. The unary minus function is used to perform this conversion on a table or an object. It can be used to perform negation on complex objects; for example, a table of values.

```
t = setmetatable({},{__unm=function() return -3 end})
print(t - 5)
print(5 - -t)
```

> **Note**   In this example, we are returning a fixed number, –3. In your program, you might want to calculate the value to return.

__add

This function is the normal addition function; it is called when adding a variable to a table object using the + operator. Overriding this can be very useful when trying to add objects that do not have a numeric value that can be simply added.

The first example that comes to mind is that of fractions. This is perhaps one of the most common examples of operator overloading with C++ and using addition between two objects that are nonnumeric.

```
t = setmetatable({},{__add=function(tbl, val) return 5+val end})
print(t+5)
```

> **Caution**   Do *not* call this as print(5 + t), which can lead to stack overflows. The table has to be the leftmost value for this to work, as the function __add expects the first parameter to be a table value.

__sub

This function is the normal subtraction function, which is called when subtracting a variable from a table object using the – operator. Overriding this can be very useful when trying to subtract objects that do not have a numeric value that can be simply subtracted.

```
t = setmetatable({},{__sub=function(tbl, val) return 5-val end})
print(t-3)
```

> **Note**   Again, do not call this as print(3 - t), which can lead to stack overflows. The table has to be the leftmost value for this to work, as the function __sub expects the first parameter to be a table value.

__mul

This function is the normal multiplication function, called when multiplying a variable from a table object using the * operator. Overriding this can be useful when trying to multiply objects that do not have a numeric value that can be simply multiplied. A good example is when trying to get a dot product of a matrix or a vector.

```
t = setmetatable({},{__mul=function(tbl, val) return 2^val end})
print(t * 3)
print(2 * 2)
```

In this example, depending on the value we multiply by, we are returning 2 to the power of that number; this is an example of how we can have functionality that is closest to operator overloading in Lua.

__div

This is the normal division function, called when dividing a variable from a table object using the / operator. Overriding this can be very useful when trying to divide objects that do not have a numeric value that can be simply divided.

```
t = setmetatable({},{__div=function(tbl, val) return 1/val end})
print(t/3)
```

__pow

This is the normal exponential function, called when using the ^ operator. Overriding this can be useful when trying to execute operations that do not have a numeric value that can be used simply.

```
t = setmetatable({},{__pow=function(tbl, val) return 7^val end})
print(t^3)
```

__concat

This is the concatenation function, which is called when the concatenation operator (..) is used to concatenate two or more table values.

```
t = setmetatable({}, {__concat=function(tbl,val) return "Hello " .. val end})
print(t .. "Jayant")
```

__eq

This is the equal operator (==); it can be used to help compare two table values that are not easily comparable. The not (a==b) is equivalent to a~=b.

__lt

This is the *less-than* operator (<); it can be used to help compare two table values that are not easily comparable.

__le

The *less-than-or-equal-to* operator (<=) is also useful for comparing two table values that are not easily comparable.

A Useful Example

Let's look at a sample that demonstrates the practical use of the functions just described and their use with tables. The + operator works well between numbers. If we try to add two tables using the + operator, it will not work. We can create the functions that can be used to manage operations such as adding these tables. In the following example, we override the __add function, which allows us to add two tables using the + operator.

```
thePos = {}

thePos.__add = function (a, b)
    local res = {
        a[1] + b[1],
        a[2] + b[2]
    }
    setmetatable(res, thePos)
    return res
end

function make_pos(x,y)
    local res = { x, y }
    setmetatable(res, thePos)
    return res
end
```

```
p1 = make_pos(5,6)
p2 = make_pos(2,4)
p3 = p1 + p2
print(p3[1], p3[2])
```

Object-Oriented Lua

Lua is not an object-oriented language, but it has functionality that allows for it to be used like one. I described this in Chapter 2, where functions can be added to a table, called with the : operator, and passed to the function.

We had a look at deepcopy earlier—a way to create a copy of a table other than just passing a pointer to memory. We also had a look at tweaking the metatable to override some of the functionality of tables.

The logic programming language Prolog has features that help to create relationships and thereby connections between data, and then look this information up using predicates. In the most basic manner, Lua can provide similar functionality.

First, here's an example of how we can create the relationships:

```
-- Create the relationships
company(Jayant, OZApps)
language(CoronaSDK, Lua)
language(GiderosStudio, Lua)
language(Moai, Lua)
language(XCode, ObjectiveC)

-- Query the relationships
print(is_language(CoronaSDK, ObjectiveC))
print(is_company(Jack, OZApps))
print(is_company(Jayant, OZApps))

-- additionally
father(Vader, Luke)
father(Vader, Leia)
brother(Luke, Leia)
sister(Leia, Luke)

print(is_sister(Leia, Luke))
print(is_sister(Leia, Han))
```

All of this can be run from the terminal. One of the challenges in this is that Lua does not have commands that help associate these relationships; the first thing you will get if you type father (Vader, Luke) in the terminal window is an error that states that there is no global called father. This happens because there is no function or variable called father, Vader, or Luke. To rectify this situation, we take the help of metatables. As described previously, whenever Lua tries to retrieve a missing value, it calls the __index function. Let's see what happens when we set an __index metamethod and try to invoke father(Vader, Luke):

```
setmetatable(_G, {__index =
    function(tbl, name)
```

```
            print("Retrieving the variable :", name)
        end
})
```

```
what(was, this)
```

Notice that we still get an error that the global variable what was not found. When we access a member from the table, the member is returned, but if the member is not present, the __index function is used to calculate or determine the data to be returned. If there is no __index function, then we get the error.

We can rectify that by using rawset and making sure that there is a global function (if it is not found) similar to an autodeclare, where the variable would get declared if not declared already.

```
setmetatable(_G, {__index =
    function(tbl, name)
        print("Retrieving the variable :", name)
        rawset(tbl,name,{})
    end
})
```

```
what(was, this)
```

While this should have removed the error, we find that this doesn't rectify the situation, even though a new global variable called what is declared. This fails because what is a table, not a function, and we are trying to invoke it like a function.

An easy way to rectify this is to replace the rawset(tbl, name,{}) with rawset(tbl, name, function() end. This way, we return a function that can be called without invoking errors in Lua. The most important point here is that the __index metamethod has to return something expected in the context.

```
setmetatable(_G, {__index =
    function(tbl, name)
        print("Name :", name)
        rawset(tbl,name,function() end)
        return rawget(tbl, name)
    end
})
```

```
what(was, this)
```

This is fine; however, since Vader and Luke are also not defined, we cannot have them converted into functions. One logical solution is to identify that all variable names starting with a lowercase letter are functions and all uppercase names are variables. So, in the case of father(Vader, Luke), Vader and Luke would be variables, while father would be a function.

```
setmetatable(_G, {__index =
    function(tbl, name)
        if name:match("^[A-Z]") then
            rawset(tbl, name, {} )
        else
```

```
                rawset(tbl, name, function() end)
            end

            return rawget(tbl,name)
        end
})
```

what(was, this)

Now we are able to create as many relationships as we want—the preceding code will check if the words begin with uppercase or lowercase letters; if uppercase, then it will create a function, and if not, then it will simply create an empty table. However, despite all of this, we still need to create relationships between the two elements.

```
setmetatable(_G, {__index =
    function(tbl, name)
        if name:match("^[A-Z]") then
            rawset(tbl, name, {} )
        else -- create a rule here
            local rule = create_rule(name)
            rawset(tbl, name, rule)
        end

        return rawget(tbl,name)
    end
})
function create_rule(name)
    return function(a,b)
        a[name .. "_of"]=b
        b[name]=a
end
```

What this little tweak does is create two link keys: one that has an _of suffixed to the end of the relationship we are setting.

If we are unable to query the relationships that we are attempting to create, then the code will return an error. So, we add a little bit of checking and see if we have a prefix of is_ to query the relationship.

```
function make_predicate(name)
    local rule = name:match("^is_(.*)")
    return function(a,b)
        return b[rule]==a
    end
end
```

We also add a little change to our metamethod:

```
setmetatable(_G, {__index =
    function(tbl, name)
        if name:match("^[A-Z]") then
            rawset(tbl, name, {} )
```

```
        elseif name:match("^is_") then
            local pred = make_predicate(name)
            rawset(tbl, name, pred)
        else --create a rule here
            local rule = create_rule(name)
            rawset(tbl, name, rule)
        end

        return rawget(tbl,name)
    end
})
```

We can now safely try setting and querying the relationships we set:

```
-- Create the relationships
company(Jayant, OZApps)
language(CoronaSDK, Lua)
language(GiderosStudio, Lua)
language(Moai, Lua)
language(XCode, ObjectiveC)

-- Query the relationships
print(is_language(CoronaSDK, ObjectiveC))
print(is_company(Jack, OZApps))
print(is_company(Jayant, OZApps))
```

This could be daunting, especially given that this is actually quite advanced-level manipulation of metatables. However, it also demonstrates how metatables can be used to change the way the app works with Lua.

But What's the Object?

In the preceding exercise, we had a bit of fun with metatables and created our own metafunctions to manage the objects. Depending on how you use them, metatables can be useful in your apps. Next, I'll discuss another thing that is most certainly useful in your apps: working with objects. Before we embark on making objects, however, let's look at what objects are and how they are managed in Lua.

Here are some important things to remember about objects:

- All Lua objects are tables.
- All objects that have functions have them as their member functions.
- Objects can have a custom metatable.

Using these few bits of information, let's create an object:

```
vehicle = {}
function vehicle:isVehicle()
    print("Yes!")
end
```

```
vehicle:isVehicle()

car = {}
function car:name()
    print("Car")
end

car:name()

carTable= { __index = vehicle}
setmetatable(car, carTable)

car:isVehicle()
car:name()

vehicle:name()
```

In terms of an object-oriented language, a *virtual* (or *abstract*) class has functions that are common, and each object that inherits from this class (see Figure 6-1) has all the functions of the class. Further, you can add more functions that are specific for the new inherited class, as shown in Figure 6-2.

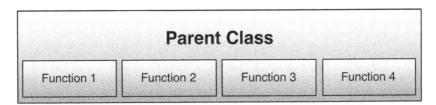

Figure 6-1. An abstract or virtual (parent) class

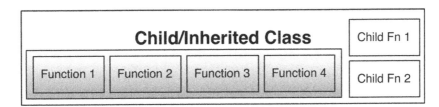

Figure 6-2. An inherited or child class

In the preceding code example, we create a virtual class called vehicle and add the function isVehicle as a member function of the class; the function prints Yes when called. Then we create a new object called car, which has a member function called name that prints Car when called. Let's revisit that piece of code:

```
vehicle = {}
function vehicle:isVehicle()
    print("Yes!")
end
```

```
vehicle:isVehicle()

car = {}
function car:name()
    print("Car")
end
carTable= {__index = vehicle}
setmetatable(car, carTable)

truck = {}
function truck:name()
    print("Truck")
end
truckTable = {__index = vehicle}
setmetatable(truck,truckTable)
```

This way, we can create multiple vehicle objects. To make it easier, we can create a *factory function*. This is like a factory that will create objects en masse.

```
function newObject()
    local newVehicle = {}
    local theTable = { __index = vehicle }
    setmetatable(newVehicle, theTable)
    return newVehicle
end
```

So, every time we call the function, we get a new object that is of type vehicle. We can also use this function to set the default values of the object, such as the name of the vehicle in the preceding sample.

```
Vehicle = {}
function Vehicle:isVehicle()
    print("yes")
end

function newObject(theName)
    local newVehicle = {}
    newVehicle._name = theName
    setmetatable(newVehicle, {__index=Vehicle})

    function newVehicle:name()
        print(self._name)
    end

    return newVehicle
end

car = newObject("Car")
truck = newObject("Truck")
car:name()
truck:name()
car:isVehicle()
```

Summary

In this chapter, we had a look at coroutines, which are the equivalent of threading for Lua. Coroutines are like subroutines that we can call and exit from in between the call, or resume from at the last point from which we exited.

We also had an advanced look at tables and metatables, and how they help us change or alter the behavior of the tables, including using them to create Lua objects.

With this chapter, we conclude our brief look at Lua; I hope you are now ready to use Lua for coding. The next chapter offers various tips and tricks for working with Lua.

Chapter 7

Tips and Tricks

The dilemma that many developers face is, as the old saying goes, there are many ways to skin a cat. In simple terms, while there are many ways to achieve an outcome, many developers face the issue of how to and where to start. This chapter will help you with those starting points. It will offer the tips and tricks that can be applied across most of the frameworks. The main differences to note are the native display objects as used by the frameworks and some quirks associated with those.

Generic Lua Functions

This section addresses some generic functions that help developers and can be used across all frameworks. Most of these are related to tables for storage, retrieval, and indexing, and math relevant to game development.

Using the printf Function

Lua has a `print` function, but it does not allow for formatted output like the C `printf` does. It is always nice to have outputs that are formatted and read like a sentence, as opposed to pieces of information stuck together. "There are 5 boys and 4 girls in the Math class" rather than "Boys: 5 Girls: 3, Class: Math" which could have been outputted using the code

```
print("Boys:", boys, "Girls:", girls, "Class:", className)
```

The `printf` function is quite simple, and can be used as follows:

```
function printf(format, ...)
  print(string.format(format, ...))
end
```

Here's an example of the function in use:

```
local boys = 5
local girls = 3
local className = "Math"
print("Boys:", boys, "Girls:", girls, "Class:", className)
printf("There are %d boys and %d girls in the %s class", boys, girls, className)
```

Counting the Number of Elements in a Table

Tables were introduced in Chapter 2. Tables that are stored as arrays can return the number of elements present via the # (length-of) operator. But when dealing with tables that are not arrays or a combination of arrays, this functionality does not work as expected. To remedy this, we can write a quick function to get the length of any table type:

```
function tableLen(theTable)
  local count = 0
  for i,j in pairs(theTable) do
    count = count + 1
  end
  return count
end
```

We simply iterate through every element in the table, increment our count variable, and then return the count value as a result.

Using IsEmpty

Sometimes, you want to know if a variable is empty. But the definition of *empty* depends on the type of variable it is. A numeric variable holding a zero value would be considered empty, a string with no characters would be empty, a table with no elements would be empty, and all of these, if nil, could also be considered empty. We can use the function tableLen (which we just created in the preceding example) to determine the length of a table-type variable.

```
function isEmpty(var)
    if var == nil then return true end

    local varType = type(var)

    if varType == "number" and var == 0 then
        return true
    elseif varType == "string" and #var == 0 then
        return true
    elseif varType == "table" and tableLen(var)==0 then
        return true
    end

    return false
end
```

Knowing the Index of an Element

When working with a table (array object), we can get the element if we know the index of the element (e.g., if we have a list of names and we know that the fifth element is Jayant, then we can access it as arrTable[5]). However, there are cases when we would have no clue about the index, but might know the value. If we wanted to know what element in the table has the value of Jayant, we can use the indexOf function:

```
function indexOf(arrTable, theValue)
    for i, j in pairs(arrTable) do
        if j == theValue then
            return i
        end
    end
end
```

This will also work for non-array tables, but the return value will not be a numeric index, but a key of type string.

Determining Whether a Table Is an Array

There could be a scenario when you need to know if a table is a hash table or an array. We can determine this because the # operator returns the number of elements in an array, whereas for a table it returns 0 or the count of elements that it can determine as an array. A non-array table will be one that has more elements than the # operator can return.

```
function isArray(arrTable)
  return #arrTable == tableLen(arrTable)
end
```

Setting Default Values

If you have been developing with other languages, you might be used to checking for values and ensuring that they are set, as missing values can cause errors. You may be familiar with something like the following:

```
function foo(bar)
  if bar == nil then
    bar = "Untitled"
  end

  print("We got :", bar)
end
```

While working with Lua, this is not really an issue; we can get rid of all these conditional statements like so

```
function foo(bar, baz, faz)
  local bar = bar or "Bar"
  local baz = baz or "Baz"
  local faz = faz or "Faz"

  print("We got", bar, baz, faz)
end
```

Notice that we set the default values of variables by simply using or. A good idea is to use a local variable with the same name.

Not only is this helpful in assigning default values to variables that are unassigned (i.e. are nil), but also in creating blank tables, as you can use it like this:

```
local theTable = theTable or {}
```

Copying Tables

One word of caution while copying tables is that tables are like pointers, so when you assign a new variable with the table variable, it just makes a copy to the location where the table is stored, not a copy of the table.

```
function copyTable(table 1)
  local res = {}
  for i, j in pairs(table 1) do
    res[i] = j
  end
  return res
end
```

Please note that the preceding function is called a *shallow copy*, as it does not copy the embedded tables, so if the table has any nested tables, those are not copied. To make an exact copy, we need to perform what is called a *deep copy*.

Performing a Deep Copy

As mentioned in the preceding section, to completely create a copy of a table, we need to perform a deep copy. This will copy all elements recursively and also set the metatables as required. Normal copying does not set the metatable.

```
function deepcopy(t)
  if type(t) ~= 'table' then
    return t
  end
  local mt = getmetatable(t)
  local res = {}
  for k,v in pairs(t) do
    if type(v) == 'table' then
      v = deepcopy(v)
```

```
    end
    res[k] = v
  end
  setmetatable(res,mt)
  return res
end
```

> **Note**   If you have cyclic references in your tables, these are not handled by this function.

Copying Array Components

In some cases you might want to only copy the array component, not the entire table, as follows:

```
function copyList(table 1)
  local res = {}
  for i,j in ipairs(table 1) do
    res[i] = j
  end
  return res
end
```

Just in case you think that the two preceding functions are the same, note that in the first function we are using the function pairs, while in the second one we are using ipairs.

Copying Non-Array Components

If you need to copy the non-array component and leave the array alone, then you can do so with the following:

```
function copyHash(table 1)
  local res = {}
  local size = #table 1
    for i, j in pairs(table 1) do
      if type(j) ~= "number" or i<= 0 or i> size then
        res[i] = j
      end
    end
  return res
end
```

Merging Two Tables

If you need to merge two tables, you can do so using

```
function mergeTables(table 1, table 2)
  for i,j in pairs(table 1) do
    table 2[i] = j
  end
end
```

Note that if you have array values, the values in table 2 will overwrite these.

Determining Whether a Value Exists in a Table

If you need to check if a value exists in a table or not, here's how you can do it:

```
function isValueInTable(theValue, theTable)
  for i,j in pairs(theTable) do
    if j == theValue then
      return true
    end
  end
  return false
end
```

Finding the Difference Between Two Tables

In your game, you might have the player collect items, so that you can display the items collected at the end of the level. But you might also want to display the items that the could have collected but did not. An easy way to do so is to use two tables—one with the items collected and one with all of the items that could have been collected. Then, using the following function, you can determine the items that exist in table 2 but not in table 1:

```
function differenceOfTables(table1, table2)
  local res = {}
  for i, j in pairs(table1) do
    if not isValueInTable(j,table2) then
      table.insert(res, j)
    end
  end
end
```

Getting a Return Value As a Table

In some cases you expect to get a table, but if the return value is a number or a string, it just breaks your code and causes errors. You can ensure that you get returned a table value with the following:

```
function getTable(theValue)
  if type(theValue) == "table" then
```

```
    return theValue
  else
  return {theValue}
  end
end
```

Sorting on Elements of a Table

The `table.sort` function is a very handy function for sorting tables with single dimensions and that have numeric or string values. If we were given a table that was a record with the structure as follows, the generic `sort` function would not work:

```
{
name = "Jayant",
subject = "IT",
grade = "A"
}
```

We might want to sort these records according to one of the three fields: `grade`, `name`, or `subject`. As this is sorting on more than one dimension, the `sort` function would not work.

We sort a table using the function `table.sort(theTable, functionToSort)`. In the case of this example, we can use

```
function sortOnField(theTable, theField)
  table.sort(theTable,
    function(a,b)
        return a[theField] < b[theField]
    end)
end
```

If the table is a multidimensional array, you can simply pass the dimension instead of the field name, and it should work.

Determining Frequency of an Item in a Table

The table can be used as a storage space. For example, you could save all the items that the player collects during the game to be used in calculating an end-of-level score, using a multiplier based on the collected items. To do so, you might want to know how many items of a particular type there are in the table. If these were plain numbers, you might want to know the frequency of the numbers in the table.

```
function getCount(theTable, theValue)
  local count = 0
  for i,j in pairs(theTable)
    if j == theValue then
      count = count + 1
    end
  end
  return count
end
```

Converting Numbers into Roman Numerals

If you ever need to translate number into Roman numerals, you use the toRoman function, as follows:

```
function toRoman(theNumber)
  local res = ""
  local romans = {
      {1000, "M"}, {900, "CM"}, {500, "D"}, {400, "CD"}, {100, "C"},
      {90,   "XC"}, {50, "L"}, {40, "XL"}, {10, "X"}, {9, "IX"},
     {5,    "V"}, {4, "IV"}, {1, "I"}
     }
  local k = theNumber
  for i,j in ipairs(romans) do
    theVal, theLet = unpack(j)
    while k >= theVal do
      k = k - theVal
      res = res .. theLet
    end
  end
  return res
end
```

Creating Linked Lists

There are more efficient ways to manage data in Lua than the ones we have seen so far. However, if you would like to implement linked lists in Lua, here's how (note that you need to place this code in a file called linkedlist.lua):

```
local _lists = {}

function _lists:create(theVal)
  local root = { value = theVal,  next = nil}
  setmetatable(root, {__index = _lists })
  return root
end

function _lists:append(theVal)
  local _node = { value = theVal, next = nil}
  if(self.value == nil) then
    self.value = _node.value
    self.next = _node.next
    return
  end

  local currNode = self

  while currNode.next ~= nil do
    currNode = currNode.next
  end
```

```
  currNode.next = _node

  return
end

function _lists:delete(theVal)
  if type(theVal) == "table" then
    print("Cannot remove a table value from the list")
    return
  end

  local currNode = self

  if(self.value == theVal) then
    local temp = self.next
    if temp ~= nil then
      self.value = temp.value
      self.next = temp.next
    else
      self.value = nil
      self.next = nil
    end
    return
  end

  lastVisited = currNode

  while currNode ~= nil do
    if currNode.value == theVal then
      lastVisited.next = currNode.next
      currNode = nil
      return
    end

    lastVisited = currNode
    currNode = currNode.next
  end

  return

end

function _lists:displayList()
  local currNode = self
  if(self.value == nil) then
    print ("No entries in this list")
    return
  end
  while currNode ~= nil do
    print(currNode.value)
    currNode = currNode.next
  end
end
```

Expanding Tokenized Variables

In many RPG-style games, while the story is unfolding, you may be asked for your name, after which the story continues using your name from that point forward. One way to manage this is to store the name in a variable and templatize it using the `printf` function, as follows:

```
printf("The %s Wizard looks at you and says, %s, you are worthy", wizardAdjective, yourName)
```

This works, but it requires that you place the variables at precise locations so that they match each of the tokens required. If you missed the `wizardAdjective`, you would receive an error as the code requires two additional arguments, not one. If you had them accidentally swapped, and yourName was Damon and the `wizardAdjective` was `apprentice` ,then it would display as The Damon Wizard looks at you and says, apprentice, you are worthy, instead of the correct output of, The apprentice Wizard looks at you and says, Damon, you are worthy.

```
local sentence = expandVars("The $adj $char1 looks at you and says, $name, you are $result",
{adj="glorious", name="Jayant", result="the Overlord", char1="King"})
print(sentence)
```

The entire sentence can be built as required. The only catch is that if the variable cannot be expanded, it will show up as the variable name itself, e.g. `result` instead of `the Overlord`.

```
function expandVars(tmpl,t)
  return (tmpl:gsub('%$([%a_][%w_]*)',t))
end
```

You can also use it like this:

```
print(expandVars('welcome $USER?',os.getenv))
```

Padding Zeros to a String

In many games, it can be interested to display scores with leading zeros (e.g., 0003 instead of 3)—for instance, to make the score look like old-style games, many of which used this type of display. This can be used to create many interesting effects—for example, you could have an odometer-type display roll the numbers as the score increases.

Here's how you can pad numbers with zeros:

```
function paddWithZero(theNumber, numOfDigits)
  return string.rep("0", numOfDigits - string.len(theNumber)) .. theNumber
end
```

Getting the Month As a String

There are times when you might want the name of the month as a string, as shown in the code below. You can also adapt this to have the full names (January, February, etc.), and then return the first three characters if you want the short name.

```
function getMonthName(theMonth)
  local months = {"Jan", "Feb", "Mar", "Apr", "May", "Jun", "Jul", "Aug", "Sep", "Oct",
"Nov", "Dec"}
  return months[theMonth]
end
```

Accessing Strings Like an Array

In some other programming languages, string can be accessed using square brackets. However, in Lua, we use the `string.sub` function. The flexibility of Lua allows for a few alterations and provides us this functionality such as

```
getmetatable('').__index = function(str,i)
    return string.sub(str,i,i)
end
```

After we have declared this function, we can test it out quickly, as follows:

```
theString = "abcdef"
print(theString[4])
```

Finding the Distance Between Two Points in One or Two Dimensions

This is almost a no-brainer. When dealing with two points on the same axis, we can use simple subtraction to find the distance between them, like so:

```
function getDistance(pos1, pos2)
  return pos1 - pos2
end
```

However, if we're trying to find the distance between two points, we have to resort to trigonometry. Here's an example:

```
function getDistanceBetween(ptA, ptB)
  return math.sqrt((ptA.x - ptB.x)^2 + (ptA.y - ptB.y)^2)
end
```

Determining the Angle Between Two Points

If you're creating a tower defense–style game, for example, you might need to turn a player, gun, or other object to point in the direction of an approaching enemy or rotate a the object to a point where the screen has been touched. To do this, you need to determine the angle between two points: the center point where the turret or player is, and the point of touch or where the enemy currently is. The angle between two points can be determined again using trigonometry, as follows:

```
function angleBetween(ptA, ptB)
    local angle = math.deg(math.atan2(ptA.y - ptB.y, ptA.x - ptB.x))
    angle = angle + 90
    return angle
end
```

Keeping a Number in a Given Range

There could be a scenario when you might want to keep a value within a given range. In this way, rather than having several if...then statements for each value, we can create a function that keeps the value within a range.

```
function keepInRange(theVal, low, high)
  return math.min(math.max(low, theVal), high)
end
```

The alternative method, using if...then statements, looks like this:

```
function _keepInRange(theVal, low, high)
  if theVal < low then
    return low
  end
  if theVal > high then
    return high
  end
  return theVal
end
```

Performing Linear Interpolation

No matter what framework you use for your game, the game might have some form of transition—for example, a fade in or a movement. The simplest form way to accomplish a transition is to apportion a value over time equally (linearly). Using the following function, you can retrieve a value over a given time by designating the starting and ending values. Here, we are calling the retrieved value thePercent, which is a value between 0 and 1, indicating the state of progress—0 being the start and 1 being completed.

```
function getLinearInterpolation(theStartValue, theEndValue, thePercent)
  return (theStartValue + (theEndValue - theStartValue) * thePercent)
end
```

Getting the Sign of a Value

Sometimes it's important to determine if a value is a negative number of not. It is easy to check whether a number is less than 0, but when performing a calculation, it might not be possible to use if...then statements. Instead, you can create a function. To keep things organized, you should add it to the math namespace.

```
function math.sign(theValue)
 return theValue > 0 and 1 or theValue < 0 and -1 or 0
end
```

The preceding function is equivalent to

```
function math.sign(theValue)
  if theValue > 0 then
    return 1
  elseif theValue < 0 then
    return -1
  else
    return 0
  end
end
```

Collisions

One of the basic things that you will need for your games is the ability to check if two objects on the screen have collided. For example, in PAC-MAN, you would need to determine collisions between PAC-MAN and the ghosts and fruit. In Space Invaders, you would need to determine collisions between alien bullets and the player's shield and the player itself. However one point to note is that real world objects are not rectangular stamps, and therefore are not always rectangular in shape. Therefore, we have various methods, described in this section, which we can use to check for collisions between two circles, two rectangles, a rectangle and a circle, and so on.

Using isPointInRect

This is the most commonly used function in the UIs that we use every day. Each button in a UI has a rectangular boundary, and programs check whether a touch point is inside of this boundary to determine if that button was tapped or not.

The way it works is that the point defined by x and y should be contained in the rectangle—that is the x value should be greater than or equal to the value of the rectangle's x-coordinate, and the point x should be less than or equal to the rectangle's x point plus the width (and similarly on the y axis too).

```
function isPointInRect( x, y, rectX, rectY, rectWidth, rectHeight )
  if x >= rectX and x <= rectX + rectWidth and
     y >= rectY and y<= rectY + rectHeight then
    return true
  end

  return false
end
```

Using pointInCircle

In the tower-defense genre of games, each defense tower or structure has a range; this range is displayed in the form of a circle around the center of the structure. We can check whether the midpoint of the enemy is inside of this circle to determine if the enemy is in the range of this structure or not, as follows:

```
function pointInCircle( ptX, ptY, circleX, circleY, radius )
  local dx = ptX - circleX
  local dy = ptY - circleY
  if dx * dx + dy * dy <= radius * radius then
    return true
  end

  return false
end
```

Determining Whether a Rectangle Is Within Another Rectangle

This can be useful in games where you have to wait for an object to reach a safe zone. in such a case, when the second rectangle is completely contained in the first one, it can be determined that the event has taken place.

```
function rectInRect( rect1X, rect1Y, rect1Width, rect1Height, rect2X, rect2Y, rect2Width,
rect2Height )
  if rect1X >= rect2X and rect1X + rect1Width <= rect2X + rect2Width and
    rect1Y >= rect2Y and rect1Y + rect1Height <= rect2Y + rect2Height then
    return true
  end

  return false
end
```

Determining Whether a Circle Is Within Another Circle

Similarly, you might want to check whether a circular shape is completely contained inside another one. Here's the function to use for this:

```
function circleInCircle( circle1X, circle1Y, circle1Radius, circle2X, circle2Y, circle2Radius )
  local dx = circle1X - circle2X
  local dy = circle1Y - circle2Y
  local rx = circle1Radius - circle2Radius
  if dx * dx + dy * dy <= rx * rx then
    return true
  end
  return false
end
```

Identifying Overlapping Rectangles

The rectOverlaps function can be used to determine if two rectangles are overlapping. For example, this could be used to determine whether the player is in contact with a spike or some other object on the screen, and trigger an event accordingly.

```
function rectOverlaps( rect1X, rect1Y, rect1Width, rect1Height, rect2X, rect2Y, rect2Width,
rect2Height )
  if rect1X + rect1Width >= rect2X and
     rect2X + rect2Width <= rect1X and
     rect1Y + rect1Height >= rect2Y and
     rect2Y + rect2Height <= rect1Y then
       return true
  end

  return false
end
```

Identifying Overlapping Circles

This can be used to determine if two circles are overlapping.

```
function circleOverlaps( circle1X, circle1Y, circle1Radius, circle2X, circle2Y, circle2Radius )
  local dx = circle1X - circle2X
  local dy = circle1Y - circle2Y
  local rx = circle1Radius + circle2Radius
  if dx * dx + dy * dy <= rx * rx then
    return true
  end

  return false
end
```

Determining Whether a Circle Overlaps a Rectangle

This can help determine if a circle overlaps a rectangle.

```
function circleOverlapsRectangle( rectX, rectY, rectWidth, rectHeight, circleX, circleY,
circleRadius )

  if rectX <= circleX and rectX + rectWidth >= circleX then
    if rectY + rectHeight >= circleY - circleRadius and
       rectY <= circleY + circleRadius then
         return true
    else
         return false
    end
  elseif rectX <= circleY and rectX + rectHeight >= circleY then
```

```
    if rectX + rectWidth >= circleX - circleRadius and
       rectX <= circleX + circleRadius then
          return true
    else
          return false
    end
  else
    if rectX < circleX then
      if rectY < circleY then
        return pointInCircle( rectX + rectWidth, rectY + rectHeight,
            circleX, circleY, circleRadius )
      else
        return pointInCircle( rectX + rectWidth, rectY,
            circleX, circleY, circleRadius )
      end
    else
      if rectX < circleY then
        return pointInCircle( rectX, rectY + rectHeight,
             circleX, circleY, circleRadius )
      else
        return pointInCircle( rectX, rectY, circleX, circleY, circleRadius )
      end
    end
  end
end
```

Using pointInTriangle

In some cases, triangles will suit your needs better than rectangles or circles. There are plenty of methods for checking the bounding values of a triangle. However, the one described following is the simplest. It simply extends lines from each of the triangle's vertices to the point we are checking, thereby dividing the triangle into three triangles; it then calculates the area of each of these triangles. If totalArea is the same as the area of the three new triangles created, then the point can be said to be in the bounding triangle. Here's the function that determines whether a point is inside a triangle:

```
function triangleArea( pt1x, pt1y, pt2x, pt2y, pt3x, pt3y )
  local dA = pt1x - pt3x
  local dB = pt1y - pt3y
  local dC = pt2x - pt3x
  local dD = pt2y - pt3y
  return 0.5 * math.abs( ( dA * dD ) - ( dB * dC ) )
end

function pointInTriangle(ptx, pty, pt1x, pt1y, pt2x, pt2y, pt3x, pt3y)
  local areaT = triangleArea(pt1x, pt1y, pt2x, pt2y, pt3x, pt3y)
  local areaA = triangleArea(ptx, pty, pt1x, pt1y, pt2x, pt2y)
  local areaB = triangleArea(ptx, pty, pt3x, pt3y, pt2x, pt2y)
  local areaC = triangleArea(ptx, pty, pt1x, pt1y, pt3x, pt3y)
  return (areaT == (areaA + areaB + areaC))
end
```

Using pointInPolygon

You can also determine whether a point is inside a polygon. The following code (adapted from the functions in the articles "Determining if a point lies on the interior of a polygon," by Paul Bourke [http://paulbourke.net/geometry/insidepoly/] and "Point in Polygon Strategies," by Eric Haynes [http://erich.realtimerendering.com/ptinpoly/] enables you to do this:

```lua
function pointInPolygon(x,y,poly)
  n = #poly
  inside = false

  p1x,p1y = poly[1], poly[2]
  for i=1,n-2, 2 do
    p2x,p2y = poly[i+2], poly[i+3]
    if y > math.min(p1y,p2y) then
      if y <= math.max(p1y,p2y) then
        if x <= math.max(p1x,p2x) then
          if p1y ~= p2y then
            xinters = (y-p1y)*(p2x-p1x)/(p2y-p1y)+p1x
          end
          if p1x == p2x or x <= xinters then
            inside = not inside
          end
        end
      end
    end
    p1x,p1y = p2x,p2y
  end
  return inside
end
```

Other Generic Functions

This section examines some additional functions that you might find useful in your Lua development projects.

Comparing Boolean Values

Another common task that you might want to accomplish in Lua is comparing Boolean values. At first glance, you might think that these two commands are the same:

```lua
if someValueOn then print("On") end
```

and

```lua
if someValueOn==true then print("On") end
```

In the first case, someValueOn will return true as long as someValueOn is not nil or false. However, if someValueOn were −1 or "Off", the statement would still evaluate to true, whereas in the second line, someValueOn==true would return a true only if the value were true, and in no other circumstance.

Translating C/Java Like Loops to Lua

If you come from a Java/C/C++ or JavaScript background, you should be used to loops like this:

```
for (initialize; condition; iteration){
}
```

where multiple values can be set in initialize, each separated with a comma. The condition can be made up of a compound condition, and the iterator can have multiple operations.

For example, consider this loop:

```
score =  110   --something
for (i=20, k = 120; i> -1 && score < 100; --i, --k ){
}
```

In Lua, this would be written as follows:

```
score = 110
k = 120
for i=20, 0, -1 do
  if score < 100 then
      break
  end

  -- Do whatever here
  k = k - 1
end
```

Applying Friction to an Object

The easiest way to move an object around the screen is to move it at constant speed (i.e., increase or decrease the axis value by the same value over time). This behavior is of course quite unrealistic. For example, in the real world, when a box is pushed across the hall, it moves fast at first and then it gradually slows down until it finally stops. One shortcut that a lot of developers prefer is to use a physics object; it works, but we can simulate friction without using a physics object with the help of a little math.

```
local speed = 20
local friction = 0.9
repeat
  print(speed)
  speed = speed * friction
until speed <= 1
```

Depending on the framework, you can reduce the y value by this speed value. This will give the illusion of a slide or flick upward with friction. The object will slide quickly at first, and then slow down till it comes to a complete halt.

Note that this example uses a repeat loop. If you are working with display objects, you need to have a nonblocking mechanism that allows for updates to be made. In other words, you need to use something like the draw function, which is called every so often, or the enterFrame events, so that the new position is set at each frame, and you can see the transition of the object. If you want the transition to be super-smooth, try a maximum value of 0.99. This can be used to simulate flicks, sliding an object across the screen with inertia, and so on.

Simulating a Jack-in-the-Box

When you open a jack-in-the-box, the spring-loaded "Jack" springs out with full force, and then bobs more slowly over time, until it stops. We can simulate a jack-in-the-box with the help of a little bit of trigonometry.

> **Note**   Since we aren't using a GUI-based framework, the code here is generic and will produce x and y values that can be applied to display objects in a GUI to simulate the visual effect. For the purpose of this function, however, we shall display the values to the console.

```
frequency  = 5.0
amplitude  = 35
decay      = 1.0
time       = 0

function jackInTheBox(time)
  y = amplitude * math.cos(frequency * time * 2 * math.pi) / math.exp(decay * time)
  return y
end
```

To use this function, we need to call the function and pass it a time value. If you were to use this in a loop, you would increment the time variable in increments (e.g., of 0.01, or another value that suits the delay of your calling function).

Using a Sine Scroller

The preceding function makes use of a cosine wave. Similarly, you can vary the parameters and even use sine waves. These were most commonly used in the 1980s on sine scrollers and to animate waves of attacking aliens (e.g., in games like R-Type, Zynaps, and Crosswise). In a similar fashion, the following function shall calculate the x and y values, which can be used to set the x- and y-coordinates of a display object to simulate the visual effect.

```
amplitude = 55
frequency = 0.6
speed     = frequency

function sineScroll(time)
    y = (amplitude * math.sin(frequency * time * 2 * math.pi) )
    return y
end
```

To make the object move, you would also need to manipulate the x position. With every call of this function, you'd alter the x value by either increasing it or decreasing it by the frequency (speed). To understand better how the amplitude and frequency would affect the output, you can play with the settings. As in the previous function, a good time increment to start with is 0.01.

Placing a Tile on a Board with No Other Tile in the Same Row and Column

Sometimes in a board game you might need to quickly check the board for empty squares, or squares that might share a row or a column. This function will help identify if a tile that we place on the board shares a row or a column with another tile.

```
N = 8
board = {}
for i=1, N do
  board[i] = {}
  for j=1, N do
    board[i][j] = false
  end
end

function allowedAt(x,y)

  for i=1, N do
    if board[x][i] == true or board[i][y] == true then
      return false
    end
  end

  return true
end
```

This can be expanded to solve other problems like the N-Queen, or the N-Rook.

Using Arrays to Output Large Amounts of Text Using Templates

The children's poem "There Was an Old Lady Who Swallowed a Fly," in which a woman swallows increasingly larger animals to catch the previously swallowed one, is a good example to rebuild using arrays. We have a series of animals that she swallowed and each has a corresponding output line.

```
animals = {
  {"fly"   , "But I don't know why she swallowed a fly, \nperhaps she will die"},
  {"spider", "That wriggled and jiggled and tickled inside her"},
  {"bird"  , "quite absurd"},
  {"cat"   , "Fancy that"},
  {"dog"   , "what a hog"},
  {"pig"   , "Her mouth was so big"},
  {"goat"  , "she just opened her throat"},
  {"cow"   , "I don't know how"},
  {"donkey", "It was rather wonky"},
  {"horse" , "She's dead, of course!"},
}
line1 = "I knew an old lady who swallowed a %s,"
line2 = " She swallowed the %s to catch the %s,"

function printf(format,  ...)
  print(string.format(format,  ...))
end

for i=1, #animals do
  if i==1 then
    printf(line1, animals[i][1])
  else
    printf(line2, animals[i][1], animals[i-1][1])
  end
  print(animals[i][2])
end
```

Parameter Handling

You can write functions to break longer and repetitive tasks making them modular. To make them work for you, these functions need to be sent parameters. In some C-type languages, functions with the same name but different parameter types can be declared. For example, you can have this:

```
function one(int, int)
```

and also this:

```
function one (int)
```

With Lua, the function can accept anything, including varargs, as mentioned earlier when we saw the printf function. There are three types of parameters you can pass to the function:

- *A primitive*: This can be a number, a string, a Boolean, or nil.

- *A table*: This can be an array or a hash table.

- *A vararg*: This is an arbitrary number of arguments, represented by three dots (...).

In the function, you can check for the type of parameter by using the type function, which will return the type of variable the parameter is.

Fixed Parameters

The default convention for passing parameters to a function is using fixed parameters. These tell the function how many parameters there will be and the order of the parameters. When using fixed parameters, you know what to expect from the function, and based on the values of the parameters passed, you can take appropriate action.

```
function listParams(one, two, three)
  print("We got :", one, two, three)
  if one=="one" then
    print("Something")
  else
    print("Nothing")
  end
end
```

While calling this function, the first parameter has to be one, the second two, and the third three.

Variable Parameters

You can use variable parameters (passed as a table) when we want to pass multiple parameters. An alternative would be to use varargs; both approaches act as a table of parameters.

```
function arrayParams(arrTable)
  print("We got :")
  for i, j in pairs(arrTable) do
    print("", i, j)
  end
end
```

Variable Named Parameters

You can use variable named parameters when you do not know what is passed, but you want to check for certain parameters. This is also a table like in the example above, but instead of having table items, it has named items, which can be referenced by name rather than an index.

```
function namedArrayParams(arrTable)
  if arrTable.debug == true then
    print("We are now in Debug Mode")
  else
    print("We are not in Debug Mode")
  end
  if arrTable.color then
    print("We got the color as ", arrTable.color)
  else
    print("We shall use the default color")
  end
end
```

The way to pass parameters to this type of function is as follows:

```
namedArrayParams({debug=true, 56,"One", color="red", false})
```

> **Note** When calling a function in Lua with a table—for example,
> someFunction({one=1,two=2})—you can also call it as follows: someFunction {one=1, two=2}.
> This can only be used if the table is the only parameter being passed to the function. It cannot be used
> for any type of parameter other than a table value being passed.

Using Varargs

Varargs are similar to variable parameters, as described previously, but instead of a variable name, they are defined by a special combination of three dots. Though they may seem a lot like table arrays, they are different in the way that you can interact with them.

```
function passvarargs(...)
  local a, b = ...
  print(a, b)
end
```

a and b get the first and the second parameter passed; this is not possible with table arrays.

You can create a list of elements from the varargs by simply enclosing them in curly brackets, like so: local tbl = {...}. This is now a table array.

With the return... command, you can return all of the received vararg parameters.

> **Note** As mentioned earlier, the ... is also available as a named variable, arg, of type table, which
> is the equivalent of {...}.

Parsing a List of Passed Parameters

Some functions have optional parameters, like so:

```
function addObjectAtPosition( [parent,] object, [x [, y [,position ] ] ] )
```

The values in square brackets are optional. In this function, the first parameter (parent) is optional, the second (object) is not, and the third and fourth (x and y) are optional (but if either x or y is set, the other must be set as well). The last parameter(position) is optional.

Parsing this could get a bit difficult, but Lua makes it easy. Here's how it can be done. We know that the parent and the object are table-type variables, x and y would be numeric, and the position is a string. First, we check for the number of parameters passed—if only one is passed, we know it must be the required parameter, object. If two are passed and the second one is of type table, the first one is the parent and the second the object. If the second is of type `string`, then it is `position`. Otherwise, it is the x position.

```lua
function addObjectAtPosition(param1, param2, param3, param4, param5)
  local  lstPassed = {param1, param2, param3, param4, param5}
  -- set the default values
  local parent = nil -- or default value if you want to set any
  local object = nil
  local x =0
  local y = 0
  local position = "left"

  local numPassed = #lstPassed
  if numPassed == 1 then
    object = lstPassed [1]
  elseif numPassed == 2 then
    if type(lstPassed[2])=="number" then
      x = lstPassed[2]
      object = lstPassed[1]
    elseif type(lstPassed[2])=="string" then
      position = lstPassed[2]
      object = lstPassed[1]
    elseif type(lstPassed[2])=="table" then
      object = lstPassed[2]
      parent = lstPassed[1]
    end
  elseif numPassed == 3 then
    if type(lstPassed[2])=="number" then
      object = lstPassed[1]
      x = lstPassed[2]
      y = lstPassed[3]
    else
      parent = lstPassed[1]
      object = lstPassed[2]
      x = lstPassed[3]
    end
  elseif numPassed == 4 then
    if type(lstPassed[4])=="string" then
      object = lstPassed[1]
      x = lstPassed[2]
      y = lstPassed[3]
      position = lstpassed[4]
    else
      parent = lstPassed[1]
      object = lstPassed[2]
      x = lstPassed[3]
      y = lstpassed[4]
    end
  else
    parent = param1
    object = param2
    x = param3
```

```
    y = param4
    position = param5
  end
end
```

This can help create very flexible parsing methods. The idea is to check the type of parameters to determine the parameters passed. While the preceding example was somewhat complex, there are simpler examples. For instance, take the following function, in which the first parameter is optional:

```
parseParams( [parent, ] theMessage, theTime )
```

We can easily parse this as follows:

```
function parseParams( param1, param2, param3 )
  local lstPassed = {param1, param2, param3}
  local parent = nil
  if type(lstPassed[1]) == "table" then
    parent = lstPassed[1]
    table.remove(lstPassed, 1)
  end
  theMessage = lstPassed[1]
  theTime = lstPassed[2]
end
```

In this function, if the first parameter is the parent, we remove it from the table, and the rest of the function can access the parameters as required.

Making Read-Only Tables

There may be times when you want portions of your table to be read-only and other portions modifiable. This is all fine till the numerous if...then statements start to plague your code. The metatable modifications make for a lot of interesting hacks and tricks.

```
function readonlyTable(theTable)
  return setmetatable({}, {
    __index = table,
    __newindex = function (table, key, value)
      --Do not update or create the key with the value
    end,
    __metatable = false
  })
end
```

If you want to keep a portion of your table unlocked, you can keep a table-type member that is not locked via the readonlyTable function, and you can add data to this as follows:

```
local myRO = readonlyTable{
    name = "Jayant",
    device = "iOS",
```

```
      model = "iPhone5",
      apps = {},
}
```

With this, the name, device, and model cannot be changed; however, the apps table can be altered using the various functions.

```
print(myRO.name)
RO.name = "Something Else"
print(myRO.name)
```

If for some particular reason you want to overwrite a value in the read-only table, there is a way (but if you have to use it, then the whole point of using read-only tables would be lost). The way to do this is to bypass the metatable functions of __newindex and set the value directly, as follows:

```
function overrideValue(theTable, theKey, theValue)
   rawset(theTable, theKey, theValue)
end
```

Implementing a Stack

In your game you might want to create a stack, place objects on the stack (i.e., *push* them onto the stack), and later remove them (i.e., *pop* them from the stack). The usage scenarios for a stack can vary based on how you write the logic and code. In some scenarios, you can place all the items you collected on a stack, and then at the end of the level, you can award points based on what was collected, while removing the items from the stack. To try out this example, place this code into a file called stacks.lua.

```
local _stack = {}

-- Create a table with stack functions
function _stack:create()

  local theStack = {}
  theStack._entries = {}

  -- push a value onto the stack
  function theStack:push(...)
    if  ... then
      local tArgs = {...}
      -- add these values
      for i,v in pairs(tArgs) do
        table.insert(self._entries, v)
      end
    end
  end


  -- pop a number of values from the stack
  function theStack:pop(num)
```

```lua
    -- get num of values from stack
    local num = num or 1

    -- return table
    local entries = {}

    -- get values into entries
    for i = 1, num do
      -- get last entry
      if #self._entries ~= 0 then
        table.insert(entries, self._entries[#self._entries])
        -- remove last value
        table.remove(self._entries)
      else
        break
      end
    end
    -- return unpacked entries
    return unpack(entries)
  end

  -- get the number of entries on the stack
  function theStack:getn()
    return #self._entries
  end

  -- print the list values on the stack
  function theStack:list()
    for i,v in pairs(self._entries) do
      print(i, v)
    end
  end

  return theStack
end
```

And using it is as simple as this:

```lua
myStack = _stack:create()
myStack:push("A","small","world")
print(myStack:pop(2))
myStack:list()
print(myStack:pop(1))
```

Converting Between Parameters and Tables

Sometimes functions take a variable number of parameters and sometimes they take tables. A simple example would be in the case of colors that are specified as a tuple, but in some functions they would be required to be given as r, g, and b values instead of the table.

```
local theColor = {255,0,0}
--[[
  this is easier to specify than
  theColorR = 255
  theColorG = 0
  theColorB = 0
--]]
```

The functions that accept the color generally take four variables, as in the following function:

```
setTheColor(r, g, b, a)
```

theColor, which is a table, cannot be passed to the function, as the function expects numbers, not a table. This is easily fixed with the unpack function, as follows:

```
setTheColor(unpack(theColor))
```

Converting values into a table is perhaps the easiest approach; we can add them to the table using table.insert, like so:

```
table.insert(theTable, param1); table.insert(theTable, param2); table.insert(theTable, param3)
```

or by enclosing them in the curly braces, as follows:

```
theTable = {param1, param2, param3}
```

Vector 2D

This section demonstrates a set of functions that help perform tasks using vectors. This book will not get into explaining vectors; however, if you are looking for some good reading points, the Vectors for Flash site, at http://tonypa.pri.ee/vectors/index.html, is a good starting point. Place this entire code into a file called vectors.lua.

```
_vec2D = {}

function _vec2D:new(x, y)
  local _newVec = {x = x, y = y}
  setmetatable(_newVec, { __index = _vec2D } )
  return _newVec
end

function _vec2D:magnitude()
 return math.sqrt(self.x * self.x + self.y * self.y)
end

function _vec2D:normalize()
  local t = self:magnitude()
  if t > 0 then
    self.x = self.x / t
    self.y = self.y / t
  end
end
```

```
function _vec2D:limit(theLimit)
  if self.x > theLimit then
    self.x = theLimit
  end

  if self.y > theLimit then
      self.y = theLimit
  end
end

function _vec2D:equals(theVec)
  if self.x == theVec.c and self.y == theVec.y then
    return true
  else
    return false
  end
end

function _vec2D:add(theVec)
  self.x = self.x + theVec.x
  self.y = self.y + theVec.y
end

function _vec2D:sub(theVec)
  self.x = self.x - theVec.x
  self.y = self.y - theVec.y
end

function _vec2D:multiply(scalar)
  self.x = self.x * scalar
  self.y = self.y * scalar
end

function _vec2D:divide(scalar)
  self.x = self.x / scalar
  self.y = self.y / scalar
end

function _vec2D:dot(theVec)
  return self.x * theVec.x + self.y * theVec.y
end

function _vec2D:dist()
  return math.sqrt((self.x * self.x) + (self.y * self.y))
end

function _vec2D:Normalize(theVec)
  local tmpVec = _vec2D:new(theVec.x, theVec.y)
  local vecMag = tmpVec:magnitude()
  if vecMag > 0 then
```

```lua
      tmpVec.x = tmpVec.x / vecMag
      tmpVec.y = tmpVec.y / vecMag
    end
    return tmpVec
end

function _vec2D:addVec(theVec, theVec2)
  local tmpVec = Vector2D:new(0,0)
  tmpVec.x = theVec.x + theVec2.x
  tmpVec.y = theVec.y + theVec2.y
  return tmpVec
end

function _vec2D:subVec(theVec, theVec2)
  local tmpVec = Vector2D:new(0,0)
  tmpVec.x = theVec.x - theVec2.x
  tmpVec.y = theVec.y - theVec2.y
  return tmpVec
end

function _vec2D:multiplyVec(theVec, scalar)
  local tmpVec = Vector2D:new(0,0)
  tmpVec.x = theVec.x * scalar
  tmpVec.y = theVec.y * scalar
  return tmpVec
end

function _vec2D:divideVec(theVec, scalar)
  local tmpVec = Vector2D:new(0,0)
  tmpVec.x = theVec.x / scalar
  tmpVec.y = theVec.y / scalar
  return tmpVec
end

function _vec2D:distance(theVec, theVec2)
  return math.sqrt((theVec2.x - theVec1.x)^2 + (theVec2.y - theVec1.y)^2)
end

return _vec2D
```

Summary

The functions described in this chapter represent only a small selection of the functionality you might need when creating your games. Some of the most frequently used functions were included here, and they can be used in many ways. The tips and tricks mentioned in this section are generic and do not rely on any particular framework, which means that they will work with every Lua-based framework mentioned in this book. After you finish reading the next few chapters, which introduce the various frameworks, Chapters 13 and 14 will provide you more details on framework-specific libraries and third-party applications to get things done.

Chapter 8

Corona SDK

If you have embarked on the journey to develop cross-platform apps for mobile devices, you will have heard of Corona SDK, from Corona Labs (previously called Ansca Mobile). It is available for both Windows and Mac OS X (though running it on Wine is not reported as stable). A trial version of Corona SDK allows for unlimited testing and building for the device (although it includes a trial message). Once you purchase a license, you can deploy the apps on the app stores.

Setting Up Corona SDK

To start using Corona SDK, you will need to download the trial edition, either as a `.dmg` file (for the Mac) or an `.msi` file (for Windows), from `https://developer.coronalabs.com/downloads/coronasdk`.

To be able to download the file, you will have to register with Corona Labs. You can convert the trial version into a full version at any time by simply purchasing an appropriate license. There are several licensing options that you can choose from. The Indie license ($199) allows you to run one platform, either iOS or Android, the Pro license ($399) allows you to run both iOS and Android, and the Enterprise license (in the range of $3,000—pricing is on demand from Corona Labs). Details on the Enterprise Edition can be found towards the end of the chapter.

If you have no previous experience with Corona SDK, the first impressions can be quite intimidating, as there is no IDE or editor whatsoever.

How Corona SDK Works

Corona SDK is offered as *Corona terminal* and *Corona simulator*. It is advisable to launch Corona SDK using Corona terminal. This will start up a terminal (where you can see all the debugging output), and this will in turn start Corona simulator. The welcome screen for the SDK is shown in Figure 8-1.

From here you can navigate to the directory where your project files are and the simulator will run your code.

Figure 8-1. The welcome screen when you start Corona SDK

The entry point for a Corona SDK project is the `main.lua` file. This, along with the other project files, is used to run the project.

Hello World for Corona SDK

The architecture of Corona SDK, shown in Figure 8-2, is as follows: the Corona SDK engine runs in the simulator or on the device and runs with all the resources that make up the project, including the code, artwork, sound, and so on. These resources all reside in a directory from which the simulator looks for the entry point. The entry point is in the form of the `main.lua` file that is opened and executed.

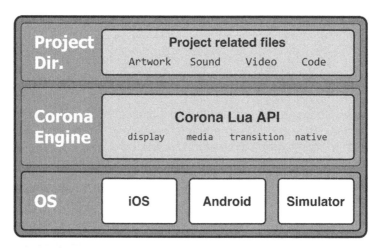

Figure 8-2. The Corona SDK architecture

First, create a new directory, Proj_01, and with the text editor of your choice, type the following code and save it as main.lua in the Proj_01 directory.

```
-- Hello world for Corona SDK
print("Hello World")
```

Now start Corona SDK and click Simulator. Then navigate to the directory you just created and click Open. This will start the simulator with a blank screen, but if you look at the terminal window, you'll see the text Hello World displayed.

Graphic Version

The Corona Engine is made up of the basic Lua libraries and other libraries that are responsible for display, audio, video, etc. Table 8-1 provides a list of the libraries that are available with Corona SDK that make up the Corona Engine.

Table 8-1. The Namespaces Available in Corona SDK

Library	Description
ads	All ad-displaying libraries
analytics	All functions relating to using analytics
audio	All audio-related functions
credits	All functions related to virtual currency
crypto	All crypto-related functions
display	All functions related to display elements
easing	All easing-related options used in transitions
facebook	All Facebook-related functions
gameNetwork	All functions relating to Apple Game Center and OpenFeint/Gree
graphics	All graphics-related functions that help with the display elements
json	All functions related to reading and writing JSON data
lfs	The Lua file system library for dealing with files and folders
media	The media functions to display video and audio
native	The functions to deal with native functionality of the devices
network	The functions related to the network and data communications
physics	The Box2D-related physics libraries
socket	The LuaSocket library to allow for all TCP and UDP socket communication
sprite	The functions to work with sprite libraries
sqlite3	The functions that allow for SQLite3 database access
store	All functions related to in-app purchases
storyboard	All functions related to storyboards
timer	All functions related to timers
transition	All functions for performing transitions
widget	All functions for creating widgets

For more details on the libraries and functions, the online API reference found on the Corona Labs web site is quite useful (see `http://docs.coronalabs.com/api/`). It lists the API and if there are any additions, this online reference provides all of the latest updates to the API.

Hello World on the Screen

In this exercise, let's display "Hello World" on the device for the world to see (Figure 8-3). We shall use an alert box to display "Hello World" on the device, instead of the terminal.

```
native.showAlert("Hello World", "via the showAlert", {"OK"})
```

Figure 8-3. "Hello World" displayed in an alert dialog on the iOS device

This is the easiest and the quickest way to display information to the user without the hassle of creating display objects. The best part is that this adapts natively to the platform you are running the app on.

Hello World on the Device

The display namespace has functions to create basic display objects, including images, text, rectangles, rounded rectangles, circles, lines, groups, and so forth. To begin, we'll create a text object and display it on the screen.

```
local lblText = display.newText("Hello World",10,50)
```

This one line will place a new text object with the text Hello World on the screen at locations 10 and 50 in the default system font as can be seen in Figure 8-4. The syntax of the function newText is as follows:

```
display.newText( [parentGroup,] string, left, top, font, size )
display.newText( [parentGroup,] string, left, top, [width, height,] font, size )
```

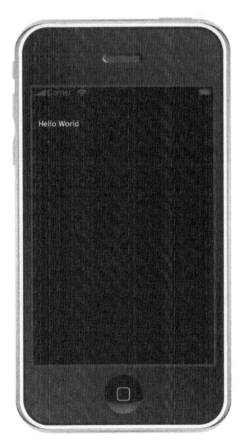

Figure 8-4. "Hello World" displayed as a label on the device

At any point, you can build the application for the device and run it on the device rather than running it in the simulator. To be able to upload a built app onto an iOS device, you will need to be enrolled in Apple's iOS Developer Program and have the necessary certificate to sign the app to be able to upload to the device. On Android, this should not be an issue, and you can build an APK that can be uploaded to the Android device.

Beyond Hello World: Creating a Rectangle on the Screen

In the same manner, we can create a rectangle on the screen, as shown in Figure 8-5.

```
local rect_01 = display.newRect( 50, 50, 200, 200 )
```

Figure 8-5. A rectangle on the device with the default fill colors

This shall create a rectangle on the screen that is placed at position 50, 50 and has the dimensions 200×200. The display elements, when created, are assigned the default settings; therefore, we see a white rectangle on the screen even if we do not specify a fill.

We can change some of the attributes, such as the fill color, outline color, and alpha (transparency), as well as the scale and the rotation of the rectangle. Let's modify the rectangle to manipulate all of these.

```
rect_01:setFillColor(255,0,0)
```

setFillColor takes the color as four values: red (R), green (G), blue (B), and the optional alpha (A). The values for the colors are in the range of 0 to 255, and the alpha is opaque (255) by default.

We can add an outline to the rectangle by specifying the stroke color and the stroke line width, as follows:

```
rect_01.strokeWidth = 2
rect_01:setStrokeColor(0,255,0)
```

strokeWidth sets the width of the stroke line (outline); setting it to 0 is equivalent to specifying no border or outline for the object. setStrokeColor is similar to setFillColor in terms of the arguments it takes. These are colors specified in the RGBA format.

We can scale the rectangle using the scale function.

> **Note**   You can adjust an object's scale using either the scale() function or the xScale and yScale properties, although they work somewhat differently. The function scales the object relative to the current scaling, and the properties assign absolute scale values to the object.

In this exercise, we'll simply use the xScale or yScale method to scale the rectangle. The advantage is that we can scale an object on one axis when required with the scale property, whereas with the scale() function, we need to specify the scales for both the x- and y-axis.

```
rect_01.xScale = 0.5
```

Rotating the object is equally simple—we can simply use the rotation property or the rotate() function. Similar to the scaling function and method, rotate and rotation also work with relative or absolute rotation. If we were to call the rotate() function on the object three times with a value of 30, that would rotate the object to 90 degrees (i.e., 30 degrees × 3), whereas calling the rotation property with 30 any number of times would rotate it to an absolute value of 30 degrees.

```
rect_01.rotation = 30
```

Here's the code all together:

```
 local rect_01 = display.newRect( 50, 50, 200, 200 )
rect_01:setFillColor(255,0,0)
rect_01.strokeWidth = 2
rect_01:setStrokeColor(0,255,0, 128)
rect_01.xScale = 0.5
rect_01.rotation = 30
```

Figure 8-6 shows what it would look like after applying all of the transformations just described.

Figure 8-6. *Transformations applied to the rectangle*

Groups

All display elements can be placed in a group. Think of a group as a container that can hold display elements. The advantage of a group is that by manipulating the position and display attributes of the group, you can affect all of the display elements held in the group together. You can move, rotate, and scale them, and you can change their alpha property and the visibility.

```
local grp = display.newGroup()
local text1 = display.newText("One", 10, 10)
local text2 = display.newText("Two", 10, 30)
local text3 = display.newText("Cha-Cha Cha", 10, 50)
```

When we run this, three lines of text are displayed on the screen. We can relocate any one of them by modifying the x or y position of the elements. Add the following code to the end of the preceding code. To rerun or refresh, simply press ⌘+R on the Mac or Ctrl+R on Windows. Corona SDK also monitors the directory for changes and will offer the option to relaunch the project if it is changed.

```
text2.y = 90
```

After running this, "Two" is now displayed below the "Cha-Cha Cha" text, and the place where "Two" was displayed is now blank, or empty.

Let's add the text "One" to the group:

```
grp:insert(text1)
```

When we refresh, everything should look the same as before. Let's try to position the group that contains the text "One."

```
grp.x = 100
grp.y = 20
```

On refreshing the simulator, the text "One" moves, as shown in Figure 8-7. It is now in the position where the text "Two" used to be, but a bit more to the right. Although we modified the position of the group, the text moved because it is contained in the group.

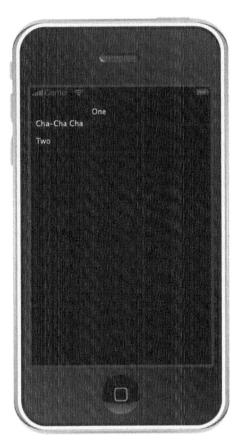

Figure 8-7. Displaying text in a group

By default, everything has a parent, or a group in which it is contained. The root, or parent, group of all elements created is referred to as the *stage*. We can access that via the `display.getCurrentStage()` function.

Images

One of the advantages of choosing Lua over languages such as C, C++, or Objective-C is that the need for allocating and deallocating memory is made redundant. The wrappers that the frameworks provide allow for easier coding compared to native code. When using Corona SDK, we can load and display images on the screen with ease.

To load an image, we use the newImage function in the display namespace:

```
local img = display.newImage("image1.png")
```

Alternatively, we can also provide the coordinates where we might want the image to be located:

```
local img = display.newImage("image1.png", 50, 50)
```

This will now load an image called image1.png and place it at the position 50, 50 on the screen.

Event-Based Processing

In the days of DOS and character-based terminals, when computers were primitive even in comparison to digital TV sets, program flow used to be linear. The code would run from the first line and continue until it reached the last line and the program ended. This worked best for the technology of the times. However, with today's touch screens and GUI-based apps, the linear flow model does not fit. We might have a touch or an event at any point in time, so applications are no longer necessarily synchronous in their flow. Events can occur and need to be handled at various times in an app's life cycle.

To enable us to use GUI-based applications, the concept of *event-based programming* was introduced. As shown in the diagram in Figure 8-8, in this type of processing, an event occurs and is passed to the application to be processed, and based on the event type, the application does what's necessary. In our case, the most commonly used event that we shall be working with is the touch event. That is the primary source of all input to the application. To allow the code to listen to the events that occur, the program has to register itself as a listener for a particular event and also pass a handler to the program that is called when the event occurs.

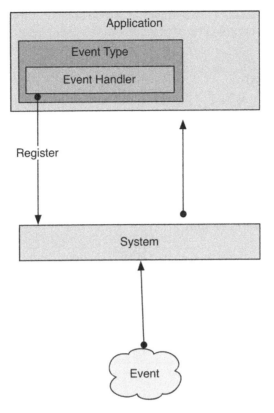

Figure 8-8. Architecture of an event process in Corona SDK

We can register the program to listen to specific events using the addEventListener function on the object on which we want to listen to the events, and we can pass it a function that will handle the event when passed to it.

OBJECT:addEventListener(*EVENT, HANDLER*)

In this code, *EVENT* is one of the many events that we can register to listen for, and *HANDLER* is the function that is invoked when the event is received.

Input: Touches

We can place images and text on the screen using the methods mentioned. However, we also need to handle the various forms of input, such as touches on the touch screen. These are equivalent to mouse clicks on the desktop. Generally, touch events are associated with a display element; you can touch the display element and trigger a touch phase. However, Corona SDK also allows you to have a generic touch handler that is associated with the Runtime object, which triggers the touch event for all objects.

When the user places a finger on the device, a touch event is triggered. As shown in Figure 8-9, this touch event has a couple of attributes, or members. A touch event starts with the finger touching the screen, and the event sets the value of phase to began. It also sets the target to the object that has been touched and the x and y to the coordinates of point where the user placed the finger on the screen.

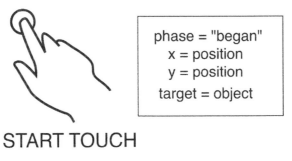

phase = "began"
x = position
y = position
target = object

START TOUCH

Figure 8-9. The touch "began" event and its members

If the user, while keeping the finger touching the screen, drags the finger, an event is triggered, but this time the value of phase is set to move. The target, x, and y still contain the values of the object touched and the current position of the finger. If the user moves the finger across the screen, as shown in Figure 8-10, a series of touch events are triggered, with phase set to move, and the x and y will reflect the coordinates as the finger moves across the screen.

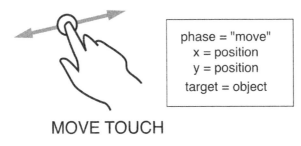

phase = "move"
x = position
y = position
target = object

MOVE TOUCH

Figure 8-10. The touch "move" event and its members

When the user lifts the finger off the screen, a touch event is triggered with phase set to ended, as shown in Figure 8-11. The other three attributes reflect the target and the x and y position where the touch ended.

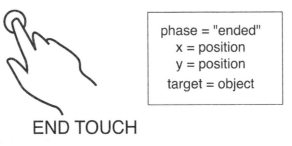

phase = "ended"
x = position
y = position
target = object

END TOUCH

Figure 8-11. The touch "ended" event and its members

The `cancelled` phase is triggered when a touch event is interrupted after it triggers the `began` phase but does not complete with the `ended` phase. This interruption can be due to an incoming phone call, a system-triggered message, a notification, and so on.

Let's write some code to display the touch events (what we have just read about):

```
function handler( event )
  print( "touch phase=" .. event.phase .. " at x=" .. event.x .. ", y=" .. event.y)
end
Runtime:addEventListener( "touch", handler )
```

On running this code, we can look at the terminal window for the output.

Similar to the `touch` event, there is a `tap` event can be handled. The difference between a touch and tap is that a touch starts with the `began` phase and ends with the `ended` phase. A tap event, on the other hand, is triggered when the user begins the touch and ends it without moving the touch. The tap event has a property numTaps that indicates the number of taps associated with that touch event.

```
function onTap( event )
  print( "Taps :".. event.numTaps )
end
Runtime:addEventListener( "tap", onTap )
```

Physics

The feature that brought Corona SDK into the limelight and made it popular with developers was its ability to integrate physics into its code in about eight lines or so. You can make any display object into a physics object simply by assigning it as a physics body using the function `physics.addBody()`.

```
local ground = display.newRect( 0, 40, 320, 20)
```

On running this code, rectangle is displayed on the screen. In order to make this a `physics` object, we need to include the physics library. I described in earlier chapters that the you can include libraries by using the `require` keyword, like so:

```
local physics = require "physics"
physics.start()
```

These two lines are of utmost importance: the first one gets a handle on the `physics` library, which allows us to call the physics-related functions from the `physics` namespace, and the second line actually starts the physics engine. Making the objects physics objects does not make a difference until `physics.start` is called. This is mostly used in games that allow the user to position the objects on the screen and then invoke the `physics.start` function to start the physics simulation interacting with the placed objects. Some examples that use this are Bubble Ball and Angry Orange (not made with Corona SDK).

However, even after adding these two lines, the rectangle we created doesn't yet act as a physics body, because we have not as yet marked it as a physics body. To do so, add the following line of code:

```
physics.addBody( ground )
```

Upon refreshing the project in the simulator, the rectangle starts to obey gravity and falls down, off the screen.

Let's create another object that falls; for simplicity's sake, we'll create another rectangle. To do this, we'll alter the first line of the preceding code and place the ground object close to the bottom of the screen rather than toward the top of the screen.

```
local physics = require "physics"
physics.start()
local ground = display.newRect( 0, 460, 320, 20 )
local rect1 = display.newRect( 140, 0, 40, 40 )
physics.addBody(ground)
physics.addBody(rect1)
```

Notice that both the objects start to fall off the screen. However, we don't want the ground to fall off the screen—what if we do not make that a physics object? Then will it stay as we expect it to? If we comment out or remove the line that makes the ground a physics body, notice that the rect1 object simply falls through the ground object.

Before we proceed, we need to know a few things. Creating a physics body is easy, but there are a few different types of physics bodies that we can create, and their differences are important. A physics body does not interact with other display objects; it can only interact with other physics bodies. There are three main types of physics bodies: static, dynamic, and kinematic. The default type of physics object is *dynamic*, which means that the moment we start the physics engine, this object will start to obey the rules of gravity. The second type is *static*; objects of this type stay in place and do not obey gravity, but they still interact with physics objects. The last type is *kinematic*, in which the velocity affects the objects but gravity has no effect on it. A kinematic object moves under the influence of its own velocity.

With this knowledge, we can write the following code:

```
local physics = require "physics"
physics.start()
local ground = display.newRect( 0, 460, 320, 20 )
local rect1 = display.newRect( 140, 0, 40, 40 )
physics.addBody( ground, "static")
physics.addBody( rect1 )
```

Now, as shown in Figure 8-12, the rectangle for the ground does not fall off the screen, and the rect1 rectangle bounces when it hits the ground.

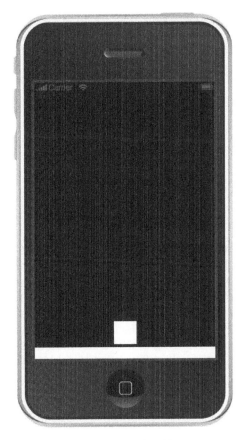

Figure 8-12. *A dynamic physics object interacting with a static physics object*

The rectangle can be replaced with a *skin*—that is, a graphic—and this is a very easy:

```
local physics = require "physics"
physics.start()
--
local ground = display.newRect( 0, 460, 320, 20 )
local rect = display.newImage( "DominoTile.png" )
--
physics.addBody( ground, "static")
physics.addBody( rect1 )
--
```

Timing Is Everything

Many games offer special powers to their players. For example, games like Arkanoid (Breakout) offer get lasers, multiple balls, and so on. In other games, you might get super-speed or strength for a limited time, depicted on the screen in the form of a timer, whereby the powers disappear when the time is up. What if for our game we wanted something similar? For example, say we want to track or provide some special abilities for a short period of time.

The timer comes to our rescue. Though the word *timer* might bring to mind something like an alarm that goes off at the end of a specified time, in Lua, the timer is more like a heartbeat—one that we can control the beat of. And we can decide what we want the program to do when that timer beats.

Setting up a timer is easy—we simple use the following:

```
local heartbeat = timer.performWithDelay(1000,
    function()
      print("tick")
end, 0)
```

When you run this, you'll see the words *tick* outputted to the terminal once per second. The function sits in the Timer namespace and has four functions: `timer.performWithDelay()` to create a new timer, `timer.cancel()` to cancel a timer, `timer.pause()` to pause the timer from firing further, and `timer.resume()` to continue from the point where the execution was paused.

Of the timer-related functions, `performWithDelay` takes a single parameter, which is the handle to the timer that has been created. The function `performWithDelay`, when called, returns a handle to the instance that shall run that code. The function takes three arguments: `delay`, `listenerFunction`, and `iterations`. The first parameter, `delay`, specifies the frequency that the timer event is fired in milliseconds. In plain words, this simply means that we should do something every time there is a heartbeat. The second parameter is the `listenerFunction`; this points to a Lua function and is the function that is called every time the event occurs. The last parameter is optional, and its default value is 1. It signifies the number of times that this event should invoke this function.

Here's how to print a list of numbers from 1 to 10 using the timer:

```
local counter = 1
  function printNumber(event)
      print("Counter is :".. counter)
    counter = counter + 1
end
timer.performWithDelay(1000,printNumber, 10)
```

Frames

While the workings of televisions and movies may seem complex, the way they work is actually quite simple. The movie or TV screen displays a series of static images in rapid succession, fast enough that our eyes perceive these images as continuous movement. This is also how animators create animation. They draw a series of frames with the images, and when the images are then played back to us in rapid succession, it provides us the illusion of movement. If the images are played back too slowly, we can catch the changing of images between frames; if they're played too fast, everything appears abnormal and sped up. Now, what does that have to do with development? Everything!

Most animation software works with a timeline. The timeline is generally the blueprint of the animation, which determines the position and transformations of the objects over time or frames. The app starts at frame 1 and iterates through a set number of frames to provide the illusion of movement, till it reaches the end of the frames, when it stops. However, in some cases, the timeline may *wrap*—that is, start again from the beginning as if in a loop. The numbers of frames that are displayed in a second is referred to as the *frame rate*. The more frames you can display in a second, the smoother the movement. Most software uses the terminology *frames per second (fps)*, which is used to describe the frame rate of animated objects on the screen.

Think of this as the heartbeat of the app. For example, you can set the heartbeat to either 30 fps or 60 fps, the latter providing a smoother animation. However, a higher frame rate will be harder on the CPU, especially in an app that triggers some processing, so in certain cases a lower frame rate is a better choice.

When you create animations in Lua, Corona SDK allows you to set your app to either 30 or 60 fps.

For simplicity's sake, we'll write a handler to catch an event and simply print a message.

```
function ticker( event )
    print ( "tick" )
end
--
Runtime:addEventListener ( "enterFrame", ticker )
```

When run, this will output a lot of lines that display "tick" in the terminal window.

> **Note** The enterFrame event is dispatched prior to the screen render taking place.

Making a Health Bar

If you have played any real-time strategy or tower-defense games, you know that each character has some amount of health, and every time the character is hit, the health bar reduces or changes color.

In this example, we'll create a bar using a rectangle, as shown in Figure 8-13. Then we can modify the size of the rectangle by manipulating the height of the rectangle at the enterFrame event.

```
local bar = display.newRect ( 100, 300, 20, 70 )
bar:setFillColor (100,100,200,200)
local theText = display.newText( "value", 140, 300, nil, 20)
theText:setTextColor( 255, 255 ,255 )
--
local time = 20
local counter = 0
local direction = 1
local isStopped = false
--
function toggleMove ( event )
  isStopped = not isStopped
end
--
function move ( event )
  if isStopped == true then return end
  counter = counter + direction
  if counter>=time or counter<=0 then
   direction = -direction
  end
```

```
    bar.height = 8 * counter
    bar:setReferencePoint(display.BottomLeftReferencePoint)
    bar.y=300
    theText.text = counter
end
--
Runtime:addEventListener ( "enterFrame", move )
Runtime:addEventListener ( "tap", toggleMove )
```

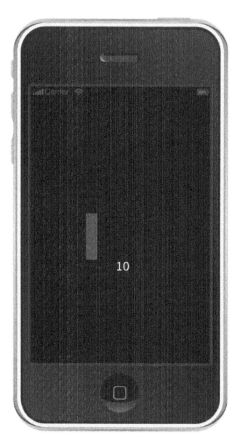

Figure 8-13. The health bar on the device (or simulator), with the value displayed

Notice that the bar starts to bob, increasing at first and then decreasing. The health bar bobs to demonstrate how an object can be modified each time the enterFrame function is called. This can be used for animation, such as changing the location of the object on the screen or changing the dimensions of the object.

Animating Using enterFrame

As shown in Figure 8-14, we can use enterFrame to move an object on the screen. In Chapter 4, you learned about constraining an object to a particular dimension on the screen. We are definitely not in the matrix where we have be able to understand things by looking at numbers, so we'll create a GUI version of the same code.

Figure 8-14. Using the enterFrame handler to make a red circle bounce around the screen

```
local point = {x=0,y=0}
local speed = {x=1,y=1}
local dimensions = {0,0,320,480}

local ball = display.newCircle(0,0,20)
ball:setFillColor(255,0,0)

function positionBall(thePoint)
    print("ball is at" .. thePoint.x .. " , ".. thePoint.y)
    ball.x = point.x
    ball.y = point.y
end
```

```
function moveBall()
  local newX, newY = point.x + speed.x, point.y + speed.y
  if newX > dimensions[3] or newX < dimensions[1] then speed.x = - speed.x end
  if newY > dimensions[4] or newY < dimensions[2] then speed.y = - speed.y end
  point.x = point.x + speed.x
  point.y = point.y + speed.y
end
function loop_it_all(event)
    positionBall(point)
    moveBall()
end
Runtime:addEventListener ( "enterFrame", loop_it_all )
```

You can speed up the movement by changing the speeds in the second line, like so:

```
local speed = { x = 1, y = 1 }
```

Back to Health Bars

Many real-time strategy and tower-defense games include an indicator that shows a character's remaining health. Each time the character takes a hit, this health level is reduced, and the bar may change color to reflect the lost health.

In this exercise, we'll create a similar bar. First, we'll create a bar, color it green to indicate full health, and give it a health value of 10. Each time we tap the screen, we'll reduce the health by 1, and the bar will correspondingly get shorter. The bar will also change color from green to orange to red, indicating the severity of the situation.

```
local barSize = 200
local barHeight = 30
local healthBar = display.newRect ( 10, 100, barSize, barHeight)
  healthBar:setFillColor ( 0, 255, 0 )  -- make this green
  healthBar.health = 10 -- a dynamic var for the healthBar
--
function updateHealth()
  local theHealth = healthBar.health - 1
  if theHealth <0 then return end
  healthBar.health = theHealth
  --
  if theHealth > 6 then --GREEN
    healthBar:setFillColor ( 0, 255, 0 )
  elseif theHealth > 4 then      --ORANGE
    healthBar:setFillColor ( 180, 180, 0 )
  elseif theHealth > 0 then      --RED
    healthBar:setFillColor ( 255, 0, 0 )
  elseif theHealth == 0 then     --BLACK
    healthBar:setFillColor ( 0, 0, 0 )
  end
```

```
   if theHealth > 0 then
      healthBar.width = (barSize * theHealth/10)
   end
end
Runtime:addEventListener ( "tap", updateHealth )
```

On running this code, as shown in Figure 8-15, a green bar is displayed on the screen. It gets smaller every time we tap the screen and changes color from green to yellow to red. In a real game, this health bar might be smaller and linked to each character, and multiple bars might be used—one linked to each character.

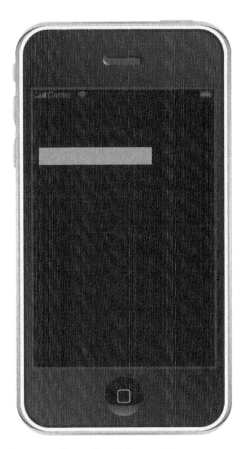

Figure 8-15. *A health bar displayed on the screen (currently at full capacity)*

To make the bar smaller, you can simply tweak the barSize and barHeight to the values of your choice. You can also pass the healthBar to the updateHealth function to manage multiple health bars. Finally, you may want to create a healthBar object that is self-contained and works with its own set of functions and properties, like a widget. I'll leave these last options for you to try on your own.

Using Transition Functions

Next, we'll look at some *transitions*. These are handy functions that help us modify the visible attributes of an object and provide us with the illusion of animation.

Note   In the world of Adobe Flash, these types of transitions are called *tweens*.

Transitioning an object is similar to moving an object to a new position over a period of time. In the earlier example of the bouncing ball, we could have used transitions; however, transitions require a start and an end, so we would have had to define those. Transitions are carried out over a specific period of time, during which the transitioning code calculates each of the intermediate steps between the first state and the last state.

Let's move a simple circle from the bottom of the screen to the top of the screen:

```
local ball = display.newCircle ( 160, 480, 50 )
transition.to ( ball, {time=1000, y = 0})
```

We can slow it down by increasing the time or speed it up by decreasing the time. Here, we have called the transition function and asked it to modify the y position of the object ball to the position of 0 over a period 1,000 ms (i.e., 1 second).

The following code colors this ball red, makes it grow as it moves, and makes it fade in as it appears, like the morning sun.

```
local ball = display.newCircle ( 160, 480, 50 )
ball:setFillColor(255,255,0)
ball.alpha = 0.5
ball:scale(0.5,0.5)
transition.to ( ball, {time=2000, y = 80, alpha = 1, xScale = 1.2, yScale = 1.2})
```

We can use a transition to scroll some text on the screen:

```
local theText = display.newText("Hello, hope you are enjoying your journey with Lua so far",0,440)
theText.x = theText.contentWidth
transition.to(theText,{time=8000, x = -theText.contentWidth})
--
```

You will see the text scrolling at the bottom of the screen. Also notice that the other transitions go about at their own speeds irrespective of the scrolling text. In short, they do not affect each other. You can have multiple transitions on the screen at the same time, independent of each other.

In a game, if we use transitions, we also need to also know when they have completed, because we might want to do something when the transition is finished. With the transition function, there are two parameters that we can use to carry out specific actions when the transitions start and end. These are aptly named `onStart` and `onComplete`.

In this exercise, we'll have the sun rise like we did in the preceding code, and then after 2 seconds, we'll make the sun set.

Since Lua is flexible and not very fussy, you can write the code in several ways. To keep it readable and simple, we'll split the code chunk into a function.

```
--
local ball = display.newCircle ( 160, 480, 50 )
ball:setFillColor(255,255,0)
ball.alpha = 0.5
ball:scale(0.5,0.5)
--
local theText = display.newText("Hello, hope you are enjoying your journey with Lua so far",0,440)
theText.x = theText.contentWidth
transition.to(theText,{time=8000, x = -theText.contentWidth})
--
function sunset()
    transition.to ( ball, {delay=2000, time=2000, y=480, alpha=0.5, xScale = 0.5, yScale = 0.5})
end
--
function sunrise()
    transition.to ( ball, {time=2000, y=80, alpha=1, xScale = 1.2, yScale = 1.2, onComplete = sunset})
end
--
sunrise()
```

Notice that in the sunset function, we have a new parameter: delay. This tells the transition function to wait for the duration specified before starting the transition.

> **Note**   Any value assignable to the object can be transitioned over the time specified. If you create your own custom display objects, like widgets, you can animate them by modifying their values in a transition function.

The transition namespace has a couple of functions. The one that is used the most is transition.to, and the other is transition.from.

When transition functions are called, depending on the to or the from, the object being transitioned is modified based on the attributes specified to be transitioned. If we use transition.from, the object is at first set to the attributes provided and then transitioned to the current settings of the object. So, if we were to use transition.from as transform.from(theObject, {time=500, alpha=0}), the alpha setting for the theObject would be first set to 0, and then the transition would end by setting the current attributes to theObject.

On the other hand, if we use `transition.to`, theObject is transitioned from the current settings to the settings that we specify in the transition. This is also the reason that this transition is used more often than the `transition.from`.

Both of the transition functions return a transition handle that we can capture. This handle can be used with the `transition.cancel` function to cancel the transition.

> **Tip**   One good way to manage the transition handle and transitions without creating additional variables is to save the transition into the object itself. This way, you can cancel the transition without having to look very far before you can delete the object especially if the object is halfway through the transition.

The way it works is that when we set a transition, the function returns a handle. In the majority of cases, programmers do not capture this handle, as it wouldn't be necessary in the case of a one-off transition. In the example of our scrolling text, the transition goes on for about 8 seconds, whereas our sunrise and sunset takes a total of 6 seconds. If in our app the user taps the screen to move to the next set of transitions, the scrolling transition will still continue, as it is active. If our code removes the text object from memory, the transition function will try to set the next position for the text object, and finding it gone, it will throw an error. To avoid such an error, we can cancel our transitions so they do not get left behind and cause problems.

```
local theText = display.newText("Hello, hope you are enjoying your journey with Lua so far",0,440)
theText.x = theText.contentWidth
theText.trans = transition.to(
    theText,{time=8000, x=-theText.contentWidth})
--
local ball = display.newCircle ( 160, 480, 50 )
ball:setFillColor(255,255,0)
ball.alpha = 0.5
ball:scale(0.5,0.5)
--
transition.to (ball, {time = 2000, y = 80, onComplete=function()
    transition.cancel(theText.trans)
  end} )
```

Notice that the moment the sun reaches the top of the screen, the transition stops the text-scrolling transition by canceling it.

There is another parameter that you can pass to these transition functions, and that is `delta`. This is a Boolean value that is either `true` or `false`. The default value is `false`, and it specifies whether the values passed are absolute values or relative to current values.

The transitions do not have to be linear (i.e., uniform in the steps) while sliding the text off the screen; for example, you can give your transition the effect of acceleration or deceleration as it reaches its target position. This type of acceleration and deceleration behavior is knows as *easing in* and *easing out*, respectively. There are a few easing options that are available with Corona SDK.

```
local theText = display.newText("Hello, hope you are enjoying your journey with Lua so far",0,440)
theText.x = theText.contentWidth
theText.trans = transition.to(
    theText,{time=8000, x=-theText.contentWidth})
--
local ball = display.newCircle ( 160, 480, 50 )
ball:setFillColor(255,255,0)
ball.alpha = 0.5
ball:scale(0.5,0.5)
--
transition.to (ball, {time = 2000, y = 80, transition = easing.outExpo, onComplete=function()
    transition.cancel(theText.trans)
  end} )
```

In this code, transition = easing.outExpo causes the ball to slow down and then speed up as it moves toward the top of the screen.

You can also add other interesting effects by simply writing your own easing function. Such a function is declared as follows:

easing.function(t, tMax, start, delta)

In this declaration, t is the time since the start of the transition, tMax is the overall length of the transition time, start is the initial value, and delta is the change in the value at the end of the transition. The final value should always be start + delta.

Here's an example of easeOutBounce, with the result illustrated in Figure 8-16.

```
function easeOutBounce(t,b,c,d)
    t,d,b,c= t,b,c,d;
    t=t/d;
    if (t<(1/2.75)) then
        ret=c*(7.5625*t*t)+b
    elseif (t<(2/2.75)) then
        t=t-(1.5/2.75)
        ret=c*(7.5625*(t*t)+.75)+b
    elseif (t<(2.5/2.75)) then
        t=t-2.25/2.75;
        ret=c*(7.5625*t*t+.9375)+b
    else
        t=t-2.625/2.75;
        ret=c*(7.5625*t*t+.984375)+b
    end
return ret;
end
```

This code is taken from the LHTween library on GitHub, authored by logHound.

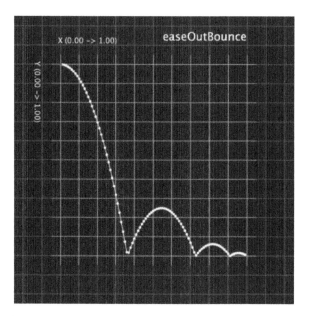

Figure 8-16. *The graph plot of the easeOutBounce function*

Removing Objects from the Screen

You just learned how to stop a transition. However, the object still remains on the screen. If this were a screen that displayed the score between levels, for example, we would want it to disappear. In the simplest way, we could just turn off the visibility of the object by setting the isVisible property to false. However, with this method, the object would still remain in memory (though not visible on the screen) and would be created again; if you were to play a game with a substantial number of levels, there would be quite a few objects on the screen taking up valuable memory.

A better way to remove these objects is to remove them from the stage. When we create an object, it is added to the stage or the parent object automatically. To remove an object, we simply pass the object handle to the remove() function in the display namespace. For instance, to remove the text in the preceding example , we just pass it the following:

```
display.remove(theText)
```

Another way to remove the objects—which seems simpler and more direct—is to call the removeSelf function of the display object:

```
theText:removeSelf()
```

> **Note**   If the object is already removed or is nil, then the removeSelf function will fail and give an error. However, the display.remove function exits gracefully without any errors if the object being removed has previously been removed.

Creating Sound

While we've covered the visual and tactile parts of game play, to complete the experience, we need to have some sound. This sound can be simple, such as the sound when an element on the screen is touched, or it can be more complex, such as the sound of explosions or pulsating music. We might also want to include a video for advertising purposes, as a replacement for a help feature, or for helping transition the game's story from one part to another. We'll look at creating video in the next section.

Let's Make Some Noise

Corona SDK has two sets of namespaces that can be used for audio. Initially it used the media namespace, but it's now pushing toward making media redundant, and wants developers to use the audio namespace with OpenAL (for maximum Android compatibility). OpenAL stands for Open Audio Library, a cross-platform audio library. The API style and conventions resemble those of OpenGL. OpenAL also provides multiple simultaneous channels for playing sounds, so you can really layer sounds. For example, you could simulate the sound of sitting at a café outside on a lovely day—hearing a person singing and playing a guitar, the chatter of other people talking, traffic, and so on, all at the same time.

To start with the basics, let's say we want to play a click sound, and the audio file we have is click. wav. We can simply use the playSound function from the media namespace:

```
media.playSound ( "click.wav" )
```

We can also use the playEventSound function to play a short sound (between 1 and 3 seconds). This requires that we load the sound prior to playing it. This function does not take a file name, but instead takes a handle to the loaded sound data.

```
local snd = media.newEventSound ( "click.wav" )
media.playEventSound ( snd )
```

The playSound function can also be provided additional parameters that allow for the sound to be looped or a function be called when the sound stops playing.

This can be used to create a simple MP3 jukebox, like so:

```
local listMP3 = {
   "track1.mp3",
   "track2.mp3",
   "track3.mp3",
   "track4.mp3",
   "track5.mp3",
   "track6.mp3"
}
local currentTrack = 0
--
```

```
function getfilename(thisFile)
  local thePath = system.pathForFile( thisFile, system.ResourceDirectory)
  return thePath
end
--
function playNextTrack()
  currentTrack = currentTrack + 1
  if currentTrack > #listMP3 then currentTrack = 1 end
  media.playSound(getfilename(listMP3[currentTrack]), playNextTrack)
end
--
playNextTrack()
```

In this code, we had to include another function, getfilename, which returns the file path to the track, instead of just the file name. All of our tracks are placed in the root directory of the project, and they would then get placed into the ResourceDirectory on the mobile device. So, with the system.pathForFile function, we get the full path, prefixing the file with the passed directory. The function generates an absolute path based on the directory that we pass along with the file name. The two arguments passed are the file name and the directory name; the function is essentially the equivalent of returning the directory name, plus /, plus the file name.

Manipulating the Sound

While the sound is playing, we can pause it or stop it. The media namespace offers an easy way to do so:

```
media.stopSound()
media.pauseSound()
```

We can also increase or decrease the volume by using the following functions:

```
media.getSoundVolume()
media.setSoundVolume()
```

The volume is expressed as a real number that has the range from 0 to 1.0, with 0 being silent and 1.0 being the loudest possible volume. Here's some code to increase or decrease the volume in increments of 10 percent:

```
function increaseVolume()
  local currVol = media.getSoundVolume ( )
  if currVol >= 1.0 then return end -- Already at the max volume
  media.setSoundVolume ( currVol+0.1 )
end
--
function decreaseVolume()
  local currVol = media.getSoundVolume ( )
  if currVol <= 0 then return end -- Already at the min volume
  media.setSoundVolume ( currVol-0.1 )
end
```

As an exercise, try to make a UI that can display the name of the current track being played, and place some buttons on the screen for playing, pausing, and skipping to the next or previous track.

Using OpenAL Sound

The audio namespace includes the OpenAL functions, which might eventually replace the media. playSound and media.playEventSound functions.

With OpenAL, you need to load the sound and then dispose of it once you are done. If you don't, you can end up leaving sounds in memory and soon run out of memory.

```
local snd = audio.loadSound( "click.wav" )
local channel = audio.play( snd )
```

We have 32 channels on which we can play our sounds. Each time we use the function audio.play, the API looks for a free channel and starts to play the sound on that channel, and it returns the channel number back to us. It is with this channel number that we can pause or stop the sound from playing on that channel. We can also query the channel to determine the state of the channel, using any of the following:

```
audio.isChannelActive
audio.isChannelPaused
audio.isChannelPlaying
```

Once we have finished playing the sounds, we are responsible for disposing of (freeing up the memory used for) the sound using the audio.dispose function.

```
audio.dispose ( snd )
```

Setting the Volume

With OpenAL, we can set not only the master volume, but also the volume for each of the channels. Similar to the volume in the media namespace, the level ranges from 0 (silent) to 1.0 (loudest).

```
function increaseVolume()
  local currVol = audio.getVolume ( )
  if currVol >= 1.0 then return end -- Already at the max volume
  media.setVolume ( currVol+0.1 )
end
--
function decreaseVolume()
  local currVol = media.getVolume ( )
  if currVol <= 0 then return end -- Already at the min volume
  media.setVolume ( currVol-0.1 )
end
```

Notice that we are using the same name for the function that we used previously, and we're substituting the media functions with the audio functions to manipulate the volume. This way, if the code is encapsulated within a generic function, we can use the functions increaseVolume and decreaseVolume from our app. Since these can be written for any framework, our code will be quite portable. One of the basic mistakes a lot of developers (especially those starting off) make is that of directly accessing the framework functions. Due to the fact that the code becomes tightly integrated with the framework, it becomes difficult to port it.

Working with Videos

We have just had a look at how to work with sound; let's look at how to work with video. The media namespace has an easy-to-use API and makes it quite simple to play video:

```
function done(event)
  print( "The video has finished playing" )
end
media.playVideo ( "video1.mov", true, done )
```

The syntax of the playVideo function is

```
media.playVideo( path, showControls, listener )
```

The first parameter is the path to the video file. The second parameter, showControls, indicates whether the playback UI should be displayed. The user can tap the screen to bring up this UI and then adjust the playback. However, setting this to false will disable the display of this interface. The last parameter is the function that is called when the playback completes. On the iOS platform, playing the video is an asynchronous operation, which means that any code following the playing of the video will be run while the video is being played. So you might want to pause everything and wait for the video to finish playing and then resume execution. You would want to do this, for example, when you play an intro video at the start of a game and you didn't want the game to start playing till the video finished playing.

Corona SDK has another video-playing API, which is not cross-platform, but allows for advanced manipulation on the iOS platform. This is available as native.newVideo.

The objects created via this API can be rotated, assigned as a physics body, and manipulated as a display object.

```
local video = native.newVideo ( 0, 0, 160, 240 )
--
function theHandler( event )
  print(event.phase, event.errorCode)
end
--
video:load ( "theVideo.mov", system.ResourceDirectory )
video:addEventListener( "video", theHandler )
video:play()
```

> **Note** This function might not be available as a public release yet, so if you have a trial version of Corona SDK, you might not be able to run this particular code.

Creating an Elevator

You might come across a scenario while making a game where the character has to ride an elevator to move to a different level. Though this is conceptually very simple, it's important to understand the specifics.

For this example, we shall have four objects: the up and down buttons, the platform, and the character/player. For simplicity, as shown in Figure 8-17, we will use rectangles. When the program starts, the character, which is a physics body, will fall, and the platform will absorb the fall and prevent the object from bouncing. The buttons will move the platform up and down.

```lua
local physics = require("physics")
physics.start()

display.setStatusBar(display.HiddenStatusBar)
local beam = display.newRect(50,300,200,50)
physics.addBody(beam,"static",{friction=1,density=1,bounce=0})
beam:setFillColor(0,255,0)
local box = display.newRect(120,120,40,40)
physics.addBody(box,{friction=1})
box:setFillColor(255,0,0)

function moveUp()
    box.bodyType="static"
    transition.to( box,
        {time=300, y=-100, delta = true,
          onComplete=function() box.bodyType="dynamic" end})
    transition.to(beam,{time=300,y=-100, delta=true})
end
function moveDown()
    box.bodyType="static"
    transition.to( box,
        {time=300, y=100, delta=true,
          onComplete=function() box.bodyType="dynamic" end})
    transition.to(beam,{time=300,y=100, delta=true})
end
local btnUp = display.newRect(10,10,20,40)
local btnDn = display.newRect(10,60,20,40)

btnDn:addEventListener("tap",moveDown)
btnUp:addEventListener("tap",moveUp)
```

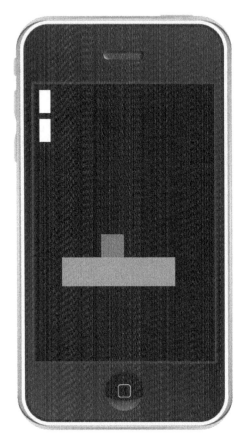

Figure 8-17. *The physics-based elevator that responds to the up and down buttons*

> **Note**   The use of delta=true allows for relative movement, so the platform will move 100 pixels up
> or down relative to the current position.

Zooming Out for an Overview

Many games use a camera mode to show the entire area, and then zoom in to the player to start playing. We'll attempt to re-create that effect. The way it works is that the elements are placed on the screen in the place that they need to be at. This world space could be larger than the screen size, so they might reside outside of the visible screen area. We'll allow the user to zoom out for an overview by touching the screen, and on releasing the touch, the screen will zoom back in to the original position.

```
local _H = display.contentHeight
local _W = display.contentWidth
--
function position(theObject, xPos, yPos, refPoint)
  local refPt = refPt or display.TopLeftReferencePoint
```

```
    theObject:setReferencePoint(refPt)
    theObject.x = xPos
    theObject.y = yPos
end
--
local back
local function zoomer(event)
    local phase = event.phase
    local target=event.target

    if phase=="began" then
        display.currentStage:setFocus(target)
        transition.to( back,{time=200,xScale=0.5, yScale=0.5} )
    elseif phase=="ended" then
        display.currentStage:setFocus(nil)
        transition.to( back,{time=200,xScale=1, yScale=1} )
    end
end
--
back = display.newGroup()
local wallpaper = display.newImage( back, "wallpaper.jpg", 0, 0, true )
local i
for i=1, 10 do
    local rect = display.newRect( back, i*50, i*50, 40, 40 )
    rect:setFillColor( 255-(i*10), 0, 0 )
end
position ( back, _W/2, _H/2, display.CenterReferencePoint )
local  button = display.newRect( 10, 400, 50, 50 )
button:setFillColor(255,0,0,100)
button:addEventListener( "touch", zoomer )
```

There are some interesting new API features that we have used; let's look at them first before discussing how it all works together.

Each of the display objects has a dimension; this is accessible to us via code using the height and width properties. When we scale the object, the dimensions do not change. However, visually the object changes size based on the scaling factor. So, if we have a rectangle that is 100 pixels in width and we scale it by setting xScale to 0.5, the width of the rectangle still remains 100, but on the screen it looks smaller—50 pixels. When we need to get the size of this object on the screen, width does not return the correct size. This is where contentWidth and contentHeight come in handy. These two properties reflect the actual dimensions of the object with the scaling applied. This is available for every display object. The display namespace also has contentHeight and contentWidth properties, which correspond to the device screen size. display.contentWidth would return 320 for iPhone 3, 640 for iPhone 4, and 768 for the iPad.

At the start of the program, we save the values of the screen size in the variables _H and _W; these are then used throughout the program as the width and height of the device screen.

We can position an object by simply manipulating the x and y members. However, each time we change the x- or the y-coordinate, the object's reference position is set to center (i.e., the object is centered around this position). This causes extra lines of code where you have to set the x- and y-coordinates and then set referencePoint to TopLeft. The best way to manage this is to have a function that positions the object. That way, you will only have to call the function, and you can use the same function name with any framework.

```
function position(theObject, xPos, yPos, refPoint)
  local refPoint = refPoint or display.TopLeftReferencePoint
  theObject:setReferencePoint(refPoint)
  theObject.x = xPos
  theObject.y = yPos
end
```

Next, we declare another function that will be responsible for the zooming:

```
function zoomer (event )
  local phase = event.phase
  local target = event.target
  if phase == "began"
    display.currentStage:setFocus(target)
    transition.to( back, {time=200, xScale=0.5, yScale=0.5} )
  elseif phase == "ended" then
    display.currentStage:setFocus(nil)
    transition.to( back, {time=200, xScale=1, yScale=1} )
  end
end
```

This function is basically an event handler for a touch event; we are interested in two phases: when the touch begins and when the touch ends. When the touch starts we scale the entire display area to 0.5, and on release we scale it back to 1.0. If you use this in your game, you can change these to whatever best suits you.

Now for all the display elements:

```
local back = display.newGroup()
local wallpaper = display.newImage( back, "wallpaper.jpg", 0, 0, true )
local i
for i=1, 10 do
  local rect = display.newRect( back, i*50, i*50, 40, 40 )
  rect:setFillColor( 255-(i*10), 0, 0 )
end
position ( back, _W/2, _H/2, display.CenterReferencePoint )
local  button = display.newRect( 10, 400, 50, 50 )
button:setFillColor(255,0,0,100)
button:addEventListener( "touch", zoomer )
```

Now when you touch the screen, all of the display objects scale out (since they are all part of the group), and on release they all zoom in.

More Events

We added event listeners for touch, tap, and enterFrame. Similarly, we can add listeners for other events, such as the *system* event, which raises events for system-related tasks.

We set a listener for the system event if we want to catch the events such as the following:

- The applications starts (when the user taps the icon)

- The app is placed into suspension (when the user presses the home button and the app is in the background)

- The app is resumed (when the app is started again from the previous state rather than from the beginning)

- The app exits.

```
Runtime:addEventListener("system",
    function(event)
        print("System event : " .. event.type)
    end)
```

In other instances when the device is reoriented (i.e., changed from portrait mode to landscape). We can catch that with the orientation event.

```
Runtime:addEventListener("orientation",
    function(event)
        print("Orientation changed to.. event.type)
    end)
```

> **Note**   The system events cannot be seen in the Corona simulator or terminal window, as they require the Apple iOS simulator or an actual device to function. However, the applicationStart, applicationSuspend, and applicationResume events can be generated in the Corona simulator.

Custom Events

In addition to the system events, you can also have custom events—events that you create specifically for your application. This way, you can manage the asynchronous portions of your game. Let's say the game involves a boss battle with a gigantic spider; each time you take a limb off the giant spider, you can raise an event that will add a special bonus to your score and/or make the spider do something specific at that moment. With a game in the style of a top-down plane-shooter, you could use the events to update the score as you hit each plane.

Let's say we have a function that increases the score by a specified number; these parameters are passed to the function in a table-type structure:

```
function updateScore(event)
    local score = lblScore.score +  event.points
    lblScore.text = score
    lblScore.score = score
end
```

In the function where a plane is shot down or a giant spider loses a leg, we can use the following:

```
function triggerPoint(theObject)
    local points = theObject.value
    Runtime:dispatchEvent({
        name = "score",
        points = points,
        object = theObject
    })
end
```

To tie the two together, we also need to set a listener, which is done using the addEventListener function:

```
Runtime:addEventListener("score", updateScore)
```

One thing to note is that the event dispatcher works across modules, which means that two modules in the same application can communicate with each other without even being aware of the presence of the other. Think of an event as a radio broadcasting station. The radio station will broadcast its program irrespective of how many listeners are listening. Even if there are no listeners, the broadcast carries on no differently than if there were hundreds. The only thing required of the listeners is to be able to tune in to the correct station. So, the broadcast is made using the dispatchEvent function, and the audience tunes in using the addEventListener function that listens to the score event.

> **Note** A dispatchEvent requires that the event object be provided a name; this is used to identify it when the listener filters the events and calls the appropriate handler function. You can pass any data in the event object.

Alternatives to Events

As an alternative to using events, you can use *callbacks*. The shortcoming for callbacks, however, is that instead of a radio station, it is more like a telephone conversation—a communication between two parties. When you set a callback, it is set for one module alone. This is useful in scenarios such as when we want to monitor something specific. For example, in a game, if connectivity is lost, rather than broadcast that and have every function that relies on the network connectivity try to manage the situation, we could simply have just one function that registers as the callback for that event and handle the situation accordingly. Callbacks also provide a way to communicate between the modules in the same application.

```
local theCallback = nil
local callback =
    function(event)
        print("callback called")
    end
local mainLoop =
    function()
        for i=1, 20 do
            if i==15 then
```

```
            if theCallback then
                theCallback()
            end
        end
    end
    print("Loop ended")
    end
mainLoop()  -- call the loop without a callback set
theCallback = callback  -- set the callback
mainLoop()  -- call the loop with a callback set
```

Using Maps

One of the features of the iOS platform that sparked the interest of many developers was the ability to place maps in an application, as shown in Figure 8-18. UIMapKit (created by Apple) was a bit too complicated, since it involved a series of steps to display a map on the screen.

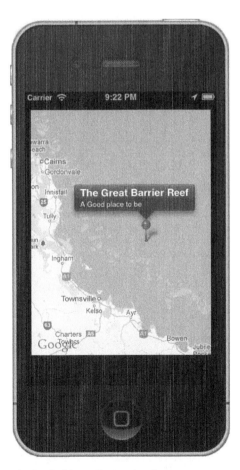

Figure 8-18. Map showing the Great Barrier Reef with a callout and a pin

Corona SDK offers an easy way to display a map on the screen:

```
local lat, lon = -18.2861, 147.7
local map = native.newMapView(10,30,300,200)
map:addMarker(lat, long, {
    title="The Great Barrier Reef", subtitle="A Good place to be"
    } )
map:setCenter( lat,lon )
```

The Internet Browser

In the earlier days, when the only way to make apps for iOS was using Objective-C, many people tried to place apps in HTML wrappers (UIWebView). They had a web browser wrapped inside of the application. This helped them cheat (in a way) to allow for templates and books, and thereby helped them make apps that were not native apps, but were not straightforward browsers either.

There are two functions that involve the process of displaying and removing the webview from the screen: `native.showWebPopup` and the `native.cancelWebPopup`. `cancelWebPopup` does not take any parameters, as there can only be one `webPopup` at any point in time. You can also use this to display a website as seen in Figure 8-19 or as a help file in your app, as shown in Figure 8-20

Figure 8-19. *A blog displayed in a web browser on the device*

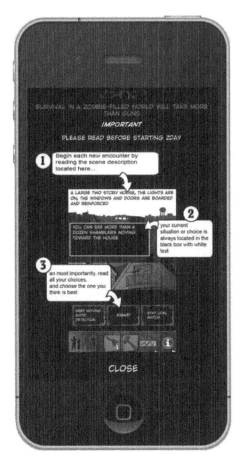

Figure 8-20. *The instructions screen from ZDAY Survival Simulator*

```
native.showWebPopup("http://howto.oz-apps.com")
```

And to remove it from the screen, use the following:

```
native.cancelWebPopup()
```

Nothing Lasts Forever

In your game, you might want to give the player some special abilities or powers that are temporary in nature, or you might want to display a bonus item on the screen for the player to get within a small window of time (like the fruit bonus in Pac-Man). If the player does not get this object within the allotted time, then the object is removed from the screen.

```
print("displaying the special object for 3 seconds")
timer.performWithDelay(3000,
    function()
        print("The object has now been removed")
    end)
```

The terminal displays text indicating that the object is being displayed for 3 seconds, and then after 3 seconds, it is replaced by text that says that the object has been removed.

```
local dot = display.newCircle(160,240,20)
dot.alpha = 0
dot:setFillColor(255,72,72)
transition.to(dot, {time=400, alpha = 1, onComplete =
    function()
        dot.timer = timer.performWithDelay(3000,
            function()
                transition.to(dot, {
                    time = 400,
                    alpha = 0,
                    onComplete =
                        function()
                            dot:removeSelf()
                            dot = nil
                        end
                })
            end)
    end})
```

This brings us to the end of our discussion of Corona SDK, but it's important to know that it includes many more features that weren't discussed in this chapter. Corona SDK also allows access to other events, such as the accelerometer, sprites for animation, gameNetwork, gyroscope, compass, maps, local notifications, in-app purchases, and scene manager, to name a few. While these are out of the scope of this chapter, you can get more information on these topics at http://docs.coronalabs.com/api/.

Enterprise Edition

The Enterprise Edition is a new offering from Corona Labs that allows developers to add features using native Objective-C or Java into their applications. This also provides the functionality of offline and automated builds. This is a rather expensive option but provides game studios with the flexibility and power that they might require when working with Corona SDK.

Summary

Corona SDK is one of the easiest-to-use frameworks that support mobile development. The API has functionality for use of the objects, display elements that one might require of a framework. Using physics is quite easy, as Corona SDK abstracts most of the Box2D functions, and you never really have to bother with fixtures and the like. It even has features that enable enterprise developers to add native code functionality.

In the next few chapters we'll explore the other frameworks and look at the basic similarities toward developing for the iOS devices.

Chapter 9

Gideros Studio

In the previous chapter, we looked at using our first Lua-based mobile framework, Corona SDK. The things that we noted while working with it was that it has no IDE and the trial version does not allow for creating an app that can be uploaded to the app store. Knowing that there comes a point at which you might want to extend the capabilities of the framework, our other offering, Gideros Studio, fills in the gap here.

License

Gideros Studio has four licenses to offer:

- *Community*: This free license provides all of the functionality of the other versions, but displays a "Made with Gideros" splash screen.

- *Indie*: At $149 per year, this license offers all of the functionality of the Community license, but allows for having your own splash screens.

- *Student*: This license is similar to the Indie license, but is discounted for students and academic staff ($79 per year).

- *Professional*: The Professional license ($449 per year) is advised for those that have an annual turnover of over $100,000.

Installing Gideros Studio

Before downloading Gideros Studio, you need to create an account. This shall then allow for downloading the binaries as appropriate for your operating system. The latest version at the moment is Gideros 2012.09.1.

However, there are some requirements for building to your mobile device. For iOS, the prerequisites are the following:

- A 64-bit Mac OS X operating system (Snow Leopard or later)

- Xcode
- An Apple Developer license

Building apps for the Android platform is a bit more involved and requires that you have the following:

- The Java SDK
- The latest Android SDK
- The Android development tools
- Eclipse IDE

If you want to install Gideros Studio on Unix, you can do so using Wine. A detailed guide can be found online at http://giderosmobile.com/DevCenter/index.php/Running_Gideros_Studio_under_Linux.

What's Included

When you install Gideros Studio, it comes with a suite of tools (shown in Figure 9-1), all ready to help you create your application. The package contains the following:

GiderosiPadPlayer.
zip
19.9 MB

GiderosiPhonePlaye
r.zip
19.9 MB

GiderosAndroidPla
yer.apk

All Plugins
5 items

Documentation
13 items

Examples
6 items

Plugins
2 items

Sdk
2 items

Gideros Font
Creator.app

Gideros License
Manager.app

Gideros Player.app

Gideros Studio.app

Gideros Texture
Packer.app

Figure 9-1. *The contents of the Gideros package*

- Gideros License Manager
- Gideros Font Creator
- Gideros Texture Packer
- Gideros Player
- Gideros Studio

It also contains a couple of folders with samples and documentation, an Android build of the player for your android device, and the source code for the iPhone and iPad players.

Setting the License

The first thing that you must do when starting to work with Gideros Studio is start up the License Manager (shown in Figure 9-2), which allows for authorizing the license with the user name you used while creating the account to download Gideros Studio. Upon entering the details and authorizing the free license, you are greeted with the license window shown in Figure 9-3.

Figure 9-2. *The Gideros Studio License Manager*

Figure 9-3. *The free license activation for Gideros Studio*

First Steps

Now you are ready to start working with Gideros Studio. Close the window and start Gideros Studio, and you'll be greeted with the IDE shown in Figure 9-4, which allows for creating a new project, opening one of the recent projects, opening an example project, and using the reference material.

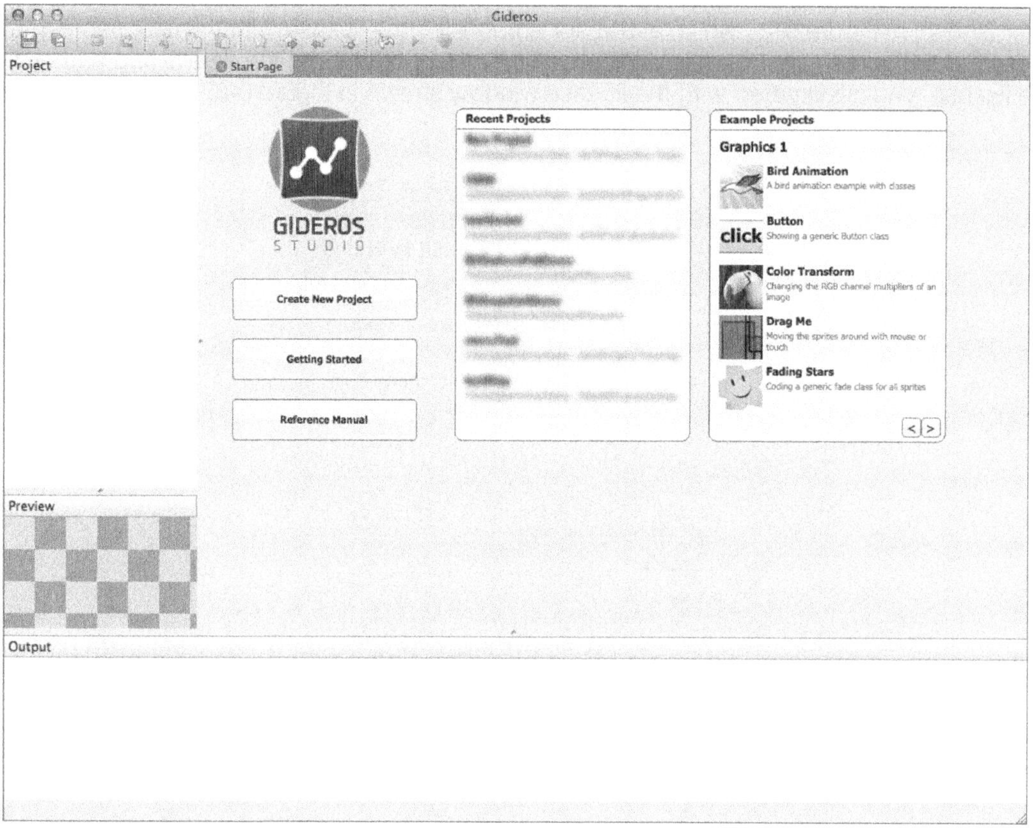

Figure 9-4. The Gideros Studio start screen

To create your first application, choose the Create New Project option; if required, we can customize the project path and the name. Following this, we are presented with a blank IDE to start our development.

The first step is to create a new Lua file, so right-click the project name and select Add New File. If you have a file that you want to add to the project from the hard drive, you can select the Add Existing File option and navigate to the file to be added.

After you add a new file, name it file `main.lua`. Leave the location set to the value displayed, and double-click the file name (`main.lua`) displayed under the project name. The editor will open for us to type our code. Start with typing the following:

```
print ("Hello World")
```

Running the Code

To run the code, we need to connect to the Gideros Player, either on the desktop or the device. We have the option of using either the desktop player or the device player to run our code. We can select Player ➤ Player Settings, which brings up the dialog box shown in Figure 9-5 and allows us to set the IP address of the player device. If you want to use the desktop player, check the Localhost check box, which sets the IP address to 127.0.0.1 (localhost). When the player app starts (either on the device or the desktop), it displays some basic information, including the version number and the IP addresses, as shown in Figure 9-6.

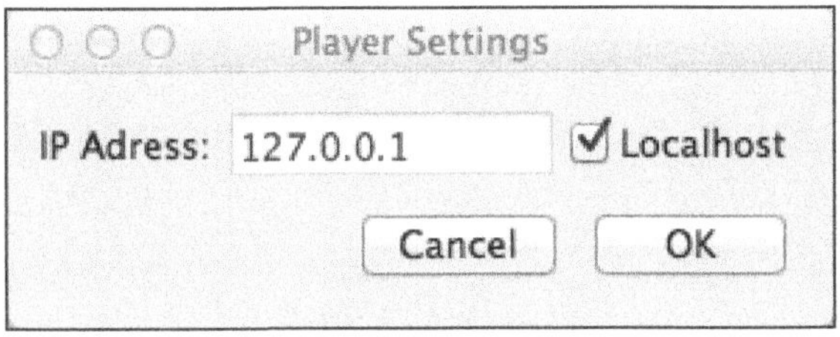

Figure 9-5. The Gideros Player settings

Figure 9-6. The Gideros Player ready for connecting

If you have already set up the player or are using the default desktop player's settings, click the icon that looks like an Xbox controller, which will start the Gideros desktop player. The player (both the desktop and the device player) displays the IP address on the screen. This IP address can be used to connect to a Gideros Player anywhere.

Click the blue play button (which should be enabled once the player is started, as shown in Figure 9-7).

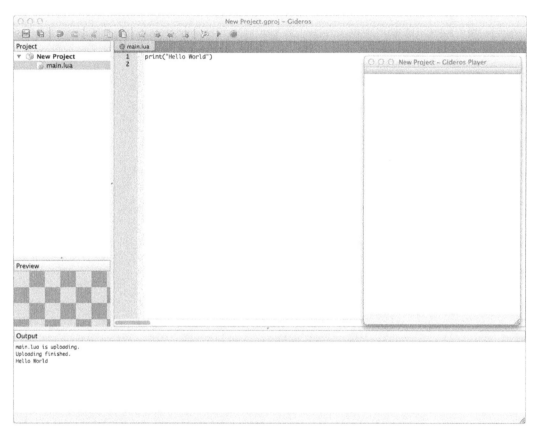

Figure 9-7. The Gideros Studio IDE

You will see that the output window has three lines:

```
main.lua is uploading.
Uploading finished.
Hello World
```

The last line is the output of the program, which we are printing from the code. The second line indicates that the uploading of the code and resources is finished. Gideros Studio copies the resources to the player (uploads them), displays each on the output panel as it's uploaded, prints a confirmation, and then executes the program.

Configuring the Project

Right-click the project name on the left-hand side of the screen and select the Properties option. This allows you to set the properties for the project. Here you can set the scale mode for the app, the logical dimensions, the orientation, the frame rate, and even the suffix for image files, if required. This is an advanced option that you probably won't use at first while you are learning Gideros Studio, but it's very useful, so I'll describe it here.

The first option, Scale Mode, sets how the app will scale when run on various devices—this is covered in more detail later in this chapter. The logical dimensions are used to set the base settings for the application; it is from these dimensions that the display scales up using the scale mode on the various devices. Apple has suffixes of @2x or @4x that allow you to load retina graphics on the new iPhone and iPad. Gideros is a multi-platform system and it extends this format for the Android platforms as well. So you can have @1.5, @2, @4, etc. as suffixes.

> **Tip**   The scaling suffix can be used not only for high-resolution graphics, but also to have a graphic for each platform without having to write any code checking for specific platforms.

The iOS tab is useful to configure a few other settings specific to iOS; for example, whether the app should consider the target device a device with a retina display, and whether autorotation should be enabled. If the logical dimensions are set to 320×480 and the retina display set to "No retina display," then the display is deemed to have dimensions of 320×480, as shown in Figure 9-8, while with the retina-display option, the device is deemed to have a 640×960 display, as shown in Figure 9-9. Both of the images are taken from the player running on the iPhone 4, which has dimensions of 960×640, but based on the project settings, the display can vary.

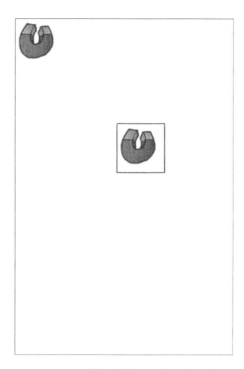

Figure 9-8. *The Gideros Player running at a resolution of 320×480 (no retina display)*

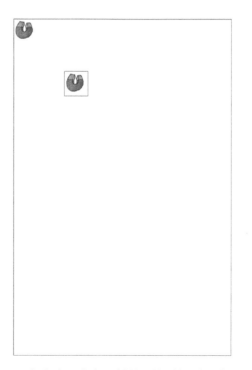

Figure 9-9. *The Gideros Player running at a logical resolution of 320×480 with retina display*

Architecture

The architecture of Gideros is similar to other frameworks. The core Gideros engine talks to Lua code on one side, and in the background it interacts with the device or desktop using OpenGL. Figure 9-10 shows the architecture of Gideros Studio. There are a couple of utilities that form the Gideros Studio family; these were discussed at the start of the chapter.

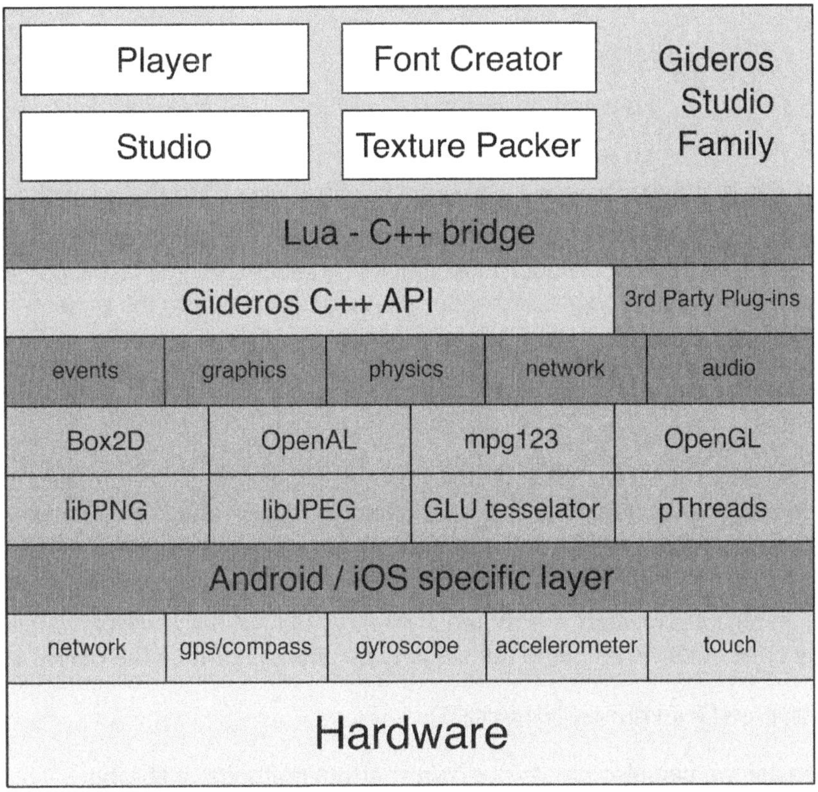

Figure 9-10. The Gideros Studio family architecture

The Lua code that we write is compiled into bytecode and executed.

Unlike Corona SDK, Gideros offers offline compilation, which a lot of developers like. The entire Gideros engine is available as a library that has to be linked to the final app (similar to the Corona SDK Enterprise offering). So, the Xcode or Android project has some wrapper code that starts off the scripts and compiles the Gideros library into the final application binary. Any plug-in is also compiled as a static library into the application.

The plug-in feature is very handy and powerful; we'll explore it later in this chapter.

The Gideros Engine

The Gideros engine is the framework that is facilitated by the Lua language for development. This contains all the specific commands that grant access to the Gideros API. This is what a developer can use to code and display an application to the device.

Gideros is object oriented, but do not let that sentence scare you. This just means that the Gideros API uses colon notation rather than dot notation—for example, it would use `image:setX(100)` instead of `image.x = 100`.

Hello Birdie

To follow up our Hello World example, we'll now display an image on to the screen.

One point to note about Gideros Studio is that having a resource in the directory means nothing; you should add each of the files that you want for the project by either adding a *new* file or an *existing* file. So, before we can use `bird.png` in our application, we need to add that to the project.

```
local texture = Texture.new("bird.png")
local image = Bitmap.new(texture)
stage:addChild(image)
image:setPosition(100,100)
```

This piece of code first creates a texture from a file called `bird.png`, and then creates a bitmap image using that texture. This image instance is the *sprite*, or the object that we display on the screen; we can reposition it as we like using the `setPosition` function.

In Gideros, when an object is created, it is stored in memory but not made visible to the user. We need to add the display object that we create to the stage to be able to see it on the device screen.

```
local image = Bitmap.new(Texture.new("bird.png"))
```

To make things easier, we can also create our own shortcut methods or library:

```
function newImage (imageName, posX, posY)
  local image = Bitmap.new(Texture.new(imageName))
  stage:addChild(image)
  image:setPosition(posX, posY)
  return image
end
```

Now, all we need to do is call this function, as follows:

```
local birdie = newImage("bird.png", 100, 100)
```

Another point to note about Gideros Studio is that it loads multiple Lua files without having to use the `require` function. We can use this to our advantage by having a separate file that houses all of the utility functions for our projects. Let's create a file, `myutils.lua`, add the `newImage` function to it, and include it in our projects.

Aligning the Images

All images have an *anchor point* on which they are hinged; when an image is rotated, it is this point that determines how the rotation takes place. The anchor point is a numerical value from 0 to 1, which represents the height or width of the image. This is illustrated in Figure 9-11. You can think of this value as a percentage: 0 being the top and 100 being the bottom on the y-axis and 0 being the left and 100 being the right on the x-axis. To get our value, we simply divide this percentage by 100.

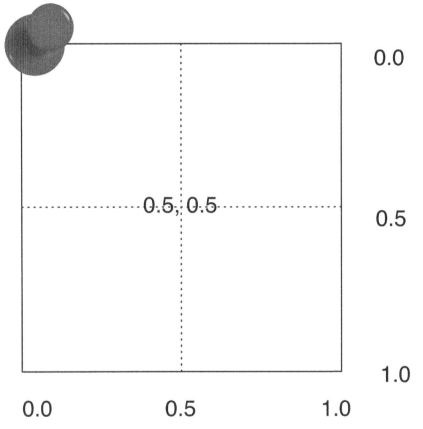

Figure 9-11. A bitmap object with the anchor point set at 0, 0

The center anchor point would be 0.5 on both x- and y-axis. Consider the following code:

```
local birdie = newImage("post-it.png", 100, 100)
birdie:setAnchorPoint(0.5,0.5)
birdie:setRotation(45)
```

Notice that the image is rotated around the center of the image when run. Now try to change the 0.5, 0.5 to different numbers to observe the effect of the anchor point.

Groups

A group is a container of different display objects. When the attributes of the group are altered, it affects all of the display objects contained in the group. The stage is a group; in fact it is the root group, which is the container for all of the other display objects. The way to add an object to a group is using the following syntax:

```
group:addChild(displayObject)
```

To remove an object from the group, you use this function:

```
displayObject:removeFromParent()
```

To create a new group, you create a new object that inherits from the Gideros class:

```
local obj = Core.class(Sprite).new()
```

Now we need to place this object on to the stage:

```
stage:addChild(obj)
```

Here's a new function to add to myUtils.lua file:

```
function newGroup()
  local obj = Core.class(Sprite).new()
  stage:addChild(obj)
  return obj
end
```

We can use this henceforth to create a group object.

We use stage:addChild to add most of the objects to the stage. We can now use this function to add an object to a group by using the group:addChild.

To get the handle of an object in a particular group, we can get it using the function getChildAt by passing it the index. Alternatively, we can get the index position by passing the object to the function getChildIndex. We can also use this to check if a particular parent group contains a display object or not by using this function by passing it the display object.

We can determine the number of objects contained in the parent by using the group:getNumChildren function.

After we are done with the group or the objects in the group, we can remove the objects from the stage or the group using the removeChild or removeFromParent function, or using the removeChildAt function, which takes the index of the display object.

```
object:removeChild()
group:removeChildAt(index)
group:removeFromParent(object)
```

There is another function, addChildAt, which allows for adding a child at a particular index position. This allows for positioning display objects that is equivalent of moving an object to the front or to the back relative to the other objects.

Displaying Text

This section will describe how to display text to the screen in your application. Gideros Studio allows you to use custom fonts in your application, and it works with both TrueType and bitmapped fonts. Note that if you want to use a custom font, then it needs to be loaded before use.

> **Note**   Gideros Studio comes with Gideros Font Creator, an application for creating bitmapped fonts that can be used with Gideros Studio.

The first thing you need to do to display text is create a text field, which you can do as follows:

```
-- To use the default font, pass a nil value for the font parameter
local text = TextField.new(nil, "Hello World")
text:setPosition(10,10)
stage:addChild(text)
text:setText("Hello from Gideros Studio")
-- Change the text
```

Here, we create a new text field with `nil` as the parameter, which will use the default font. Then we position the text on the screen. Text in Gideros is displayed using *baseline font*. Simply, the y parameter is where the base of the font is aligned, which may take a while to get used to. For example, if we do not position the text at position 10 from the top, the text might not be visible. Then we add the text to the stage and change the text displayed.

The TextField object can be modified like any other display object. The text color can be set using the function object:setTextColor(*colour*), where colour is a hexadecimal value derived from $b + g *$ $256 + r * 65536$, and r, g, and b represent the red, green, and blue values of the color, respectively.

To make the preceding text red, we use the following:

```
-- To use the default font, pass a nil value for the font parameter
local text = TextField.new(nil, "Hello World")
text:setPosition(10,50)
text:setTextColor(0xff0000)
stage:addChild(text)
text:setText("Hello from Gideros Studio")
-- Change the text
text:setScale(2,2)
```

When this is run, the player displays the text "Hello from Gideros Studio" in red and at twice the size of the default font, as shown in Figure 9-12.

Figure 9-12. Text displayed in the Gideros Player with modified text color

Drawing Shapes

Gideros Studio also has a Shape object, which you might use when you want to create vector shapes like lines, rectangles, and so on. Drawing shapes in Gideros is based on the same principles as drawing on a deviceContext in many other languages. This section will help you get started by describing how to create lines and rectangles, as well as how to fill shapes.

Lines

Lines are the simplest shapes to draw. A line is basically defined as four points: a starting x,y-coordinate and an ending x,y-coordinate. The line joins these two points.

```
function newLine(x1, y1, x2, y2)
  local obj = Shape.new()
  obj:setLineStyle(2, 0x000000)
  obj:beginPath()
  obj:moveTo(x1, y1)
  obj:lineTo(x2, y2)
   obj:endPath()
  stage:addChild(obj)
  return obj
end
```

To draw the line, we call the function as follows:

```
local line = newline(10,10,250,50)
```

This creates a line from 10, 10 to 250, 50 with a width of 2 pixels. We can set the line width and the color with the setLineStyle function. We could extend that function to also include a width and color, which could default to the standard values of 1 for the width and 0x000000 for the color.

```
function newLine(x1, y1, x2, y2, lineWidth, lineColour)
  local lineWidth = lineWidth or 1
  local lineColour = lineColour or 0x000000
  local obj = Shape.new()
  obj:setLineStyle(lineWidth, lineColour)
  obj:beginPath()
  obj:moveTo(x1, y1)
  obj:lineTo(x2, y2)
   obj:endPath()
  stage:addChild(obj)
   return obj
end
```

Now we can draw a line in pretty much the same way as earlier, but also choose our own line width and color, like so:

```
local line = newLine(10, 10, 250, 50, 4, 0x00FFFF)
```

Rectangles

A rectangle is a slightly modified form of a line. It is made up of four lines, and also includes a fill color. If we don't pass a parameter for the fill color, the rectangle will have an outline; otherwise, it will be filled in with the color passed. Figure 9-13 shows an example of the each.

```
function newRectangle(x1, y1, x2, y2, lw, lc, fc)
  local obj = Shape.new()
  local lw = lw or 1
  local lc = lc or 0x000000
  obj:beginPath()
  obj:setLineStyle(lw, lc)
  if fc then
    obj:setFillStyle(Shape.SOLID, fc)
  end

  obj:moveTo(x1,y1)
  obj:lineTo(x2, y1)
  obj:lineTo(x2, y2)
  obj:lineTo(x1, y2)
  obj:lineTo(x1, y1)
  obj:closePath()
  obj:endPath()
```

```
  stage:addChild(obj)
  return obj
end

newRectangle(10,10,200,50,1,0x0000FF)
newRectangle(100,150,250,250,1,nil, 0xFF0000)
```

Figure 9-13. An outlined rectangle (top) and a filled one (bottom)

Note   Note that there is an issue with the preceding code. Although it gives the results expected, if you try to reposition the rectangle, it will be a few pixels off. This is mainly because we are drawing the lines on the shape with respect to its position. What we should rather be doing is drawing everything at the position 0, 0 and then moving the shape to the starting x,y-coordinates.

Filled Shapes

Gideros Studio allows for filling shapes with either a solid color or an image. This can help for some interesting results like creating an image mask or seamlessly filled textures. Here's some example code for filling a shape with an image:

```
local texture = Texture.new("image.png") setFillStyle(Shape.TEXTURE, texture)
-- Sets the fill style as texture with "image.png"
```

We can use this to create a rectangle filled with a texture, handy for creating tiled backgrounds and such. Figure 9-14 shows an example.

```
function newImgRectangle(x1, y1, x2, y2, lw, lc, imgName)
  local obj = Shape.new()

  -- The image for the fill
  local img = Texture.new(imgName)
  local lw = lw or 1
  local lc = lc or 0x000000

  local wd, ht = x2-x1, y2-y1

  obj:clear()
  obj:setLineStyle(lw, lc)
  obj:setFillStyle(Shape.TEXTURE, img)

  obj:beginPath()
  obj:moveTo(0,0)
  obj:lineTo(0, ht)
  obj:lineTo(wd, ht)
  obj:lineTo(wd,0)
  obj:lineTo(0,0)
  obj:closePath()
  obj:endPath()

  obj:setPosition(x1, y1)

  stage:addChild(obj)

  return obj
end

newImgRectangle(10, 10, 70, 70, 0, nil, "myImage2.png")
```

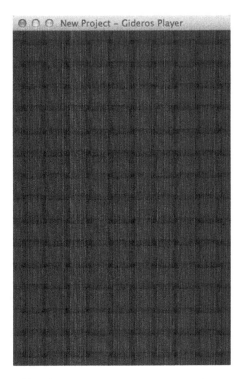

Figure 9-14. Tiling a background using a filled shape

With this example, if the rectangle were larger, we would see the image surrounded by blank space. But Gideros Studio also has an option for tiling images in the background. To use this feature, we simply modify the line in which we load our texture to the following:

```
local img = Texture.new(imgName, false, {wrap=Texture.REPEAT})
```

Now we can try the same with this example:

```
newImgRectangle(10, 10, 220, 220, 1, nil, "myImage2.png")
```

We can even create complete background images, like so:

```
newImgRectangle(0,0,application:getDeviceWidth(),application:getDeviceWidth(), 0, nil, "tile.png")
```

Drawing Other Shapes

Because Gideros Studio offers the user a canvas to draw any shape, there are no built-in API functions for lines, rectangles, circles, or arcs. However, you can use moveTo and lineTo to draw any shape you want. This allows you to create your own Bezier curves, arcs, ovals, circles, and so on.

> **Note**   When you draw something on the shape, it is retained along with any subsequent draw over whatever is already present on the shape. Therefore, it is best to start with `obj:clear()` to clear out the shape before drawing.

The Application Object

You might want to get details such as the width of the device, the height of the device, or the locale of the device, in case you are making multilingual apps. You might want to know if the device runs iOS or Android, and so on. Gideros Studio has an extensive range of functions that allow us to query the Application object to get these types of details. Here are a few examples:

```
local width = application:getDeviceWidth()
local height = application:getDeviceHeight()
local model = application:getDeviceInfo()
print("On " .. model .. " (" .. width .. " x " .. height .. " )" )
```

> **Note**   The variable that holds the Application object is application, not Application (note the lowercase *a*).

Look at the output pane in the IDE. If you are running this on a device player, the output would be the device you are running it on, and if you are running the desktop player, as in this case, you will see "Mac OS" or "Windows," depending on which is being run. In the case of a mobile device, `application:getDeviceInfo()` returns multiple values. For Android, it returns "Android" followed by the version number, and on an iOS device, it returns five values: "iOS," the version, the device type, the UI idiom, and the device model. Here's some sample output from the iPhone running the Gideros Player:

```
iOS 5.1 iPhone iPhone iPhone3,1
```

Keeping the Device Awake

If you need to perform some calculations and are worried that in that time the device might dim and then go to sleep or switch off, you can ensure that the device does not dim simply by using the following:

```
application:setKeepAwake(true)
-- Prevent the device from dimming
```

Alternatively, you can use this:

```
application:setKeepAwake(false)
-- Allow the device to dim
```

Orientation

If you need to gather how the device is held at a particular point in time, you can query the orientation of the device, like so:

```
application:getOrientation()
```

And if you need to set the orientation, you can use the following:

```
application:setOrientation(theOrientation)
```

These are the orientation options:

- `Application.PORTRAIT`
- `Application.PORTRAIT_UPSIDE_DOWN`
- `Application.LANDSCAPE_LEFT`
- `Application.LANDSCAPE_RIGHT`

> **Note** The constants for the `Application` object all begin with a capital *A*, whereas the variables begin with a lowercase *a*, as mentioned earlier.

You can use `setOrientation` to orient the device in the manner you want—for example, if you want a game fixed in landscape mode, you need to explicitly set it in the settings or change the orientation using the `setOrientation` function. Note that if you set this function, it overrides the project settings.

Scaling

One of the challenges faced by developers is ensuring that all screen resolutions are supported. One way that many developers still address this is by setting the resolutions of the project to 320×480 and then using autoscaling for higher resolutions. The scale mode can be set from the project properties window, but it can also be set via code using `application:setScaleMode(theMode)`. Figure 9-15 shows the scaling options and how they affect the display.

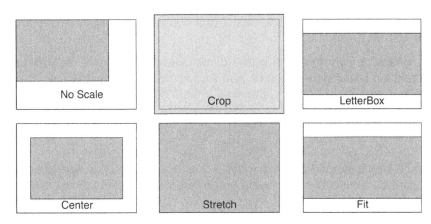

Figure 9-15. *An illustration of the various scaling options*

This will scale the screen to fit an entirely different resolution, and the settings to choose from are

- `Application.NO_SCALE`: No scaling is applied and the screen is aligned to the top-left corner. On a device with a larger screen, the area beyond the size of the project screen is left blank.

- `Application.CENTER`: No scaling is applied but the screen is centered and displayed.

- `Application.PIXEL_PERFECT`: The screen is set to the exact pixels that are available on the device.

- `Application.LETTERBOX`: The screen is displayed in letterbox mode with banding on the sides.

- `Application.CROP`: The excess area when scaled is cropped off

- `Application.STRETCH`: The screen is stretched to fit the device resolution, and the aspect ratio is *not* considered.

- `Application.FIT_HEIGHT`: The screen is scaled to the height of the device's screen.

- `Application.FIT_WIDTH`: The screen is scaled to the width of the device's screen.

Adding Sound Effects

If you're creating a game, it's important to include sound effects—for example, thumping beats to create suspense or soothing melodies to accompany calmer moments. This section will describe how to include sound effects for your game.

The Gideros Studio sound library is condensed into a couple of functions; these are enough to achieve what we just discussed.

The first thing to note while playing sound with Gideros Studio is that there are two distinct objects: the Sound object and the SoundChannel object. The Sound object provides the data that needs to be played, whereas the SoundChannel object actually plays the sound.

```
local mySound = Sound.new("sound.wav")
local theChannel = mySound:play()
```

If you want to play a long track and perhaps loop through the file, you can also specify the point from where you want the sound to start playing and whether you want to loop the sound.

```
local channel = mySound:play(startTime, loops)
```

startTime is 0 by default, and loops defines how many times you want the sound to be looped. A loops value of 0 (the default) means that the sound will not be looped but just played once, 1 means that it will be looped once, a value of 2 looped twice and so on. If you want the sound to loop infinitely, you can use math.huge.

You can control the sound further (pausing, stopping, changing the volume, etc.) with the soundChannel object. Here's an example of using the soundChannel object to manipulate the volume on a per-channel basis:

```
channel:setVolume(0.5) -- Sets the channel volume to half
```

Events

Like most frameworks, Gideros has an asynchronous way of processing things. Events are raised when certain things happen—for example, when the user touches the screen, when the frame is updated, and when system events occur (e.g., when the application starts, or is suspended, resumed, or exited). Table 9-1 lists the events that are handled by Gideros Studio.

Table 9-1. Events Handled by Gideros Studio

Event Type	Events Handled
Touch	TOUCHES_BEGIN TOUCHES_MOVE TOUCHES_END TOUCHES_CANCEL
Frame and stage	ENTER_FRAME ADDED_TO_STAGE REMOVED_FROM_STAGE

(continued)

Table 9-1. (continued)

Event Type	Events Handled
System and application	APPLICATION_START APPLICATION_RESUME APPLICATION_SUSPEND APPLICATION_EXIT
Sound and timer	COMPLETE TIMER TIMER_COMPLETE
Mouse	MOUSE_DOWN MOUSE_UP MOUSE_MOVE
URL loader	COMPLETE ERROR PROGRESS
Physics	BEGIN_CONTACT END_CONTACT PRE_SOLVE POST_SOLVE

Touch

An application needs to set an event listener to be able to listen to a particular event. The event listener can be attached to any display object.

```
local image = newImage("myImage.png")
function handler(object, event)
 print("Got an event")
end

image:addEventListener(Event.TOUCHES_BEGIN, handler, image)
```

The event listener takes the event, the handler, and an additional parameter that allows for passing data to the event handler. The event handler gets two parameters: the extra data that we pass to the handler and the event object that contains the event-related data.

> **Note**   The parameters passed to the function are different for the mouse events than for the touch events. The touch event has a record called `touches`, which is not present in a mouse event. This is mainly because the user can place multiple fingers on the screen—so, each `touches` record has an x,y-coordinates and ID, while the mouse event does not.

The touch event contains two records, `touches` and `allTouches`. `touches` is the current touch that contains the x,y-coordinates and the ID, whereas `allTouches` is an array that contains all of the `touches` records. To get the object that triggered the touch event, you can use the function `event:getTarget()`.

Enter Frame

You can set the enter frame event to perform a frame-by-frame animation, like so:

```
local _W = application:getLogicalWidth()
local _H = application:getLogicalHeight()

local xD, yD, speed = 1, 1, 10
local img = newImage("myImage2.png",0,0)
local wd, ht = img:getWidth(), img:getHeight()

function onEnterFrame(event)
local xP, yP = img:getPosition()
xP = xP + xD*speed
yP = yP + yD*speed
if xP >= _W-wd or xP == 0 then xD = -xD end
if yP >= _H-ht or yP == 0 then yD = -yD end
img:setPosition(xP, yP)
end

img:addEventListener(Event.ENTER_FRAME, onEnterFrame)
```

The enter frame event has a `frameCount` property, which returns the number of frames that have passed since the start of the application. `time` returns the time in seconds since the start of the application, and `deltaTime` contains the time difference between the last frame and the current frame. This can be used in animation and can help to coordinate time-sensitive animation.

System Events

The `stage` object is present for the lifetime of the application. We can set up listeners on the `stage` object just like we can on other display objects. The suggested way to manage system events is to set them on the `stage` object. However, system events are like a broadcast, they are sent to every object that sets up a listener, not exclusively to one.

```
stage:addEventListener(Event.APPLICATION_START,
    function(event)
      print("Started")
    end)
```

You can also monitor the time when the application is suspended or resumes, so you can save the state of your app and then load it again when the app is resumed.

Timer

You can set the timer in Gideros Studio by using the Timer.new function and then adding an event listener to listen for when the timer fires. You can also listen for the timer-complete event, which occurs after all of the timer loops have fired. The default value for loops is 0, which is the same as indicating infinite loops for the timer.

```
local theTimer = Timer.new(1000, 5)
theTimer:addEventListener(Event.TIMER,
    function(event)
        print("Timer fired")
    end)
theTimer:addEventListener(Event.TIMER_COMPLETE,
    function(event)
        print("All timer loops completed")
    end)
```

This code creates a new timer that fires at a set frequency and runs a specified number of times. In this case, the frequency is 1,000 ms and the loop runs five times. The timer then has to be started using the start function.

```
theTimer:start()
```

Now you can see the results in the output window, showing that the timer fires every 1 second (1,000 ms) and completes after firing five times.

The timer has a currentCount property (a read-only property) that holds the number of times the timer has fired. repeatCount holds the number of times the timer should repeat, and the timer stops once the currentCount value reaches the repeatCount value. We can use the reset function to set the currentCount to 0. You can set repeatCount to use the setRepeatCount function, and you can alter the delay using the setDelay function.

The timer can be finely controlled using the start, pause, and stop functions. Further, all of the active timers can be paused, stopped, or resumed using the pauseAll, resumeAll, and stopAll functions, respectively. The timer can also be queried using the isRunning function, which returns whether the timer is running or not.

If you need to trigger a function after a delay, you can use the Timer.delayedCall function. This function takes three parameters: a delay time (after which the function is invoked), a function, and a custom parameter that you can pass to the function.

```
Timer.delayedCall(1000,
    function(msg)
        print("Hello "..msg)
    end,
    "Gideros")
```

Custom Events

You can also create your own events that can be dispatched and set up a listener for these custom events, as follows:

```
local theTimer = Timer.new(1000, 5)
theTimer:addEventListener(Event.TIMER,
  function(event)
    theTimer:setRepeatCount(10)
    if theTimer:getCurrentCount() == 4 then
      evt = Event.new("hi")
      stage:dispatchEvent(evt)
    end
  end)

theTimer:addEventListener(Event.TIMER_COMPLETE,
  function(event)
    print("All timer loops completed")
  end)

theTimer:start()

stage:addEventListener("hi",
  function()
    print("Hello")
  end)
```

The way to manage custom events is to set up an event listener for a particular type of event using addEventListener. After creating an event using the Event class with Event.new(eventName), when we want to raise the event, we can use the dispatchEvent function.

Removing Events

Events can be removed using removeEventListener in a manner similar to how they're added using addEventListener. To add an event handler, you can use the following:

```
object:addEventListener(EventName, evtHandler)
```

Similarly, here's how to remove an event handler:

```
object:removeEventListener(EventName, evtHandler)
```

Additional data can also be added to the events and passed to the handler. Here's an example:

```
local myEvent = Event.new("myEvent")
        myEvent.data1 = "Data One"
        myEvent.data2 = "Data Two"

function theFunc(param)
  print("Invoked with \n\t" .. param.data1 .. ", " .. param.data2)
  stage:removeEventListener("myEvent", theFunc)
end

function raiseEvent(msg)
    print(msg)
    myEvent.data1 = msg
    stage:dispatchEvent(myEvent)
end

stage:addEventListener("myEvent", theFunc)

-- Invoke the event
print("------------\nInvoking the event")
Timer.delayedCall(1000, raiseEvent, "first time")
Timer.delayedCall(5000, raiseEvent, "second time")
Timer.delayedCall(10000, raiseEvent, "third time")
```

When the program is run, the timer initially fires at 1,000 ms, and this calls the raiseEvent handler. The program then prints the message "first time," and that in turn dispatches the custom event. When the custom event is fired, it prints the data1 and data2 members of the parameter passed to the handler, and finally the event handler is removed.

After 5,000 ms, the raiseEvent function is called again, the message "second time" is printed, the custom event is dispatched. However, because we removed the event listener the last time, the theFunc function is not called.

After 10,000 ms, the message "third time" is printed, and since the event listener is no longer in effect, nothing happens.

Now you know how to set up an event listener, dispatch custom events, and also remove event listeners.

Querying Events

If you have set an event listener or would like to know if a particular event listener is set on an object, then you can use the function hasEventListener.

```
print(stage:hasEventListener("noEvent"))
```

> **Tip**   Custom or standard events can be dispatched using the `dispatchEvent` function. This can be used to simulate touch events, as in a tutorial. So, the data can be read and saved in an array or table, which can then be passed to simulate the user interacting with the app.

Animations

Gideros Studio offers the `MovieClip` class for creating animations. It allows for creating frames and the animation plays based on these frames. Here's a code example:

```
Local image = newImage("myImage2.png")
local mc = MovieClip.new{
    {1, 100, sprite, {x = {0, 200, "linear"}}}}
```

This creates a 100-frame animation that tweens the sprite linearly on the x-axis from 0 to 200. To play the animation, we can use the `play` function. The animation starts to play automatically as soon as we create the movie clip.

```
mc:play()
```

We can also set a frame to go to after the animation reaches a particular frame. Normally the animation proceeds to the next frame in the sequence, but we can set it to another frame number. This could, for example, be used to create and play animations infinitely, as in the following example:

```
mc:setGotoAction(100, 1)
```

This command indicates that on reaching the 100th frame, the movie clip will loop back to the first.

Similar to gotoAction, you can set `stopAction`, which stops the animation when a certain frame is reached; this can be used to split the animation into multiple parts. You can stop the activity of gotoAction and stopAction by using the `clearAction` function. Similarly, there are the gotoAndPlay and the gotoAndStop function which start playing from the frame specified in gotoAndPlay or stop at the frame specified in gotoAndStop.

Networking and the Internet

In your game, you might want to open a link to your web site, or upload or download some data. In other cases, you might want to send an e-mail or dial a phone number. This section will describe how to do these things.

The simplest way to navigate to a site is by using the function `application:openUrl(THE_URL)` where the URL can be any of the following `http:`, `https:`, `tel:` and `mailto:`

To open a web page, you can use the following:

```
application:openUrl("http://www.oz-apps.com")
```

To send an e-mail, you can use this:

```
application:openUrl("mailto:dev.ozapps@gmail.com")
```

You can also add a subject and message as follows:

```
application:openUrl("mailto:dev.ozapps@gmail.com?subject=Hello Gideros&body=This is a test ")
```

If you running the app on the iPhone, then you can also dial a number by using the following:

```
application:openUrl("tel:555-7827-9277")
```

In a game, you might want to download a file, some JSON, or a text file containing some level data. This cannot be achieved with the openUrl function. We can, however, use the UrlLoader class. Here's an example:

```
local loader = UrlLoader.new("http://example.com/image.png")

local function onComplete(event)
    local out = io.open("|D|image.png", "wb")
    out:write(event.data)
    out:close()

    local b = Bitmap.new(Texture.new("|D|image.png"))
    stage:addChild(b)
end

local function onError()
    print("error")
end

local function onProgress(event)
    print("progress: " .. event.bytesLoaded .. " of " .. event.bytesTotal)
end

loader:addEventListener(Event.COMPLETE, onComplete)
loader:addEventListener(Event.ERROR, onError)
loader:addEventListener(Event.PROGRESS, onProgress)
```

In this code, we first create a new instance of UrlLoader, which will start the download. The default is method for UrlLoader is UrlLoader.GET. The other options are POST, PUT, and DELETE. When using POST or PUT, headers and data can be passed to the URL.

```
local url = "http://www.[yourDomain].com/application.php?userid=gideros&login=guest"

local loader1 = UrlLoader.new(url)
local loader2 = UrlLoader.new(url, UrlLoader.GET) -- Same as the previous line
```

```
local loader3 = UrlLoader.new(url, UrlLoader.POST, "my post data")
local loader4 = UrlLoader.new(url, UrlLoader.PUT, "my put data")
local loader5 = UrlLoader.new(url, UrlLoader.DELETE)

local headers = {
    ["Content-Type"] = "application/x-www-form-urlencoded",
    ["User-Agent"] = "Gideros Browser",
}
local loader6 = UrlLoader.new(url, UrlLoader.PUT, headers, "key=value")
```

We can set up listeners that listen for progress events, complete events, and error events. Each time a chunk of data is received, the progress event is fired and the event object passes bytesLoaded and bytesTotal. This can be used to track and display the progress in bytes or as a percentage. If there is an error, the error event is raised, and on successful completion, the complete event is raised.

GPS and Compass

The device can be queried for the GPS location and the compass location details. We can get these readings by setting a event listener for Event.HEADING_UPDATE for the GPS and Event.LOCATION_UPDATE for compass details, as follows:

```
require "geolocation"

function onHeadingUpdate()

end

function onLocationUpdate(event)
  latitude  = event.latitude
  longitude = event.longitude
  altitude  = event.altitude
  print(latitude, longitude, altitude)
end

function onHeadingUpdate(event)
  local tHeading = event.trueHeading
  local mHeading = event.magneticHeading
  print(tHeading, mHeading)
end

geolocation:addEventListener(Event.HEADING_UPDATE, onHeadingUpdate)
geolocation:addEventListener(Event.LOCATION_UPDATE, onLocationUpdate)
geolocation:start()
```

You can check the hardware if the GPS is available or if the user has enabled the GPS capability by using the function isAvailable. You can also check for the heading details via the isHeadingAvailable function on the geolocation objects.

You can start and stop the updating of the heading and location information by using the `startUpdatingHeading` and `startUpdatingLocation` functions, and the `stopUpdatingHeading` and `stopUpdatingLocation` functions, respectively.

Accelerometer

The `Accelerometer` class is used to access the accelerometer data, if the device has an accelerometer. To be able to access the accelerometer, you need to call `require "accelerometer"`, and when this is loaded, a variable of type `Accelerometer` is created. It can be accessed as `accelerometer`. Then you can call the `start` function on the `accelerometer` object. If at any time you need to stop the accelerometer for any reason—including saving battery life or preventing unnecessary events from being triggered—you can call the `stop` function.

```
require "accelerometer"
accelerometer:start()
function onEnterFrame(event)
    local x, y, z = accelerometer:getAcceleration()
    print(x, y, z)
end
stage:addEventListener("enterFrame", onEnterFrame)
```

> **Note**   Running this code on the desktop player will just display a series of zeros, as the desktop player does not have an accelerometer. To test this code, you should run it with the device player.

Gyroscope

All new iOS devices have gyroscopes that can be read from the device. First, we use the `require "gyroscope"` command, which creates a variable called gyroscope that is of the `Gyroscope` class.

The data from the gyroscope is read using the `getRotationRate` function, which returns the rate of rotation in radians.

```
require "gyroscope"
gyroscope:start()
local angx, angy, angz = 0,0,0
function onEnterFrame(event)
    local x, y, z = gyroscope:getRotationRate()

    angx = angx + x * event.deltaTime
    angy = angy + y * event.deltaTime
    angz = angz + z * event.deltaTime

    print(angx * 180 / math.pi, angy * 180 / math.pi, angz * 180 / math.pi)
end
stage:addEventListener("enterFrame", onEnterFrame)
```

Physics

Gideros Studio offers a wrapper on Box2D for using physics. To use physics in Gideros Studio, you use require "box2d", and that creates a local variable called b2 that is of type Box2D, and offers all of the physics-related functions.

The next thing that you need to do is create a physics world in which the physics objects will reside. The following code shows an example.

> **Note**   In Gideros Studio, physics objects need to be updated to allow the dynamic physics bodies to be updated; typically this is done using an enter_frame event.

```
require "box2d"

local world = b2.World.new( 0 , 9.8) -- Set the gravity
local ground = world:createBody({})

local shape = b2.EdgeShape.new(0, 480, 320, 480)
shape:set(-20, 290, 620, 290)
ground:createFixture({shape = shape, density = 0})

local shape = b2.PolygonShape.new()
shape:setAsBox(10,10)
local fixture = {shape = shape, density = 1, friction = 0.3}

local x, y = 100, 10
bodyD = {type = b2.DYNAMIC_BODY, position={x=x, y=y}}
body = world:createBody(bodyD)
body:createFixture(fixture)

function onEnterFrame()
  world:step(1/60, 8, 3)
end

stage:addEventListener(Event.ENTER_FRAME, onEnterFrame)
```

When you run the program, notice that nothing happens. This is because we need to place an object on the screen that is updated as the physics body moves.

So, we can add an image that shall represent this physics body and also update it on the screen.

```
local img = Bitmap.new(Texture.new("image2.png"))
img:setAnchorPoint(0.5,0.5)
stage:addChild(img)
```

Then we redefine the onEnterFrame function as follows:

```
function onEnterFrame()
  world:step(1/60, 8, 3)

  img:setPosition(body:getPosition())
end
```

The image is displayed centered where the dynamic body is. The world:step function updates the body and takes three parameters. The first is timeStep, which determines the steps. The other two parameters are velocityIterations and positionIterations. The number of iterations for both velocity and position define how many calculations are needed to determine the next velocity and position of the physics body.

Plug-Ins

One advantage of Gideros Studio is that you can create your own plug-ins, thereby extending its functionality by introducing features that it doesn't currently have.

> **Note**   The BhWax plug-in (discussed in Chapter 13) provides complete access to the iOS API and you can use it to create UIWindows, UIViews, UIKit objects, practically everything that the Apple API offers.

The structure of a Gideros plug-in stub looks like this:

```
#include "gideros.h"
#include "lua.h"
#include "lauxlib.h"

static int myFunc(lua_State *L)
{
  int first  = lua_tointeger(L, -1);
  int second = lua_tointeger(L, -2);
  int result = first + second;

  lua_pushinteger(L, result);
  return 1;
}

static int luaMy_func(lua_State *L)
{
  const luaL_Reg functionlist[] = {
    {"myFunc", myFunc},
    {NULL, NULL},
  };
  luaL_register(L, "myPlugin", functionlist);
}

static void g_initializePlugin(lua_State *L)
{
  lua_getglobal(L, "package");
  lua_getfield(L, -1, "preload");

  lua_pushcfunction(L, luaMy_func);
  lua_setfield(L, -2, "test");
```

```
  lua_pop(L, 2);
}

static void g_deinitializePlugin(lua_State *L) {
}

REGISTER_PLUGIN("Test", "1.0")
```

These plug-ins can be written in C++, Objective-C, or C. First, we include the headers of the libraries that we need—namely gideros.h, which has the entry point to the Gideros Engine; lua.h, which gives us access to the Lua functions; and luaxlib.h, which provides the Lua interface functions.

We need to write two functions and a macro to register our plug-ins.

g_initializePlugIn is the entry point that initializes the plug-in for the first time and g_deinitializePlugin is called when Lua does not require the plug-in any more—for example, when it is unloaded. The macro REGISTER_PLUGIN is used to register the plug-in to be available for use in Gideros Studio.

When we initialize the plug-in, we use the package.preload function and load the function that we need. In the preceding sample code, we initialize the plug-in by invoking the luaMy_func function.

In Gideros Studio, to use this plug-in in Lua code we need to first require the library:

```
require "test"
local result = Test.myFunc(10,20)
print("The sum is : ", result)
```

To write the code for plug-ins, read up on the Lua C API found at http://www.lua.org/manual/5.2/manual.html#4). Plug-ins are similar to Lua bytecode commands, and C code can be mixed with the Lua C API.

The following Lua code

```
a = f("how", t.x, 14)
```

when written in the Lua C API, this looks like:

```
lua_getglobal(L, "f");
lua_pushstring(L, "how");
lua_getglobal(L, "t");
lua_getfield(L, -1, "x");
lua_remove(L, -2);
lua_pushinteger(L, 14);
lua_call(L, 3, 1);
lua_setglobal(L, "a");
```

> **Note** More detailed information can be found on the Lua web site (http://www.lua.org). Since C-related code is somewhat out of the scope of this book, I won't cover this in detail.

When you want to use the plug-in, you need to add it to the Gideros Player (while testing) or to Xcode and compile it in the final build. For the desktop player, the code needs to be compiled and present in the directory as a dynamic library (.dylib).

If you plan to distribute a plug-in for other users, it would need to be built as a library. The required files are

- .dll for the Windows desktop player
- .dylib for the Mac desktop player
- .so for the android device player
- .a for the iOS device player

> **Note** The choice of language also determines the platforms the plug-in can be used on. A plug-in written in C or C++ can be used on both iOS and Android devices. A plug-in written in Java can be used only on Android, and a plug-in written in Objective-C can be used only on iOS.

Summary

Gideros Studio is a package that comes complete on both Windows and Mac OS X and includes a range of tools to help develop and test applications. If the framework does not fulfill your expectations, or if you want to extend your application by adding some additional code (e.g., C, C++, Objective-C, or Java), you can do this by using the Lua API bridge and wrapping the code in a plug-in. Gideros Studio is a growing framework with a growing community. The framework is very similar to ActionScript, and hence it is an easy move for ActionScript 3 developers. Where Corona SDK positions itself as an easy-to-use framework (which it is), Gideros Studio fills the gaps providing the plug-in. While a simple task like displaying an image on the screen is a bit involved with Gideros Studio, it has the advantage of letting you keep a library of functions that allow for simpler usage, as in the examples in this chapter.

Chapter 10

Moai

In this chapter, we consider another framework: Moai. Among the options for developing cross-platform mobile applications, Moai is the tool for professional game developers. It is an open source platform that provides C++ classes wrapped in Lua. These allow for development of basic 2D and 3D games for a variety of platforms: iOS, Android, Windows, Mac OS X, and Chrome. Moai is available as the free-to-use Moai SDK, which requires a "Made with Moai" splash screen or a mention in the game's credits. Moai also offers a paid service, Moai Cloud Services, which can be integrated in apps built with or without Moai.

What Is Moai?

The idea of Moai stemmed from its developers, who were veterans in the gaming industry. It's not for hobbyists wanting to make a quick app; the learning curve on Moai can be a bit steep. This little hurdle can be overcome somewhat by RapaNui, an open source layer that offers Moai via some high-level APIs (discussed in Chapter 13). A few commercially available apps have been made with Moai, and more are in the works. Nearly all of them have the A-level excellence expected from large studios, and most have a large number of downloads. At the core of Moai are the C++ libraries that help you write cross-platform applications for mobile, browsers, and the desktop. However, the Lua interface takes away the need to deal with these complex libraries. These C++ libraries wrapped in Lua also allow for access to many low-level functions. Once you have learned the basics of app development, specifically gaming, Moai is a logical choice as a professional tool set.

Obtaining Moai

Your first step is to create an account with Moai and then download the SDK. You can choose from the following:

- SDK release version 1.3 (build 98)
- SDK developer build 1.3 (build 102)
- Moai source code

Straight out of the box, Moai has no IDE or tools like Gideros Studio does. However, it does contain the moai binary to test the Lua code with. When you unpack the ZIP file (which is the same for all platforms), the bin directory contains the libraries for all platforms, and also contains the executables (which act as the simulators to test the Moai code) for Windows and Mac OS X.

The Moai SDK

The first thing you need to start development with Moai is a text editor (some alternatives are discussed in Chapter 13), as there is no IDE that integrates development for Moai (however ZeroBrane fills in that gap, but is not included with Moai by default).

The bin directory has the executables for Windows and Mac; you can run moai in the terminal window and pass it the Lua files you want to run. For Windows, pass moai.exe main.lua; for Mac OS X, pass moai main.lua.

If you run the Hello Moai code from the samples folder, either via run.bat or run.sh, you should see the output on the screen shown in Figure 10-1.

Figure 10-1. The Moai simulator running a sample app

Hello Moai

There are a couple of things we need to do to get an app in Moai running. First, we need a window to display our application, which will double as the simulator on the desktop. We create a window using the MOAISim class and call the openWindow function. The openWindow function takes three parameters: a title, a width, and a height.

```
MOAISim.openWindow("Hello World Window", 320,480)
```

Then we need to create a viewport. Since Moai uses OpenGL, to create a drawing surface, we need to set the size of the surface that we want to use for rendering. This rectangular area is called a *viewport*. The viewport needs to be created and set before we can start rendering. Here's how:

```
viewport = MOAIViewport.new()
viewport:setSize(320,480)
viewport:setScale(320,480)
```

We can set the size to a specific size or simply use the entire surface by not passing any parameters to the setSize function. All rendering is based on units; these units are not necessarily the same as pixels. However, you can set these units using the setScale function. These units define the size of the pixels rendered by calculating them based on the size of the viewport and the scale setting. The size of the pixel is determined with the following two equations:

```
pixelsizeX = viewportSizeWidth / viewportScaleX
pixelsizeY = viewportSizeHeight / viewportScaleY
```

A size of 320×480 and a scale of 320, 480 sets the pixel size to 1. Setting a scale of 10, 15 with a size of 320×480 would give a pixel size of 32×32. The same scale of 10, 15 on a surface of size 640×960 would give a pixel size of 64×64. In this case, you would see the display stretch to fill in the space.

The coordinate system in Moai is organized with the origin (0,0) at the center of the screen. The y-axis is positive moving up the screen. A point with a value of 100 is higher on the screen than a point with a lower value like 20. You can invert the axis to have a negative scale by setting the scale with a negative value:

```
viewport:setScale(320, -480)
```

The viewport can also be changed using the setOffset function. The offset is set in a projection space that is set up to be 2×2. Setting the offset as –1, 1 moves the projection system one half to the left and one half up. This will in effect place the origin at the upper-left corner of the screen.

```
viewport:setOffset(-1,1)
```

Moai does not render any sprite, image, or a display object directly; rather, these are rendered onto a *layer*. Several layers can be stacked on top of each other. Each layer needs to be associated with a viewport.

```
layer = MOAILayer2D.new()
layer:setViewport(viewport)
```

The layer then needs to be pushed onto a render stack before it can be rendered.

```
MOAISim.pushRenderPass(layer)
```

Once we've set up the layer for rendering, we need a display object to display on this layer. In Moai, a scene graph object is called a *prop*; this is a combination of the location on the surface and the representation of the object. The geometry, or the representation of the object (e.g., a triangle, quad, or spline) is held in what is called a *deck*. A deck can hold multiple geometry items, and can also be called a *set*.

There are several types of decks to choose from:

- MOAIGfxQuad2D: This is a single textured quad.

- MOAIGfxQuadDeck2D: This is an array of textured quads (from one texture). This is similar to what we would refer to as a sprite sheet.

- MOAIGfxQuadListDeck2D: This is an array of lists of textured quads (from one texture). This can be used for advanced sprite sheets.

- MOAIMesh: This is a custom vertex buffer object (used for 3D).

- MOAIStretchPatch2D: This is a single patch that contains stretchable rows and columns.

- MOAITileDeck2D: This is used for creating a tile map and sprite sheets that are accessed via an index. The texture is divided into $n \times m$ tiles, which are all of the same size. It can be used for frame animation.

We can create a single textured quad using the MOAIGfxQuad2D class and load an image to use as the quad's texture:

```
gfxQuad = MOAIGfxQuad2D.new()
gfxQuad:setTexture("myTile.png")
gfxQuad:setRect(-32,-32, 32, 32)
```

Once the quad is created, we need to create a prop that will display the quad. We set the rect using the setRect function or the quad, which is similar to setting the dimensions of the quad:

```
prop = MOAIProp2D.new()
prop:setDeck(gfxQuad)
prop:setLoc(32,32)
```

Finally, we need to add this prop to the layer so that it is rendered:

```
layer:insertProp(prop)
```

The entire block of is shown following. When we run it, we see the image on the screen.

```
MOAISim.openWindow ( "test", 320, 480 )

viewport = MOAIViewport.new ()
viewport:setSize ( 320, 480 )
viewport:setScale ( 320, 480 )

layer = MOAILayer2D.new ()
layer:setViewport ( viewport )
MOAISim.pushRenderPass ( layer )
```

```
gfxQuad = MOAIGfxQuad2D.new ()
gfxQuad:setTexture ( "moai.png" )
gfxQuad:setRect ( -64, -64, 64, 64 )

prop = MOAIProp2D.new ()
prop:setDeck ( gfxQuad )
prop:setLoc ( 0, 80 )
layer:insertProp ( prop )
```

Compared to Corona SDK and Gideros Studio, this may seem a bit excessive for displaying an image on the screen. This is the reason why Moai is known as the tool for *professional* developers. It offers low-level access to a very rich API. However, that does not mean that hobbyist developers cannot use Moai. As mentioned previously, you can use the RapaNui library, which gives developers an easy-to-use high-level wrapper over the lower-level API of Moai. RapaNui wraps all of the Moai functions in easier-to-use functions and reduces the number of lines of code you need to write to get things done.

Quads can also be *pinned*, or as it is described in Moai, the pivot point can be set; the pivot point is used as the point around which the quad is rotated, where 0, 0 is the center (by default). This is similar to the anchorPoint with Gideros or the referencePoint with Corona

```
prop:setPiv(xCenter, yCenter)
```

Displaying Text

Text can be displayed in Moai using either TrueType or bitmap fonts. MOAITextBox is the class that allows for working with text in Moai.

TrueType Fonts

The easiest way to display text is using TrueType font. You can create a new font object using the MOAIFont class and pass it the characters to load from the font, the size (in points), and the dpi of the font.

```
charcodes = "abcdefghijklmnopqrstuvwxyzABCDEFGHIJKLMNOPQRSTUVWXYZ0123456789,.?!:()&/-"
font = MOAIFont.new()
font:loadFromTTF( 'arial.ttf', charcodes, 12, 163 )
```

Then you can create a text box to display the text using MOAITextBox:

```
textbox = MOAITextBox.new()
textbox:setFont(font)
textbox:setRect(-160, -80, 160, 80)
textbox:setLoc(0,160)
textbox:setAlignment(MOAITextBox.CENTER_JUSTIFY)
layer:insertProp( textbox )

textbox:setString( "Hello World from MOAI" )
```

> **Note** The characters passed to the MOAIFont function are created as a texture and cached, and if new glyphs are used, they are dynamically created and also cached, thereby providing faster speeds while rendering text.

Bitmap Fonts

The other way to display text is by using bitmap fonts (from an image file), in which each glyph (character) is divided by a solid-color guideline, as shown in Figure 10-2. This way it becomes easy to create bitmap fonts; however, kerning is not supported by this format.

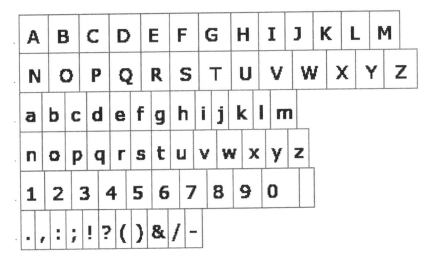

Figure 10-2. A bitmap font with an outline to indicate the dimensions of the glyph

To use the bitmap, you can use MOAIBitmapFontReader and load the glyphs using the loadPage function of the newly created bitmapFontReader object.

```
charcodes = "ABCDEFGHIJKLMNOPQRSTUVWXYZabcdefghijklmnopqrstuvwxyz1234567890 .,:;!?()&/-"
font = MOAIFont.new()

bitmapFR = MOAIBitmapFontReader.new()
bitmapFR:loadPage( "Font.png", charcodes, 16 )
font:setReader( bitmapFR )
```

If you use an app like Glyph Designer (from 71^2 ; see www.71squared.com/) to create a .fnt file containing the data related to the bitmap image file, you can use the loadFromBMFont function from the MOAIFont class, like so:

```
charcodes = "ABCDEFGHIJKLMNOPQRSTUVWXYZabcdefghijklmnopqrstuvwxyz1234567890 .,:;!?()&/-"
font = MOAIFont.new()

font:loadFromBMFont( "Font2.png" )
font:preloadGlyphs(charcodes, 64)
```

Text Attributes

A MOAITextBox can display text, which can be altered using the setString function. Note that the text can include embedded codes that alter the color of the text, similar to HTML tags:

```
textbox:setString("This text is in <c:ff0000>Red<c>, while this one is <c:00ff00>Green<c>.")
```

The tag to change the color starts with <c:*xxxxxx*> and ends with <c>. The *xxxxxx* is the color in hex (in the RRGGBBAA format). You can also use c:*xxx* and c:*xxxx* for lower-precision color codes.

Text Styles

You can alter the font, size, and color of text. We just discussed using <c> tags to change color and passing font sizes while creating a MOAIFont object. If you wanted to create text that requires different sized fonts in other frameworks, you would create multiple textbox objects with different sizes and then position them accordingly. However, with Moai, you can create styles that can be used for this, as well as for changing the font and color. These styles can be embedded in text in a manner similar to the color <c> tags:

```
function newStyle(font, size)
  local style = MOAITextStyle.new()
  style:setFont(font)
  style:setSize(size)
  return style
end
textbox:setStyle(newStyle(font, 24))
textbox:setStyle( "foo", newStyle(font, 32))
textbox:setStyle("bar", newStyle(font, 48))
text = "This text is <foo>Large</> and this is <bar>Larger</> than the normal text."
textbox:setString(text)
```

> **Note** The tags can be nested but must not overlap—that is, a child tag must be closed before closing a parent tag.

Aligning Text

After creating a MOAITextBox, you can change its properties. The text alignment can be altered using the setAlignment function. The parameters passed to setAlignment can be one of the following:

- MOAITextBox.LEFT_JUSTIFY
- MOAITextBox.RIGHT_JUSTIFY
- MOAITextBox.CENTER_JUSTIFY

Animating Text

The MOAITextBox has a spool function, which allows for the text to be revealed character by character. This provides for some interesting effects when displaying text.

```
textbox:spool()
```

Drawing Vector Primitives

Moai uses the class MOAIDeck to create a canvas on which drawing operations can be performed. All drawing is performed in the local space of the deck.

Before you can draw, you have to create an object of type MOAIScriptDeck type, as follows:

```
scriptDeck = MOAIScriptDeck.new()
```

It is important to note that the drawing coordinates of Moai are different from those of most of the frameworks. While most other frameworks have the top left as 0,0, Moai has the center as 0,0. In this way, a 320×480 screen extends 160 pixels in both directions on the x-axis and 240 pixels on the y-axis.

The scriptDeck object relies on a callback function to manage the drawing of the scriptDeck, which can be set using the setDrawCallback function. The callback has the parameters index, xOffset, yOffset, xScale, and yScale. The index determines the deck that needs to be redrawn, and the offsets and scales help in drawing.

The MOAI drawing classes allow for drawing all of the following:

- Lines
- Rectangles
- Filled rectangles
- Circles
- Filled circles
- Ellipses
- Filled ellipses
- Polygons
- Points
- Drawing attributes

Drawing Lines

A single line can be drawn using the drawRay function, the syntax for which is MOAIDraw.drawRay(x, y, dx, dy). The x and y are the absolute coordinates, and the dx and dy are the directions of the line extending from the x and y coordinates.

Drawing Rectangles

The easiest way to draw a rectangle is to use the syntax MOAIDraw.drawRect(x1, y1, x2, y2). It takes four parameters: the x and y coordinates where the rectangle starts and the endpoints that enclose the rectangle. The code below draws a rectangle on the screen as seen in Figure 10-3.

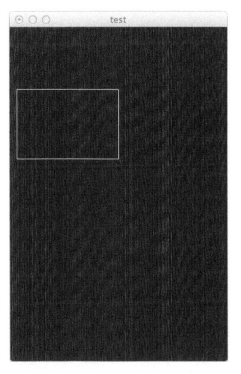

Figure 10-3. Drawing a rectangle with a stroke (border)

```
MOAISim.openWindow ( "test", 320, 480 )

viewport = MOAIViewport.new ()
viewport:setSize ( 320, 480 )
viewport:setScale ( 320, -480 )

layer = MOAILayer2D.new ()
layer:setViewport ( viewport )
MOAISim.pushRenderPass ( layer )

function onDraw ( index, xOff, yOff, xFlip, yFlip )
  MOAIDraw.drawRect(-150,-150,0,-50)
end

scriptDeck = MOAIScriptDeck.new ()
scriptDeck:setRect (-64, -64, 64, 64 )
scriptDeck:setDrawCallback ( onDraw )
```

```
prop = MOAIProp2D.new ()
prop:setDeck ( scriptDeck )
layer:insertProp ( prop )
```

Drawing Filled Rectangles

You can use the function MOAIDraw.fillRect(x1, y1, x2, y2) to draw a filled rectangle. This function takes four parameters, similar to the drawRect function. The fill color is set using the MOAIGfxDevice.setPenColor function. The code draws a filled rectangle on the screen as seen in Figure 10-4 below.

Figure 10-4. *Drawing a rectangle with a fill color and no stroke*

```
MOAISim.openWindow ( "test", 320, 480 )

viewport = MOAIViewport.new ()
viewport:setSize ( 320, 480 )
viewport:setScale ( 320, -480 )

layer = MOAILayer2D.new ()
layer:setViewport ( viewport )
MOAISim.pushRenderPass ( layer )
```

```
function onDraw ( index, xOff, yOff, xFlip, yFlip )
  MOAIGfxDevice.setPenColor(1, 0.64, 0, 1)
  MOAIDraw.drawRect(-150,-150,0,-50)
end

scriptDeck = MOAIScriptDeck.new ()
scriptDeck:setRect ( -64, -64, 64, 64 )
scriptDeck:setDrawCallback ( onDraw )

prop = MOAIProp2D.new ()
prop:setDeck ( scriptDeck )
layer:insertProp ( prop )
```

Drawing Circles

You can use the drawCircle function to draw circles. The syntax is MOAIDraw.drawCircle(xPos, yPos, radius, steps), where xPos and yPos are the center of the circle, radius determines the radius of the circle to be drawn, and the steps determines the *granularity*, or number of segments used to draw the circle. A good number for steps is 100.

```
function onDraw ( index, xOff, yOff, xFlip, yFlip )
  MOAIDraw.drawCircle(0, 0, 100, 100)
end
```

Drawing Filled Circles

You can use the fillCircle function to draw filled circles. The syntax is MOAIDraw.fillCircle(xPos, yPos, radius, steps), just like an unfilled circle. The pen color determines the circle fill color.

```
function onDraw ( index, xOff, yOff, xFlip, yFlip )
  MOAIGfxDevice.setPenColor(1, 0.64, 0, 1)
  MOAIDraw.fillCircle(0, 0, 100, 100)
end
```

Drawing Ellipses

To draw ellipses, you can use the function drawEllipse. The syntax is MOAIDraw.drawEllipse(xPos, yPos, xRadius, yRadius, steps), where xPos and yPos are the center, xRadius and yRadius determine the vertical and horizontal radii of the ellipse, and steps determines the granularity. A good number for steps is 100.

```
function onDraw ( index, xOff, yOff, xFlip, yFlip )
  MOAIDraw.drawEllipse(0, 0, 100, 100)
end
```

Drawing Filled Ellipses

Similarly, you can use the function fillEllipse to draw a filled ellipse. The syntax is the same as a regular ellipse, and the pen color determines the fill color.

```
function onDraw ( index, xOff, yOff, xFlip, yFlip )
  MOAIDraw.drawEllipse(0, 0, 100, 100)
end
```

Drawing Polygons

To draw polygons, you need define a series of vertices to pass to the drawLines function. The vertices are absolute points on the screen, not relative to the previous coordinate.

```
function onDraw ( index, xOff, yOff, xFlip, yFlip )
  MOAIDraw.drawLines(-50,50,50,50,50,-50,-50,-50,-50,50)
end
```

Drawing Points

The function drawPoints can be used to plot points at the given list of vertices. The following code gives an example of using the MOAIDraw.drawPoints function, the results of which are shown in Figure 10-5.

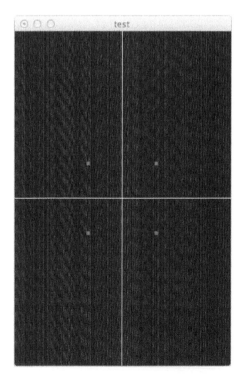

Figure 10-5. Points set in the quadrants, demonstrating the coordinate system in Moai

```
function onDraw ( index, xOff, yOff, xFlip, yFlip )
  MOAIDraw.drawRay ( 0, 0, 1, 0)
  MOAIDraw.drawRay ( 0, 0, 0, 1)
  MOAIGfxDevice.setPointSize(5)
  MOAIGfxDevice.setPenColor(1,0,0,1)
  MOAIDraw.drawPoints(-50,50,50,50,50,-50,-50,-50,-50,50)
end
```

The Drawing Attributes

The canvas on which MOAIDraw draws the vector primitives is called MOAIGfxDevice. You can query it and set certain drawing attributes, such as the color, line width, and point size. This section will describe each of these.

Color

The MOAIGfxDevice.setPenColor function is used to set the color for drawing and filling. The syntax for setting the color is setPenColor(r, g, b, a). The values for r, g, b, and a are in the range of 0 to 1. For example, the following line sets the color to green:

```
MOAIGfxDevice.setPenColor(0,1,0,1)
```

Line Width

The MOAIGfxDevice.setPenWidth function sets the width of any line drawn after the function call. The function is passed a width value, which determines how thick the line is usually expressed in positive integer units.

```
function onDraw ( index, xOff, yOff, xFlip, yFlip )
  MOAIGfxDevice.setPenWidth(3)
  MOAIGfxDevice.setPenColor(1,0,0,1)
  MOAIDraw.drawRect(-50,-50,50,50)
end
```

Point Size

The MOAIGfxDevice.setPointSize function sets the size of the points that are drawn using the drawPoints function usually expresses in positive integer units.

```
function onDraw ( index, xOff, yOff, xFlip, yFlip )
  MOAIDraw.drawRay ( 0, 0, 1, 0)
  MOAIDraw.drawRay ( 0, 0, 0, 1)
  MOAIGfxDevice.setPointSize(5)
  MOAIGfxDevice.setPenColor(1,0,0,1)
  MOAIDraw.drawPoints(-50,50,50,50,50,-50,-50,-50,-50,50)
end
```

Drawing Images

You've already learned that the way to create a display object on the screen is by creating a MOAIProp that needs to be added to a layer. Similarly, to display images, you create a MOAIProp object by creating a quad object for which you set the texture as the image you want to load. This can then be set as the deck object.

```
gfxQuad = MOAIGfxQuad2D.new ()
gfxQuad:setTexture ( "moai.png" )
gfxQuad:setRect ( -64, -64, 64, 64 )

prop = MOAIProp2D.new ()
prop:setDeck ( gfxQuad )
prop:setLoc ( 0, 80 )
layer:insertProp ( prop )
```

Drawing Custom Images

You can use the MOAIImage class to create a blank image that can be used as a canvas, like so:

```
local image = MOAIImage.new()
image:init(width, height)
```

> **Note**   The image that you create must be a power of 2—that is, the width and height must be a
> number that is a power of 2. While creating an image dynamically, if you create an image that does not
> conform to the power of 2, you can use the function padToPow2 to pad the image to the appropriate
> size as required.

This image object created can then be used to create the Quad2D object, which is then added to the layer.

```
gfxQuad = MOAIGfxQuad2D.new ()
gfxQuad:setTexture ( image )
gfxQuad:setRect ( -64, -64, 64, 64 )

prop = MOAIProp2D.new ()
prop:setDeck ( gfxQuad )
layer:insertProp ( prop )
```

This code will display nothing, as the image created is a blank image. In the following code we create a bitmap in memory and display that to the screen. This is a good way to create dynamic images via code.

```
local image = MOAIImage.new()
image:init(25, 40)
image:padToPow2()
```

```
image:fillRect(-70,-70,150,150,1,1,1,1)
image:fillRect( 20,20,50,50,1,0.6,0,1)

gfxQuad = MOAIGfxQuad2D.new ()
gfxQuad:setTexture ( image )
gfxQuad:setRect ( -64,-64,64,64 )

prop = MOAIProp2D.new ()
prop:setDeck ( gfxQuad )
layer:insertProp ( prop )
```

Loading Images

Images can be loaded onto a MOAIImage object using the load function, as follows:

```
theImage = MOAIImage.new ()
theImage:load( "myImage2.png" )
```

Once you've loaded the image, you can perform various functions on it and apply transformations.

Copying Images

You can copy an image from another image using either the copyRect or copyBits function. Note that copyBits makes a copy of the source (which cannot be scaled or flipped); a rectangular region from the source can be copied onto the destination at the position passed. Here's an example of using the copyBits function:

```
srcImage = MOAIImage.new ()
srcImage:load ( "myImage2.png" )
iWd, iHt = srcImage:getSize()
destImage = MOAIImage.new()
destImage:init(64,64)
destImage:copyBits(srcImage,0,0,0,0,iWd, iHt)
```

If you want to be able to scale or flip the image, you can use the copyRect function, which copies a rectangle from the source image to the destination image. You can flip it by reversing the min/max parameter of the rectangle. This function will draw the source image with the dimensions specified by srcMin and srcMax onto the destination space as specified by destMin and destMax. If the destination dimensions are larger, the image is scaled up and if they are smaller, the image is scaled down.

```
copyRect(source, srcXMin, srcYMin, srcXMax, srcYMax, destXMin, destYMin, destXMax, destYMax, filter)
```

Saving Images

You might need to save an image to the device or hard disk saving it for use later. The image can be saved using the `writePNG` function:

```
image = MOAIImage:new()
image:init(64,64)
-- Some drawing code here
image:writePNG("myimage.png")
```

Resizing Images

Images can be resized using the `resize` or `resizeCanvas` function. The function `resize` copies the image to an image with a new size and the function `resizeCanvas` copies the image to a canvas with a new size.

```
image:resize(width, height)
image:resizeCanvas(width, height)
```

Pixel Access for Images

You can get the color at a point in the image given the x- and y-coordinates using either the `getRGBA` function or the `getColor32` function. These return the data in RGBA or 32-bit integer format.

```
image:getRGBA(xPos, yPos)
```

and

```
image:getColor32(xPos, yPos)
```

Similarly, the pixels can be set using the `setRGBA` and `setColor32` functions:

```
image:setRGBA(xPos, yPos, red, green, blue, alpha)
image:setColor32(xPos, yPos, colour)
```

Animation

Basic frame-by-frame animation works by changing the image in the frame at a set frequency. This is called the fps or the frames per seconds. However, with other objects such as text, rectangles, and circles, modifying their attributes over time would provide the effect of animation.

To get or set the position of the prop, you can use the `getLoc` or the `setLoc` function. This is the equivalent of setting an attribute for a prop.

```
x, y = prop:getLoc()
is the equivalent of
x = prop:getAttr( MOAISprite2D.ATTR_X_LOC )
y = prop:getAttr( MOAISprite2D.ATTR_Y_LOC )
```

setLoc and getLoc are basically convenience methods that are used to access attributes from props. Another convenience method that is quite useful is moveRot, which is used to rotate the object by a particular angle over a specified period of time.

```
prop:moveRot(180, 2)
```

This code will rotate the prop 180 degrees over a period of 2 seconds.

MOAIEaseDriver can operate on attributes directly; we can simply specify the objects and attributes to operate on. MOAIEaseDriver applies simple ease curves to node attributes. Here's an example of its use.

```
ease = MOAIEaseDriver.new()
ease:reserveLinks(3)
ease:setLink(1, prop, MOAIProp2D.ATTR_X_LOC, 64)
ease:setLink(2, prop, MOAIProp2D.ATTR_Y_LOC, 64)
ease:setLink(3, prop, MOAIProp2D.ATTR_Z_ROT, 360)
ease:start()
```

This code snippet creates an ease driver, and then sets each channel to target a specific attribute of a single prop. This will rotate and move the prop from the top-left corner of the screen to a new location.

> **Note**   When you set the parent–child relation (and also a dependency) between two props (called graph nodes), the parent node is updated first and then the child node.

Tile Decks

Earlier in the chapter I described the various types of decks you can use. In this section, we'll take a closer look at MOAITileDeck2D, which helps create frame-by-frame animation. The sprite sheet for a TileDeck2D requires all of the frames to be of the same size. Then when you load the texture, you set the number of frames across and the number of frames down. Since the dimensions of all the frames are the same, when you set the size using the setSize function, the sprite sheet will be divided into an equal numbers of frames, as specified by the function. The dimensions are calculated as follows:

```
frameWidth = spriteSheetWidth / columns
frameHeight = spriteSheetHeight / rows
```

The following example shows how you can use frame animation. The results of the code are shown in Figure 10-6.

Figure 10-6. Animating a sprite in Moai using individual frames

```
_max_ = 11

MOAISim.openWindow("Tiles Deck Sample",320,480)

viewport = MOAIViewport.new()
viewport:setSize(320,480)
viewport:setScale(320,-480)
viewport:setOffset(-1,1)

layer = MOAILayer2D.new()
layer:setViewport(viewport)
MOAISim.pushRenderPass(layer)

tile = MOAITileDeck2D.new()
tile:setTexture("stick.png")
tile:setSize(_max_,1)
tile:setRect(-20,31,20,-31)

prop1 = MOAIProp2D.new()
prop1:setDeck(tile)
layer:insertProp(prop1)

curve = MOAIAnimCurve.new()
curve:reserveKeys(_max_)
```

```
for i=1,_max_ do
        curve:setKey(i, i*(1/_max_), i, MOAIEaseType.FLAT)
end

anim = MOAIAnim:new()
anim:reserveLinks(1)
anim:setLink(1, curve, prop1, MOAIProp2D.ATTR_INDEX)
anim:setMode(MOAITimer.LOOP)
anim:start()

prop1:setLoc(100,100)
```

In this example, we first create the tiles that we can use for our animation:

```
tile = MOAITileDeck2D.new()
tile:setTexture("stick.png")
tile:setSize(11,1)
tile:setRect(-20,31,20,-31)
```

Our sprite sheet has 11 frames across and 1 frame down (see Figure 10-7). The dimensions of all the frames are 40×62, which we set with setRect.

Figure 10-7. The stick.png image that we shall use for the animation

Setting a negative value for the rect dimensions in the setRect function flips the object on the axis with the negative value. Since Moai has an ascending y-axis, we change the scale to set the top-left corner as the origin (0,0), so our images will show up flipped on the y-axis. To correct that, we use the setRect function with tile:setRect(-20,31,20,-31) instead of tile:setRect(-20,-31,20,31).

```
prop1 = MOAIProp2D.new()
prop1:setDeck(tile)
layer:insertProp(prop1)
```

We create a MOAIProp2D object and set the tile we just created to the prop's deck, and then we insert that prop in the layer:

```
curve = MOAIAnimCurve.new()
_max_ = 11
curve:reserveKeys(_max_)
for i=1, _max_ do
  curve:setKey(I, I * (1/_max_), I, MOAIEaseType.FLAT)
end
```

We create a MOAIAnimCurve object and then designate the number of frames using the reserveKeys function. Then we create the frames and set the index and the time index for each of the frames, with the value of the curve at that time index. A time index is another way of looking at the animation, but instead of it being index based, we set the time index to specify the animation/transform at that point in time.

```
anim = MOAIAnim:new()
anim:reserveLinks(1)
anim:setLink(1, curve, prop1, MOAIProp2D.ATTR_INDEX)
anim:setMode(MOAITimer.LOOP)
anim:start()
```

We use the MOAIAnim class to create our animation. We set up a link between prop1 and curve on the Index attribute. We set the mode to loop as a timer. Then we start the animation with the start function.

Lastly, we reposition the prop1 object on the screen at 100,100.

We can also hook into the animation using listeners. The listeners that we can capture are:

- MOAITimer.EVENT_TIMER_KEYFRAME. This is called every time the keyframe is changed and is a callback function that has the following signature:

  onKeyFrame (MOAITimer_self, number_keyFrame, number_timesExecuted, number_time, number_value)

- MOAITimer.EVENT_TIMER_LOOP. This is called every time the function loops and has the following callback signature:

  onLoop(MOAITimer_self, number_timesExecuted)

- MOAITimer.EVENT_TIMER_BEGIN_SPAN. This is called when the timer playback mode reaches the beginSpan time set using the setSpan function; otherwise this is 0 (i.e. as soon as the animation starts). This has the following callback signature:

  onBeginSpan(MOAITimer_self, number_timesExecuted)

- MOAITimer.EVENT_TIMER_END_SPAN. This is called when the timer playback reaches the endSpan time set using the setSpan function otherwise this is set to the end of the animation. This has the following callback signature:

  onEndSpan(MOAITimer_self, number_timesExecuted)

Here's an example of using the MOAITimer.EVENT_TIMER_KEYFRAME listener:

```
function onKeyFrame(self, index, time, value)
  print("Keyframe : ", index, time, value)
end
anim:setListener(MOAITimer.EVENT_TIMER_KEYFRAME, onKeyFrame)
```

Threading

By default, all of the functions used to transform Moai objects are nonblocking and are executed in parallel. For example, if we have transforms on a prop, they will all be executed simultaneously. Here's an example:

```
prop:moveLoc(180, 180, 3)
prop:moveScl(1.2,1.2,1)
prop:moveLoc(-180,-180,3)
prop:moveScl(0.9,0.9,1)
```

Moai can perform all these transformations at the same time; if you were to run this code, you would see only the end result of the four transforms, rather than each individual one.

Moai has the concept of threads; we had a look at them and coroutines in earlier chapters. We can create blocking threads in Moai so that we can run each of the actions in blocking mode. Here's an example:

```
function threadFunction()
  action = prop:moveLoc(180, 180, 3.0)
  MOAIThread.blockOnAction(action)

  action = prop:moveScl(1.2, 1.2, 1.0)
  MOAIThread.blockOnAction(action)

  action = prop:moveLoc(-180, -180, 3.0)
  MOAIThread.blockOnAction(action)

  action = prop:moveScl(0.8, 0.8, 1.0)
  MOAIThread.blockOnAction(action)
end

thread = MOAIThread.new()
thread:run(threadFunction)
```

The blocking actions that we create can be run only for action items (transformations).

Groups

The definition of groups as described by other frameworks is that of a container—one that holds all the other display objects. Generally, groups are nonvisual display objects. With Moai, the concept is a bit different—you can set up a parent–child relation between two objects. When the parent object is modified or moved, the child object follows suit, as shown in Figure 10-8.

Figure 10-8. The Moai equivalent of groups, using traits

In Moai, this is called setting a *trait source*, where *traits* are the attributes, such as the location, transform, color, visibility, and so on. The setParent function is actually an alias to the setTraitSource.

```
MOAISim.openWindow( "Group Test", 320, 480)

viewport = MAOIViewport.new()
viewport:setSize(320,480)
viewport:setScale(320,-480)
viewport:setOffset(-1,1)

layer = MOAILayer2D.new()
layer:setViewport(viewport)
MOAISim.pushRenderPass(layer)

function newImage(imageName, xPos, yPos)
  local xPos = xPos or 0
  local yPos = yPos or 0
  local wd, ht

  local img = MOAIImage.new()
  img:load(imageName)
  wd, ht = img:getSize()
```

```
  quad = MOAIGfxQuad2D.new()
  quad:setTexture(imageName)
  quad:setRect(-(wd/2),(ht/2),(wd/2),-(ht/2))

  prop = MOAIProp2D.new()
  prop:setDeck(quad)
  prop:setLoc(xPos, yPos)

  layer:insertProp(prop)
  return prop
end

magnet = newImage("myImage2.png",40,260)
robo = newImage("myImage3.png",40,-140)

robo:setParent(magnet)

magnet:moveLoc(170,170,3)
```

Notice that the robot has a magnet that pulls the robot along with it when we move the magnet. Any operation performed will affect both the props.

Let's add some scaling at the end of the code:

```
magnet:moveScl(-0.5,-0.5,3)
```

Notice that both the magnet and the robot start to scale as they move. All of the attributes/traits are inherited from the parent object when you set it as the parent of another. The resulting action can be seen in Figure 10-9.

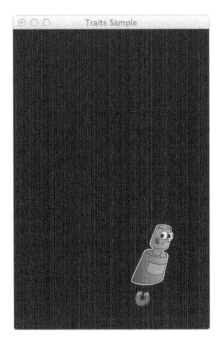

Figure 10-9. Scaling affects both the images (using traits)

Handling Input

Since Moai can generate executables from a single source for mobile devices, desktops, and web browsers, it has a very highly involved input system. This includes the keyboard, mouse, and touch.

Input is encapsulated in the MOAIInputMgr class; this depends on a callback function to handle an input event.

Keyboard Events

While developing, you will test your code on the desktop. For this you will need to capture and test the keyboard events. To capture these events, you set a callback for the MOAIInputMgr.device. keyboard object.

```
function onKeyEvent(key, down)
  if down == true then
    print("Key down : ", key)
  else
    print("Key up : ", key)
  end
end
MOAIInputMgr.device.keyboard:setCallback(onKeyEvent)
```

On an iOS device, MOAIInputMgr.device.keyboard is not present; instead, you use the MOAIKeyboardIOS class and set the listeners for the EVENT_INPUT and the EVENT_RETURN.

```
function onInput(start, length, text)
      print("on input")
      print(start, length, text)
      print(MOAIKeyboardIOS.getText())
end

function onReturn()
      print("on return")
      print(MOAIKeyboardIOS.getText())
end

MOAIKeyboardIOS.setListener(MOAIKeyboardIOS.EVENT_INPUT,onInput)
MOAIKeyboardIOS.setListener(MOAIKeyboardIOS.EVENT_RETURN,onReturn)
MOAIKeyboardIOS.showKeyboard ()
```

Mouse Events

For devices that do not have touch events, Moai offers mouse handlers. In a similar fashion to keyboard handlers, you need to set a callback on the MOAIInputMgr.device.pointer object. This captures the mouse movement events.

```
function onMove(evtX, evtY)
  print( "Pointer : ", x, y)
end
```

```
MOAIInputMgr.device.pointer:setCallback(onMove)
```

If we want to capture when the mouse buttons are clicked, you need to set callback functions for the mouse buttons, like mouseLeft, mouseRight, and mouseCenter.

```
function onMouseL(down)
  print("The Left Mouse button down is ", down)
end
function onMouseR(down)
  print("The Right Mouse button down is ", down)
end
function onMouseC(down)
  print("The Center Mouse button down is ", down)
end
MOAIInputMgr.device.mouseLeft:setCallback(onMouseL)
MOAIInputMgr.device.mouseRight:setCallback(onMouseL)
MOAIInputMgr.device.mouseCenter:setCallback(onMouseL)
```

In some cases you might not want to set callback functions on the mouse buttons. In such cases, you can query for them using the isUp and isDown functions. You can set a callback on the pointer, and in the callback also check for the button states.

```
function handleMouse( x, y )
  if MOAIInputMgr.device.mouseLeft:isUp() then
    print("Left button clicked at : ", x, y)
  end
end
```

```
MOAIInputMgr.device.pointer:setCallback(handleMouse)
```

You might have noticed the pull-to-refresh functionality in quite a few applications. With iOS 6, the mail application has a pull-to-refresh; when you pull, the circle elongates like slime, pulling down from the larger blob on the top. We can quickly re-create the same effect with Moai and the mouse. In this example, the blob reacts to the mouse pointer moving down as you move the mouse in the window. The effect is shown in Figure 10-10.

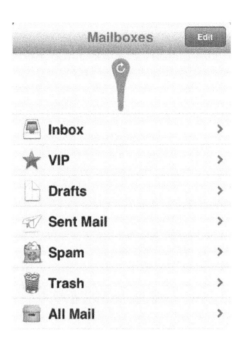

Figure 10-10. *The new pull-to-refresh organic blob, as seen in iOS 6*

First, we create the window and the viewport, and the layer on which we shall place all of our display objects:

```
MOAISim.openWindow("Slimey Blob", 320, 480)

viewport = MOAIViewport.new()
viewport:setSize(320,480)
viewport:setScale(320,-480)
viewport:setOffset(-1,1)

layer = MOAILayer2D.new()
layer:setViewport(viewport)
MOAISim.pushRenderPass(layer)
```

Then we create the scriptDeck that we can use to draw our graphics on:

```
canvas = MOAIScriptDeck.new()
canvas:setRect(-64,-64,64,64)
canvas:setDrawCallback(onDraw)

prop = MOAIProp2D.new()
prop:setDeck(canvas)
layer:insertProp(prop)
```

Finally, we need to now create the function that is responsible for all the drawing:

```
bottomOriginY = 100
bottomRadius = 10
```

```
topRadius = 25
  topOrigin = {
    x = _W/2,
    y = 30
  }

function onDraw(index, xOrg, yOrg, xFlp, yFlp)
  MOAIGfxDevice.setPenColor(1,0.64,0.1)

  MOAIDraw.fillCircle(topOrigin.x,topOrigin.y,topRadius,100)
  MOAIDraw.fillCircle(_W/2,bottomOriginY,bottomRadius,100)

  MOAIDraw.fillFan(
    topOrigin.x-currentTopRadius, topOrigin.y,
    topOrigin.x+currentTopRadius, topOrigin.y,
    topOrigin.x+bottomRadius, bottomOriginY,
    topOrigin.x-bottomRadius, bottomOriginY
  )

end
```

In our draw function, first we draw two circles, one on top and one at the bottom, as specified by topOrigin.y and bottomOriginY, with radii specified as topRadius and bottomRadius.

Next we draw a quadrangle from the middle of the upper circle to the middle of the lower circle, in effect connecting the two. To make this look a bit more realistic, this could be a curve that arches inward to give the impression of a droplet of slime expanding. However, for simplicity, we just use a quadrangle that provides a similar look.

You can make this more realistic by adding another segment, but I'll leave that as an exercise for you.

We need to position the lower blob where the mouse currently is; that way, we can simulate the effect of pulling the blob away from the larger blob.

```
function onMove(mx, my)
  bottomOriginY = my
  if bottomOriginY < 40 then bottomOriginY = 40 end
  if bottomOriginY > 400 then bottonOriginY = 400 end

  bottomRadius = 12 - ((my-currentTopRadius)/48)
end
MOAIInputMgr.device.pointe:setCallback(onMove)
```

In the mouse-move function; we first set bottomOriginY to the current y position of the mouse pointer. We also ensure that bottomOriginY remains in the range of 40 to 400. We also set the radius of the bottom circle to shrink or expand as it moves (see Figure 10-11).

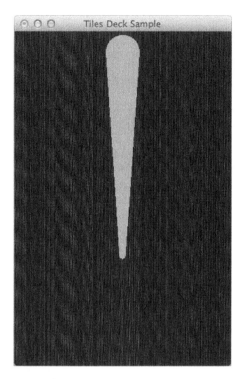

Figure 10-11. A simplified version of a pull-to-refresh blob

Touch Events

On mobile devices, which have no mouse pointer but instead react to touch, we can set the callback for touches. The object to set a callback on is MOAIInputMgr.device.touch. This captures the touch events. The callback function is passed an eventType, which can be one of the following:

- MOAITouchSensor.TOUCH_DOWN

- MOAITouchSensor.TOUCH_UP

- MOAITouchSensor.TOUCH_MOVE

- MOAITouchSensor.TOUCH_CANCEL

```
function onTouch(eventType, idx, x, y, tapCount)
  print(eventType)
end
MOAIInputMgr.device.touch:setCallback(onTouch)
```

If you run this code on the desktop, it will result in an error, as there is no touch device.

The best way to set up handlers is to ensure the existence of a device before the callback is set. Here's how to check for the existence of a device:

```
if MOAIInputMgr.device.touch then
  MOAIInputMgr.device.touch:setCallback(onTouch)
end
```

> **Note**   Setting a callback can cause an error if the device in question is not supported. It is best to check for the presence of the device before setting the callback. This is applicable to devices involving touch, mouse pointers, keyboards, and even GPS and accelerometers.

Sound

While some frameworks have an elaborate and complex audio functionality, Moai has a very simple function available in the MOAIUntzSound class. However, before you can use the audio functions, you need to initialize the MOAIUntzSystem, like so:

```
MOAIUntzSystem.initialize ()

sound = MOAIUntzSound.new ()
sound:load ( 'mono16.wav' )
sound:setVolume ( 1 )
sound:setLooping ( false )
sound:play ()
```

Displaying a Dialog

Moai allows you to display messages to the user and even get input from the user in the form of a yes/no/cancel-type dialog. In such a scenario, you can use the showDialog function from the MOAIDialogIOS class. Here's an example:

```
function onDialogDismiss(code)
  print("Dialog Dismissed")
  if (code==MOAIDialog.DIALOG_RESULT_POSITIVE) then
    print("Clicked Yes")
  elseif (code==MOAIDialog.DIALOG_RESULT_NEUTRAL) then
    print("Clicked Maybe")
  elseif (code==MOAIDialog.DIALOG_RESULT_NEGATIVE) then
    print("Clicked No")
  elseif (code==MOAIDialog.DIALOG_RESULT_CANCEL) then
    print("Clicked Cancel")
  else then
    print("Clicked Unknown")
  end
end

MOAIDialogIOS.showDialog("Sample Dialog", "", "Yes", "Maybe", "No", true, onDialogDismiss)
```

Displaying Video

If you want to play a video on the iOS device—for example, as an intro or a lead-in to a level in a game—you can use the MOAIMoviePlayer class. To play the movie, you need to initialize it with the path to the movie and then invoke the play function:

```
MOAIMoviePlayer.init (
"http://km.support.apple.com/library/APPLE/APPLECARE_ALLGEOS/HT1211/sample_iTunes.mov" )
MOAIMoviePlayer.play ()
```

Device Orientation

When it comes to orientation, many the frameworks raise an orientation-change event. However, in Moai when the device orientation is changed, the EVENT_RESIZE event is triggered. We can listen for this event by adding a listener on the MOAIGfxDevice class.

```
_W, _H = MOAIGfxDevice.getViewSize()
function onResize(width, height)
  viewport:setSize(width, height)
  viewport:setScale(width, height)
end
MOAIGfxDevice.setListener(MOAIGfxDevice.EVENT_RESIZE, onResize)
```

Notifications

In some scenarios, you might want to notify the user with some information—for example, when a task is complete (e.g., when the crops are ready to be harvested in a Farmville-type application). To enable you to do this, Moai has a MOAINotifications class that needs a listener to be added listening to the events. The code below has three distinct portions. onRegComplete is called when we try to register for a remote notification; it also informs us if it was successful or if it failed. The other function displays the notification when it occurs, based on the data passed. And the last bit sets up and registers the notification.

```
function onRegComplete(code, token)
  print("Registered")
  if code==MOAINotification.REMOTE_NOTIFICATION_RESULT_REGISTERED then
    print("Registered " .. token)
  elseif code==MOAINotification.REMOTE_NOTIFICATION_RESULT_UNREGISTERED then
  else
    print("Registration failed")
  end
end

function onRemoteNotification(event)
  print("Notification received")
  message = event.aps.alert
```

```
  local action, data, title
  if event.action then action = event.action end
  if event.data then data = event.data end
  if event.title then title = event.title end

  print("Message : " .. message)
  print("action : " .. action)
  print("data : " .. data)
  print("title : ", title)
end

MOAINotification.setListener(MOAINotification.REMOTE_NOTIFICATION_REGISTRATION_COMPLETE, onRegComplete)
MOAINotification.setListener(MOAINotification.REMOTE_NOTIFICATION_MESSAGE_RECEIVED, onRemoteNotification)
MOAINotification.setAppIconBadgeNumber(0)
MOAINotification.registerForRemoteNotification(
    MOAINotification.REMOTE_NOTIFICATION_BADGE +
    MOAINotification.REMOTE_NOTIFICATION_ALERT)
```

Networking

In your game, you might need to download level data or some other data using the HTTP or HTTPS protocol. Moai has a MOAIHttpTask class that allows for downloading data from an HTTP/S source.

```
function onDone(task, responseCode)
  print("Downloaded", responseCode)
  if task:getSize() then
    print(task:getString())
  else
    print("Got nothing")
  end
end

theTask = MOAIHttpTask.new("Download Webpage")
theTask:setCallback(onDone)
theTask:httpGet("http://www.oz-apps.com")
```

The httpGet function works synchronously; however, if you want that the data be loaded *asynchronously*, you need to call the performAsync function instead:

```
function onFinish ( task, responseCode )

  print ( "onFinish" )
  print ( responseCode )

  if ( task:getSize ()) then
    print ( task:getString ())
  else
    print ( "nothing" )
  end
end
```

```
task = MOAIHttpTask.new ()

task:setVerb ( MOAIHttpTask.HTTP_GET )
task:setUrl ( "www.cnn.com" )
task:setCallback ( onFinish )
task:setUserAgent ( "Moai" )
task:setHeader ( "Foo", "foo" )
task:setHeader ( "Bar", "bar" )
task:setHeader ( "Baz", "baz" )
task:setVerbose ( true )
task:performAsync ()
```

If you want to run some command in a blocking manner (where the entire application freezes to perform one operation and resumes once the task is completed), instead of performAsync, you use the performSync function.

HttpTask is a two-way function, which means not only can you use it for downloading using HTTP_GET, but also to upload data and set the headers. The commands that can be used with the HttpTask are

- HTTP_HEAD

- HTTP_GET

- HTTP_PUT

- HTTP_POST

- HTTP_DELETE

Using JSON

There is good support for using JSON in Moai. To decode or encode a JSON string, you can use the MOAIJsonParser object. This has just two functions, encode and decode. The decode function takes a JSON string and converts it into a hierarchy of tables, whereas encode converts a hierarchy of tables into a JSON string.

```
local test = {name="Jayant", Msg={BaaBaa="BlackSheep", Line1="Have you any wool?"}}
print(MOAIJsonParser.encode(test))
```

Using Base64

When developing a game, to send messages or upload or download data, you might need to encode data into Base64 in order to be able to send data in text format. The MOAIDataBuffer class gives you the base-conversion functionality.

```
theText = "This is plain text, but..."
encoded = MOAIDataBuffer.base64Encode(theText)
print(encoded)
decoded = MOAIDataBuffer.base64Decode(encoded)
print(decoded)
```

In some cases, you might need to work with data that is streamed; for this, you can use the MOAIStreamReader and MOAIStreamWriter classes. The stream can be used like a file, where you can open a stream, seek, and write data. Here's an example:

```
stream = MOAIMemStream.new ()
stream:open ()

data = 'Lorem ipsum dolor sit amet, consectetur adipiscing elit. Duis id massa vel leo blandit
pharetra. Aenean a nisl mi. Vestibulum ante ipsum primis in faucibus orci luctus et ultrices posuere
cubilia Curae; Nam quis magna sit amet diam fermentum consequat. Donec dapibus pharetra diam vel
convallis. Pellentesque quis tellus mauris. Sed eget risus tortor, in cursus nisi. Sed ultrices
nulla non nunc ullamcorper id venenatis urna ultrices. Cum sociis natoque penatibus et magnis dis
parturient montes, nascetur ridiculus mus. Nam sodales tellus et diam imperdiet pharetra sagittis
odio tempus. Lorem ipsum dolor sit amet, consectetur adipiscing elit. Nunc mollis adipiscing nibh
ut malesuada. Proin rutrum volutpat est sed feugiat. Suspendisse at imperdiet justo. Pellentesque
ullamcorper risus venenatis tellus elementum mattis. Quisque adipiscing feugiat orci vitae egestas.'
len = #data

print ( data )

writer = MOAIStreamWriter.new ()
writer:openBase64 ( stream )
writer:write ( data, len )
writer:close ()

stream:seek ( 0 )

reader = MOAIStreamReader.new ()
reader:openBase64 ( stream )
data = reader:read ( len )
reader:close ()

print ()
print ( data )
```

Compressing Data

When you work with online data, you might want to not only convert data, but also compress it to save on data transfer and bandwidth. The MOAIDataBuffer class allows you to compress or uncompress data using the deflate and inflate functions.

```
data = 'Lorem ipsum dolor sit amet, consectetur adipiscing elit. Duis id massa vel leo blandit
pharetra. Aenean a nisl mi. Vestibulum ante ipsum primis in faucibus orci luctus et ultrices posuere
cubilia Curae; Nam quis magna sit amet diam fermentum consequat. Donec dapibus pharetra diam vel
convallis. Pellentesque quis tellus mauris. Sed eget risus tortor, in cursus nisi. Sed ultrices
nulla non nunc ullamcorper id venenatis urna ultrices. Cum sociis natoque penatibus et magnis dis
parturient montes, nascetur ridiculus mus. Nam sodales tellus et diam imperdiet pharetra sagittis
odio tempus. Lorem ipsum dolor sit amet, consectetur adipiscing elit. Nunc mollis adipiscing nibh
ut malesuada. Proin rutrum volutpat est sed feugiat. Suspendisse at imperdiet justo. Pellentesque
ullamcorper risus venenatis tellus elementum mattis. Quisque adipiscing feugiat orci vitae egestas.'
```

```
print ( data )
print ()

print ( 'original length: ' .. #data )

data = MOAIDataBuffer.deflate ( data, 9 )
print ( 'deflated length: ' .. #data )
print ( "The compressed encoded data")
print ( MOAIDataBuffer.base64Encode(data))

data = MOAIDataBuffer.inflate ( data )
print ( 'inflated length: ' .. #data )

print ()
print ( data )
```

Physics

Physics is the most used feature in game apps, and Box2D is the library most commonly used library by most of the frameworks. Moai includes Box2D, as well as the Chipmunk library. This section will describe both.

Box2D Physics

The first thing we need to do when using physics in Moai is create a world using the MOAIBox2dWorld class.

```
MOAISim.openWindow("Physics", 640, 480)
viewport = MOAIViewport.new()
viewport:setSize(640,480)
viewport:setScale(16,0)

layer = MOAILayer2D.new()
layer:setViewport(viewport)
MOAISim.pushRenderPass(layer)

world = MOAIBox2dWorld.new()
world:setGravity(0,-9.8)
world:setUnitsToMeters(2)
world:start()
layer:setBox2DWorld(world)
```

After creating the world, we need to add a physics body. This will interact with the physics world that we have created via the addBody function as a *dynamic body*. Generally, all bodies are created as static bodies by default. *Static bodies* are immovable, i.e. forces do not act upon a static body, whereas a dynamic body reacts to forces

To get the gravity to work realistically, we need to set it to –9.8; if we set it to 9.8, the objects will start to float.

Box2D units work quite well with meter-kilogram-second (MKS) units, and the moving objects work well within a range of 0.1 to 10 meters. Although it might be tempting to use pixels as the units, this leads to some weird behavior and poor simulation.

Lastly, we need to start the physics simulation with `world:start()`. To stop the physics simulation, we can use `world:stop()`.

```
body = world:addBody( MOAIBox2DBody.DYNAMIC)
poly = {0,-1,1,0,0,1,-1,0}

fixture = body:addPolygon(poly)
fixture:setDestiny(1)
fixture:setFriction(0.3)
fixture:setFilter(0x01)
fixture:setCollisionHandler(onCollide, MOAIBox2DArbiter.BEGIN + MOAIBox2DArbiter.END, 0x02)
body:resetMassData()
body:applyAngularImpulse(2)
```

Now that we have created a dynamic body, we create a fixture that binds a shape to a body and gives the body material properties like density, friction, and restitution.

> **Note** *Restitution* deals with the way an object returns to its original shape or position after it has been deformed after a collision.

If we run our code, a physics box will appear on the screen, as shown in Figure 10-12.

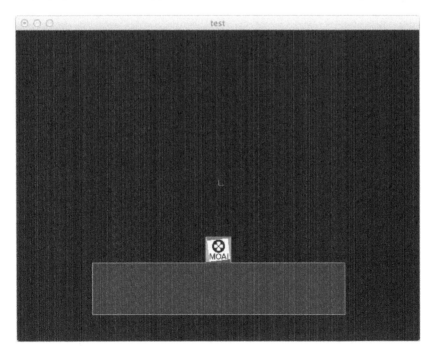

Figure 10-12. Moai Box2D physics bodies

```
body2 = world:addBody(MOAIBox2DBody.STATIC)
fixture2 = body2:addRect(-5,-5,5,-3)
fixture2:setFilter(0x02)
fixture2:setCollisionHandler(onCollide, MOAIBox2DArbiter.BEGIN + MOAIBox2DArbiter.END, 0x01)
```

This creates a static body, which acts as a ground that prevents the dynamic box from falling off the screen.

For both the body fixtures, we also set a collision handler that calls the function onCollide for the events MOAIBox2DArbiter.BEGIN and MOAIBox2DArbiter.END. The BEGIN event is triggered when a collision starts to occur and the END event is triggered when it ends. We can capture it in the onCollide function.

```
function onCollide(event)
  if event == MOAIBox2DArbiter.BEGIN then
    print("Begin!")
  elseif event == MOAIBox2DArbiter.END then
    print("End!")
  end
end
```

We can add an image to this body so that we do not see the box, but an image in its place:

```
texture = MOAIGfxQuad2D.new()
texture:setTexture("moai.png")
texture:setRect(-0.5, -0.5, 0.5, 0.5)
```

Now we need to add this image to the body:

```
image = MOAIProp2D.new()
image:setDeck(texture)
image:setParent(body)
layer:insertProp(image)
```

The polygon that we created using poly is diamond shaped; if we want it to be a square, we can use the following:

```
poly = {-0.5, -0.5, 0.5, -0.5, 0.5, 0.5, -0.5, 0.5}
```

The object does not bounce when it comes in contact with the ground. We can make both objects bouncy by setting the restitution, using the setRestitution function.

```
fixture:setRestitution(0.5)
```

and

```
fixture:setRestitution(0.7)
```

To make this little code sample more fun, let's change the gravity of the world to −1, which will make the object act like a balloon. To do this, we use world:setGravity(0,-1). The object now falls down slower. We can also add a mouse event that will make the object bounce.

```
function onClick(down)
  body:setLinearVelocity(0,0)
  body:applyLinearImpulse(0,1)
end
MOAIInputMgr.device.mouseLeft:setCallback(onClick)
```

Now every time we click the left mouse button, we reset the velocity to 0 and then apply a linear impulse of 0,1, which applies an impulse of 0 on the x-axis and 1 on the y-axis. This makes the object jump upward.

Chipmunk Physics

We can also use Chipmunk physics in Moai. The principles for this are similar to those in Box2D. We first we need to create the Chipmunk world space using the MOAICpSpace class:

```
space = MOAICpSpace.new()
space:setGravity(0,-2000)
space:setIterations(5)
space:start()
```

The iterations are the number of calculations performed to determine if bodies are in collision with each other. A larger number of iterations will provide a much smoother and better physics simulation; however, this will take up a lot of CPU time and processing. On the other hand, if we use a smaller value for iterations, less CPU power is required, but the motion may seem too bouncy and unrealistic.

To create a physics body, we can use the MOAICpBody class, which returns a Chipmunk physics body. We can then add a fixture as a polygon body to the physics body.

```
poly = {-32, 32, 32, 32, 32, -32, -32, -32}
mass = 1
moment = MOAICpShape.momentForPolygon (mass, poly)
body = MOAICpBody.new(1, moment)
space:insertPrim(body)

shape = body:addPolygon( poly )
shape:setElasticity( 0.8 )
shape:setFriction( 0.8 )
shape:setType( 1 )
space:insertPrim( shape )
```

When we run the code now, the object will fall right off the screen. Let's create a floor-type object so that the physics body doesn't fall off the screen:

```
body = space:getStaticBody()

x1,y1,x2,y2 = -320, -240, 320, -240
shape = body:addSegment(x1,y1,x2,y2)
shape:setElasticity(1)
shape:setFriction(0.1)
shape:setType(2)
space:insertPrim(shape)
```

The object will now bounce when it reaches the bottom of the screen.

We can add some code to move the object around the screen, but before that, let's create a wall around the corners of the screen so that the physics body does not fall off the side of the screen when we move it.

```
function addSegment(x1, y1, x2, y2)
  shape = body:addSegment(x1,y1,x2,y2)
  shape:setElasticity(1)
  shape:setFriction(0.1)
  shape:setType(2)
  space:insertPrim(shape)
end

addSegment(-320, -240, 320, -240)
addSegment(-320, 240, 320, 240)
addSegment(-320, -240, -320, 240)
addSegment(320, -240, 320, 240)
```

We can get the body that is present at a given point by using the function space:shapeForPoint. We can also move the point based on where the mouse is by setting a callback function on the pointer device.

```
mouseBody = MOAICpBody.new(MOAICp.INFINITY, MOAICp.INFINITY)
mx, my = 0,0
function onMove(x,y)
  mx, my = layer:wndToWorld(x,y)
  mouseBody:setPos(mx, my)
end
```

Now, as the mouse moves, the mouseBody object is placed at the location where the pointer currently is. We can also set a callback for the left mouse button function that can help pick up and move the object.

```
function onClick(down)
  if down then
    pick = space:shapeForPoint(mx, my)
    if pick then
      body = pick:getBody()
      mouseJoint = MOAICpConstraint.newPivotJoint(
        mouseBody, body, 0, 0, body:worldToLocal(mx, my))
      space:insertPrim(mouseJoint)
    else
      if mouseJoint then
        space:removePrim(mouseJoint)
        mouseJoint = nil
      end
    end
  end
end
```

We can also extend this by adding more physics objects that we can interact with using the mouse. To do so, we can create multiple objects.

```
poly = {-32, 32, 32, 32, 32, -32, -32, -32}
mass = 1

function makeObject()
  moment = MOAICpShape.momentForPolygon (mass, poly)
  body = MOAICpBody.new(1, moment)
  space:insertPrim(body)

  shape = body:addPolygon( poly )
  shape:setElasticity( 0.8 )
  shape:setFriction( 0.8 )
  shape:setType( 1 )
  space:insertPrim( shape )
end

for i=1, 15 do
  makeObject()
end
```

Notice how the objects interact with each other and can be manipulated with a mouse. We can also attach an image to the physics body; this will display the image instead of the physics body.

```
image = MOAIProp2D.new()
image:setDeck(texture)
image:setParent(body)
layer:insertProp(image)
```

Moai Cloud

When you log into your Moai account, you are greeted with the Moai dashboard, where you can set up your cloud account and select other options. The cloud service that you can create here is totally independent of whether you use Moai or any other framework or browser to consume these services.

Creating a Web Service

Let's start with creating a web service. You can create the service from the dashboard by clicking the Create Service button under Moai Cloud Services. Figure 10-13 shows the screen for creating a service; you mainly need to provide an application name while accepting the remaining default settings.

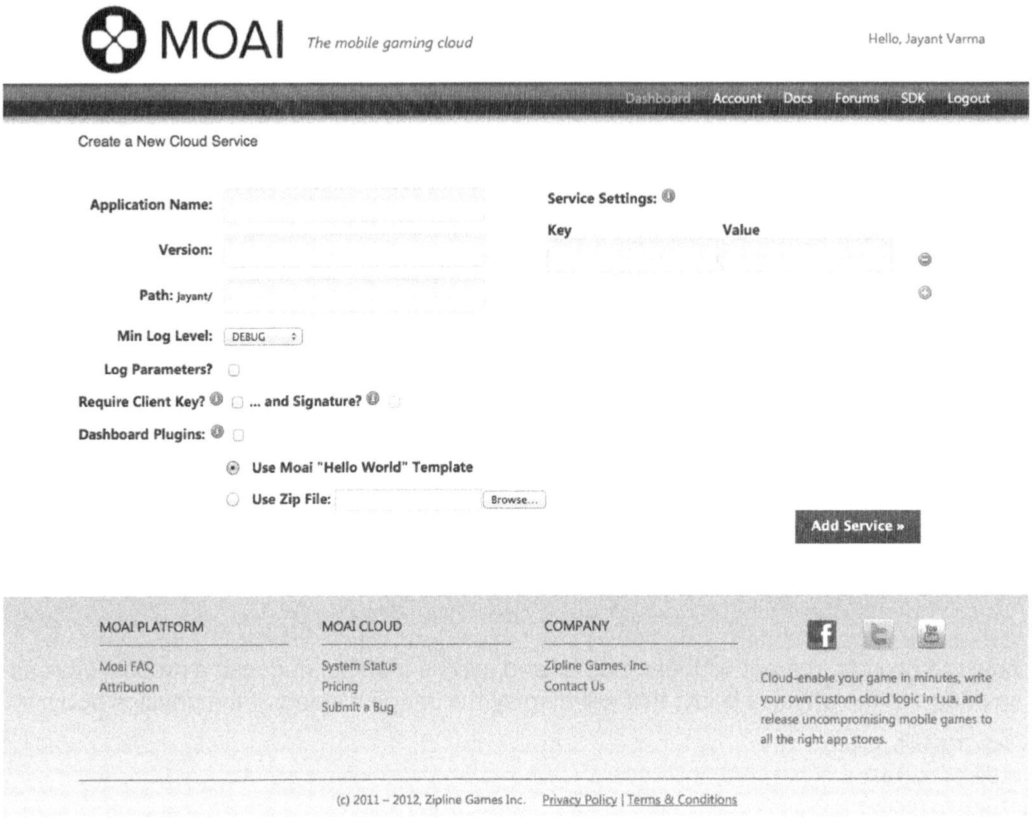

Figure 10-13. Creating a new service in the Moai dashboard

After you create a service, you are greeted with a screen that allows you to create another service or edit the existing one. Notice in Figure 10-14 that the service we called Test01 has a status of Undeployed, which means that it is unavailable on the Web. To be able to access it, we need to deploy it.

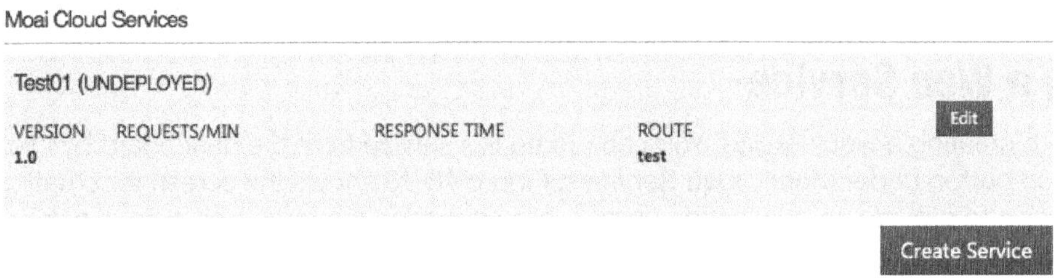

Figure 10-14. The dashboard after creating a service

Let's first click the Edit button to edit the settings for this service, as shown in Figure 10-15. For the simplest of the services, we need not change anything; we can simply click Deploy Service.

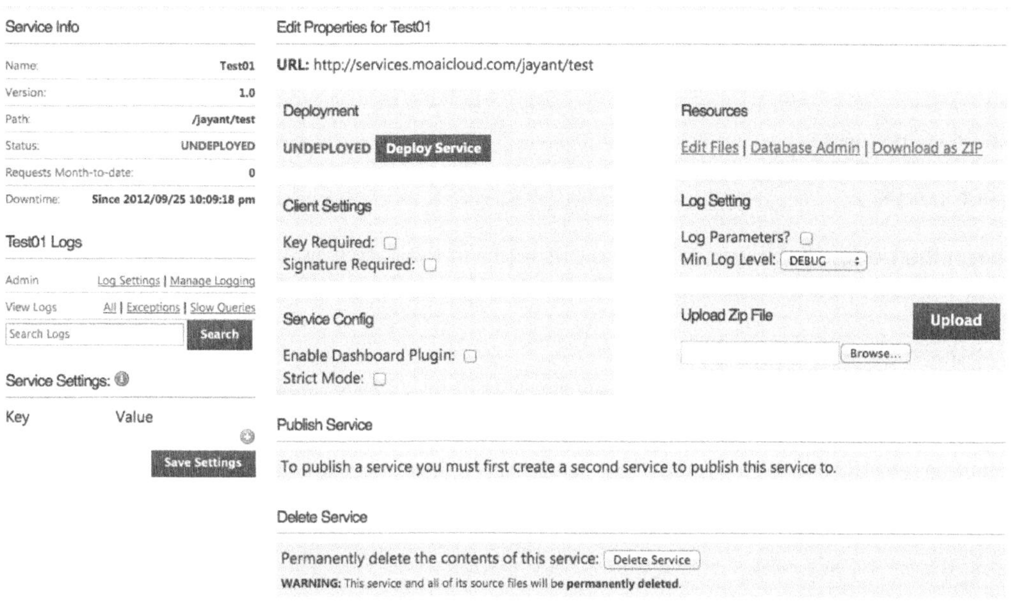

Figure 10-15. Properties of the Moai cloud service

Once we click Deploy Service, the service is available to use. Note the URL at the top; in this example, it is set as `http://services.moaicloud.com/USERNAME/test`. You need to use the URL for your own services. If you open a new browser window and navigate to that URL, you will see the text "hello world!" displayed.

If you want to modify and create a better and more useful web service, you can click the Edit Files link under Resources in the top-right corner, as shown in Figure 10-15. This shall open the code editor that allows you to work with Lua code. The only file present is `main.lua`, which has the following code:

```
function main(web,req)
    web:page('hello world!', 200, 'OK')
end
```

This is similar to the PHP and ASP environments for creating dynamic web pages, but we use the Lua language for doing so. Documentation on how to use this can be found at `http://getmoai.com/wiki/index.php?title=MoaiCloud`.

Consuming the Web Service

The web service is a simple HTTP-type service that is accessed via an URL. We shall try to access the service we created from our Moai application. Our simple code would look something like this:

```
theURL = http://services.moaicloud.com/USERNAME/SERVICENAME
MoaiSim.openWindow("Consume Web Services", 320, 480)
```

```
function getData(theTask)
    print(theTask:getString())
end

task = MOAIHttpTask.new()
task:setCallback( getData )
task:httpGet (theURL)
```

When we run the code, "hello world!" will be output to in the terminal. We can use any other language or framework that supports HTTP access to get data from the Moai cloud service.

> **Note**   The Moai cloud service has a few options (like a phone plan). All accounts created come with the Sandbox plan by default, which is free and offers 50 MB of space, 1 GB of transfer, 100,000 push notifications, and 100,000 API requests. If your needs exceed these, there are other plans to suit your requirements, ranging from $19 per month for hobbyists to $499 per month for studios.

Summary

This chapter discussed a number of features offered by the Moai framework. It covered how to change the display coordinate system. It also discussed that the app running in the Moai simulator is the desktop version of the application. So, before you can build and deploy your application for a mobile device, you can have a desktop version ready for the Mac App store (if required). It also discussed the way Moai handles input; it is easy to set up listeners for additional interfaces and check if they exist. Finally, it covered the Moai cloud, which is separate from the Moai SDK free offering, and allows developers to use the cloud features from right inside your app. While developing with Moai may be daunting at first, if you persist with it, it can provide a very pleasant development experience.

Chapter 11

LÖVE

LÖVE is an open source framework that uses Lua and OpenGL, similar to what most other frameworks offer. It's available on Windows, Mac, and Unix operating systems. Although LÖVE can't be used on iOS devices themselves, it's valuable for whipping up quick and easy prototypes of your game or app on the desktop. Another advantage of LÖVE is that it can be used to create desktop extensions to your application, which could communicate with mobile applications.

LÖVE can also be used to create a level editor for your games, and since it works with the Lua language, you can keep to the single language of choice.

The Architecture

LÖVE, unlike other frameworks, relies on specific callback functions. As with other frameworks, there is no specific structure to follow—with LÖVE there are special functions that need to be declared to allow the application to run. With these *callback functions*, the interpreter looks for these functions, and they're called if they're declared. The LÖVE application architecture is shown in Figure 11-1.

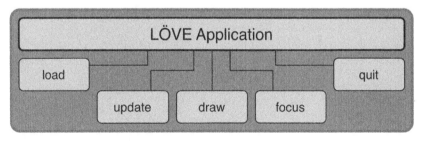

Figure 11-1. *The basic architecture of LÖVE and its callback functions*

LÖVE works on the principle of callbacks, which can be in the form of custom functions that are passed as callbacks, where the user sets them via code or as predefined functions that serve as callbacks. With LÖVE, the callbacks are predefined functions. So if you define one of the functions, it will be called as appropriate.

Installing LÖVE

LÖVE works on desktops. You can install LÖVE by downloading the source and building the binaries or downloading the prebuilt binaries. The source for LÖVE is hosted on bitbucket and can be downloaded from `https://bitbucket.org/rude/love`. The prebuilt binaries for the appropriate platform can be downloaded from `https://love2d.org/#download`.

Running LÖVE

Creating our first Hello world in LÖVE is similar to doing so in many other frameworks. We create a folder—let's call it *Love_01*—and then create a text file called `main.lua` with the following code inside it:

```
print("Hello World from Love")
```

We can get LÖVE to start our app by simply dragging and dropping the project folder onto the LÖVE executable. Or we can start a terminal and then type

```
love projectdir/main.lua
```

We'll be greeted with a blank window, and the `print` statement from our code will be displayed to the terminal. To see the text, simply add the following code in the `main.lua` file and run it again to see the output shown in Figure 11-2.

```
function love.draw()
    love.graphics.print('Hello World!', 400, 300)
end
```

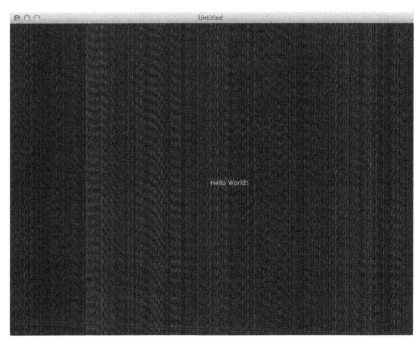

Figure 11-2. Hello World running in LÖVE

The Callback Functions

The callback functions that we can override to make LÖVE work for us are described in this section.

love.load ( )

This function is called when the game starts; it's similar to the `window_onLoad` function in JavaScript or the `main()` entry point in C. This is called only once, and it is used to perform tasks like loading the resources, setting specific settings, initializing variables, and so on. In an object-oriented setting, think of this as the constructor; it is run only once, when a LÖVE applications starts.

love.update (dt)

This function is called almost continuously. This is like an `enterFrame` event or the heartbeat of the application. The parameter passed to the function is `dt`, which is the *delta time*—the amount of time since the function was last called, in seconds. This can be a very small value—as small as 0.025714 seconds (depending on your platform). Frame rates can also affect the delta time.

love.draw ( )

This is the function where all the onscreen drawing takes place. If you have had any previous experience with development using Visual C++, MFC, ATL, OWL, or Objective-C, you will be familiar with this type of function. If any of the draw commands are called outside of this function, they will have no effect.

love.mousepressed (x, y, button)

This function is called whenever a mouse button is pressed; this function is a handler for the mouse button's down event and is passed the x- and y-coordinates of where the mouse button was pressed. It also gets which mouse button was pressed: left, right, or middle.

love.mousereleased (x, y, button)

This function is called when the mouse button is released; it acts as a handler for the mouse button's release event and is passed the x-and y-coordinates of where the mouse button was released and which mouse button was released.

love.keypressed (key, unicode)

This function is called when a key is pressed on the keyboard; this function acts as a handler for the keypress down event and is passed the key code. The key parameter holds the character of the key pressed and the `unicode` parameter holds the ASCII code of the key. If you press the key *a*, then key would be a and `unicode` would be 97.

love.keyreleased (key)

This function is called when a key that was pressed is released. This function acts as a handler for the key-release event and is passed the key code. A complete reference of the key codes can be found at `https://love2d.org/wiki/KeyConstant`.

love.focus ( )

This function is called when the user clicks on or off (any other window or desktop) the LÖVE window. This is most useful for determining if the game is in the current window or not; if it isn't, then you can pause the game or limit the processing.

love.quit ( )

This function is called when the user closes the window by clicking the Close button (the X for Windows and the red dot for Mac OS X). This can be thought of as the destructor that is called when the game has to quit; it can be used to release the memory of all loaded objects and even save the game data (if any).

LÖVE Namespaces

The LÖVE system has several namespaces, each of which has functions. The functions described in the preceding section are part of the global `love` namespace and hence are prefixed with `love`. The other namespaces are described in this section.

love.audio

This namespace provides an interface to output sound from the speakers. This namespace plays the actual sounds. All functionality associated with audio processing can be found here, including changing the volume, playing, pausing, and stopping the sound.

love.event

This namespace manages events, as we learnt earlier. All events (e.g., keypresses, mouse clicks, etc.) are part of the `love.event` namespace.

The *event queue* is used by the application to communicate within the application. This is similar to the event dispatcher and the event listener.

```
-- Using an event queue
function love.keypressed(k)
    if k == 'escape' then
        love.event.push('quit') -- Quit the game
        -- In LÖVE 7.0, you would only push 'q' to the event queue
    end
```

```
end

-- using event.poll
for event, arg1, arg2, arg3, arg4 in love.event.poll() do
    if event == "quit" then -- Quit!
        -- In LÖVE 7.0, you would look for 'q'
    end
end
```

love.event.wait is a blocking function (i.e., it will stop the application and wait till it finds an event).

```
event, arg1, arg2, arg3 = love.event.wait( )
```

> **Note**   There are some differences between LÖVE 0.7.2 and 0.8.0 regarding the number of parameters returned in love.event functions.

love.filesystem

This provides an interface to the user's file system. This is sandboxed, in a manner of speaking, and the access is granted to only two directories:

- The root folder of the .love archive (or source directory)
- The root folder of the game's *save directory*.

The write access is provided to only the game's save directory. This directory can be found in the following places on the various operating systems:

- *Windows XP*: C:\Documents and Settings\user\Application Data\Love\ or %appdata%\Love\
- *Windows Vista and 7*: C:\Users\user\AppData\Roaming\LOVE or %appdata%\Love\
- *Linux*: $XDG_DATA_HOME/love/ or ~/.local/share/love/
- *Mac*: /Users/user/Library/Application Support/LOVE/

love.font

This provides a series of functions that allow for working with fonts. The functions in this namespace allow for creating or using custom fonts.

love.graphics

This namespace provides a very large number of graphics-related functions. This is where all the functions for graphical functionality reside.

love.image

The love.image namespace has a series of functions that can be used to decode and encoded image files.

love.joystick

This namespace houses functions that act similarly to the mouse- and touchpad-related functions. The joystick is simply another input option.

love.mouse

This namespace provides an interface to the user's mouse. It has functions that can get the x,y-coordinates or the mouse cursor, show and hide the cursor, and determine the state of the mouse (e.g., if a button is pressed or not).

love.physics

This namespace houses the Box2D set of functions for including physics in the app or game. Though the interfaces to physics in most of the frameworks are easy, Box2D underneath that interface is still massive and complex.

love.sound

Not to be confused with the love.audio namespace, the functions in the sound namespace are useful for working with encoded sound files. This namespace provides the audio file encoder functions.

love.thread

This namespace offers functions for working with threading.

love.timer

This namespace is home to all the timer-related functions.

The Graphics Module

The graphics library helps create all of the lines, shapes, text, images and other drawable objects. It is also responsible for specialized objects such as particles and canvases.

There are several types of graphics objects that make up LÖVE:

- Canvas: This is the offscreen render target.

- Drawable: This comprises all the items that can be drawn.

- Font: The characters that can be drawn on the screen.

- Framebuffer: This is the offscreen render target.

- Image: This is the image that can be drawn.

- ParticleSystem: This is the particle system, which you can use to create cool effects.

- PixelEffect: This is the pixel shader.

- Quad: This is a quadrilateral with texture information.

- SpriteBatch: This stores the geometry in a buffer for drawing later.

Images

We can load an image using the newImage function; however, to display them on the screen, the code that does the drawing must be in the love.draw callback function. The code below will display the output as seen in Figure 11-3 below.

```
local theImage, x, y
function love.load()
    theImage = love.graphics.newImage("myImage.png")
    x = 50
    y = 50
end
function love.draw()
    love.graphics.draw(theImage, x, y)
end
```

Figure 11-3. Displaying images with LÖVE

In the following code, we can load an image (a texture as it would be called) and we can use this texture and display it several times without having to load it again.

```
img = love.graphics.newImage("myImage.png")
wd, ht = img:getWidth(), img:getHeight()
function love.draw()
  love.graphics.draw(img, 10, 10)
  love.graphics.draw(img, 10+wd, 10)
  love.graphics.draw(img, 10, 10+ht)
  love.graphics.draw(img, 10+wd, 10+ht)
end
```

You could use this, for example, for tile-based games, where you need to tile or repeat an image.

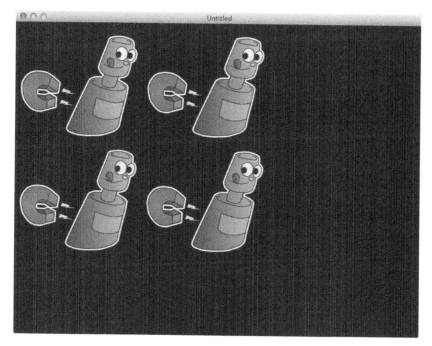

Figure 11-4. Displaying the same image multiple times

If we want to display the silhouette of the image, we can recolor the image black, as shown in Figure 11-5. This can be done with the simple function setColor.

```
local theImage, x, y
function love.load()
   theImage = love.graphics.newImage("myImage.png")
   x = 50
   y = 50
   love.graphics.setColor(0,0,0,255)
   love.graphics.setBackgroundColor(255,255,255,255)
end
function love.draw()
   love.graphics.draw(theImage, x, y)
end
```

Figure 11-5. Coloring an image black to create a mask or silhouette

You could use this technique in games for children—for example, to have children guess what an object is from its black silhouette.

Moving Around

You learned about the love.update function previously, which is the equivalent of enterFrame in other frameworks. In this exercise, we'll use this to move myImage2.png around the screen.

```
local _W, _H = love.graphics.getWidth(), love.graphics.getHeight()
local dirX, dirY = 10, 10

local theImage, x, y
function love.load()
   theImage = love.graphics.newImage("myImage2.png")
   x = 50
   y = 50
   love.graphics.setColor(0,0,0,255)
   love.graphics.setBackgroundColor(255,255,255,255)
end

function love.draw()
   love.graphics.draw(theImage, x, y)
end
```

```
function love.update(dt)
  x = x + dirX
  y = y + dirY

  if x < 0 or x > _W then dirX = - dirX end
  if y < 0 or y > _H then dirY = - dirY end
end
```

At first we get the width and height of the window. This could be different on different systems, or it could be set via the conf.lua file. We get this using the getWidth and getHeight functions, so that we know what the size is at this instance. We save the width and height in the _W and _H variables.

Next we set the speed of movement; in this case, we're setting the dirX and dirY variables to 10 and 10. This shall be used to change the position of the image at each update call.

In the function love.load, which is called only once, when the app starts, we load the image and set it to the variable theImage, and set the variables x and y to 50 and 50, which will be the starting position for this image.

In the love.draw function, we position the image at x, y.

In our love.update function, we increment the x and y by the dirX and dirY, and then we check if the position of x or y is outside of the bounds, 0,0 or width, height of the window. If the x or the y coordinates are outside of the window's bounds, we invert the dirX or the dirY accordingly, which results in creating a bounce effect and places the image back within the bounds of the window.

The Active Window

The love.focus function can be used to determine if the window is active and has focus or not. This could be used, for example, to stop processing when the current window loses focus and continue accordingly when it regains focus again.

We add a line at the top of our existing code from above:

```
local current = true
```

And then we simply add a function at the end of the code:

```
function love.focus(f)
    current = f
end
```

Finally, we redefine the update function as follows:

```
function love.update(dt)
  if current then
    x = x + dirX
    y = y + dirY
```

```
    if x < 0 or x > _W then dirX = - dirX end
    if y < 0 or y > _H then dirY = - dirY end
  end
end
```

So, whenever we move away from the window, the love.focus function is triggered, and that sets the current variable to true or false depending on if the window has focus. In the update, we increment the position of our image if the current variable is not false or nil. So, the moment we switch away from the application window, the image freezes, and when we click the window again, it starts to move.

Moving Around with the Keyboard

If we want to move the image on the screen using the keyboard instead of the love.update function, we can use the love.keypressed function.

```
local _W, _H = love.graphics.getWidth(), love.graphics.getHeight()
local dirX, dirY = 10, 10

local theImage, x, y
function love.load()
    theImage = love.graphics.newImage("myImage3.png")
    x = 50
    y = 50
    love.graphics.setColor(0,0,0,255)
    love.graphics.setBackgroundColor(255,255,255,255)
end

function love.draw()
    love.graphics.draw(theImage, x, y)
end

function love.keypressed(key, unicode)
    if key=="up" then
        y = y - dirY
    elseif key =="down" then
        y = y + dirY
    elseif key=="left" then
        x = x - dirX
    elseif key =="right" then
        x = x + dirX
    end
end
```

In this example, the image only moves when the relevant keys are pressed.

We can add another function, love.mousepressed, that is invoked every time we use the mouse. We can position the image at the location where we click the mouse. We reposition the image only if the left mouse button is pressed.

```
function love.mousepressed(x1, y1, button)
    if button == "l" then
        x = x1
        y = y1
    end
end
```

You might notice that this is not very smooth, and wouldn't be acceptable in a game setting. You need to tap the key and then release it every time to make the object move. We could, however, create some smoother movement based on the cursor keys. To do so, we can move the key-handling routine out of its own function and into the update function. That way we shall check for keypresses many more times.

```
local _W, _H = love.graphics.getWidth(), love.graphics.getHeight()
local dirX, dirY = 10, 10

local theImage, x, y
function love.load()
    theImage = love.graphics.newImage("myImage3.png")
    x = 50
    y = 50
    love.graphics.setColor(0,0,0,255)
    love.graphics.setBackgroundColor(255,255,255,255)
end

function love.draw()
    love.graphics.draw(theImage, x, y)
end

function love.update(dt)
    local key = love.keyboard.isDown
    if key("up") then
        y = y - dirY
    elseif key("down") then
        y = y + dirY
    elseif key("left") then
        x = x - dirX
    elseif key("right") then
        x = x + dirX
    end
end
```

The movement should be much smoother now.

Finally, we need to fix the image so that it can turn in the direction of our choice, instead of just moving backward as moonwalking. Here's how we can do that:

```
local _W, _H = love.graphics.getWidth(), love.graphics.getHeight()
local dirX, speed = 1, 10

local theImage, x, y
function love.load()
    theImage = love.graphics.newImage("myImage3.png")
    x = 50
    y = 50
    love.graphics.setColor(0,0,0,255)
    love.graphics.setBackgroundColor(255,255,255,255)
end

function love.draw()
    love.graphics.draw(theImage, x, y, 0, dirX, 1)
end

function love.update(dt)
    local key = love.keyboard.isDown
    if key("up") then
        y = y - dirY
    elseif key("down") then
        y = y + dirY
    elseif key("left") then
        x = x - dirX
            dirX = -1
    elseif key("right") then
        x = x + dirX
        dirX = 1
    end
end
```

This allows us to achieve the effect we want without creating a new sprite. We've done this by manipulating the scale factor. The draw function can take quite a few parameters:

```
love.graphics.draw(imgObject, x, y, angle, sx, sy, ox, oy, kx, ky)
```

Here, sx and sy are what we are interested in. By keeping them at 1, we are not changing the size of the image, but by setting it as 1 or –1, we can flip the images, so –1 is flipping the image on the horizontal axis and –1 on the vertical. Figure 11-6 shows how this mirrors our image on the x-axis.

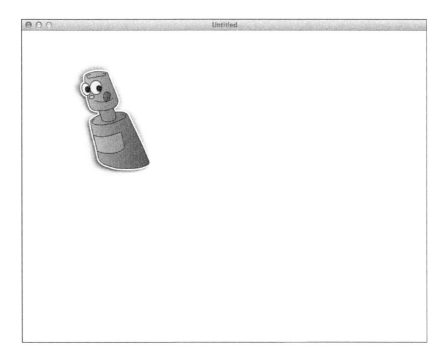

Figure 11-6. Mirroring an image

Turning the Player

In your game, you might want to rotate the player graphic based on where you click—for example, in a tower defense–type game where the player is holding a gun.

As mentioned before, the math or the code can be applied to any framework, so to determine the angle of rotation based on a point on the screen, we can use the following formula:

```
theAngle = math.atan2(posY - startY, posX- startX)
```

startX and startY are the coordinates of the player (as in our preceding example), and posX and posY are the coordinates of a point on the screen.

Using this knowledge, let's make an image on the screen that shall always point to the direction of the mouse cursor.

```
local _W, _H = love.graphics.getWidth(), love.graphics.getHeight()
local dirX, dirY = 10, 10
local theImage, x, y
local theAngle = 0
function love.load()
    theImage = love.graphics.newImage("myImage.png")
    x = 50
    y = 50
```

```
    love.graphics.setColor(0,0,0,255)
    love.graphics.setBackgroundColor(255,255,255,255)
end

function love.draw()
    love.graphics.draw(theImage, x, y, theAngle)
end
function love.update(dt)
    local mouseX, mouseY = love.mouse.getX(), love.mouse.getY()
    theAngle = math.atan2(mouseY - y, mouseX-x)
end
```

Now move your cursor around the screen, and you'll find the image turning to point toward where the cursor currently is. To make it look even better, we could add a crosshair that is displayed at the current position.

The changes that we have made to the code are hiding the cursor using the love.mouse.setVisible function, and we display the crosshair image at the current position of where the cursor should be.

```
local _W, _H = love.graphics.getWidth(), love.graphics.getHeight()
local dirX, dirY = 10, 10
local theImage, x, y
local theAngle = 0
local crosshair
function love.load()
    theImage = love.graphics.newImage("myImage.png")
    crosshair = love.graphics.newImage("crosshair.png")
    x = _W/2
    y = _H/2
    love.graphics.setBackgroundColor(255,255,255,255)
    love.mouse.setVisible(false)
end

function love.draw()
    love.graphics.draw(theImage, x, y, theAngle)
    love.graphics.draw(crosshair, love.mouse.getX(), love.mouse.getY())
end
function love.update(dt)
    local mouseX, mouseY = love.mouse.getX(), love.mouse.getY()
theAngle = math.atan2(mouseY - y, mouseX - x)
end
```

> **Note** When we set the x- and y-coordinates, this is generally the upper-left corner position, so the image is not exactly centered on the x, y coordinates.

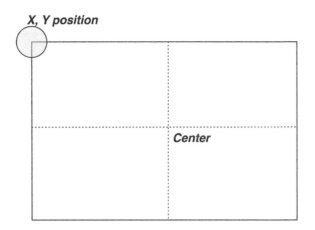

Figure 11-7. *The screen coordinates in LÖVE*

Drawing Primitives

Now that we've played around a bit with some images, we'll look at vector art—rectangles, circles, and so on. In many games, these primitives can help create the backdrops without the added overhead of additional graphics images.

Lines

The simplest of all vector-drawing objects are lines. A line is a series of points that are joined between two points. The syntax for drawing a line is

```
love.graphics.line(x1, y1, x2, y2,...)
```

You can specify a series of points and they will all be drawn. A line object can also be modified via the LineWidth and LineStyle attributes, either individually, as love.graphics.setLineWidth and love.graphics.setLineStyle, or at once, as love.graphics.setLine(width, type). In the code below, we set the line width to 2 and use the smooth type; we then draw a line from 15, 15 to 70, 90.

```
love.graphics.setLine(2,"smooth")
love.graphics.line(15, 15, 70,90)
```

Rectangles

This is the syntax for drawing a rectangle:

```
love.graphics.rectangle( mode, x, y, width, height )
```

mode can be either fill, which will fill the rectangle, or line, which will display the rectangle with an outline and no fill.

In this example, we'll put the concept of rectangles to work by drawing chessboard. The first thing about a chessboard is that it has squares of alternating color and is generally 8×8 squares in size.

```lua
local _W, _H = love.graphics.getWidth(), love.graphics.getHeight()
local smaller = math.min(_W, _H)
local tileSize = math.floor(smaller/10)   -- To allow for spacing above and below

function love.load()
    love.graphics.setColor(0,0,0,255)
    love.graphics.setBackgroundColor(255,255,255)
end

function drawBoard()
  local mode = 1
  for i = 1, 8 do
    for j = 1, 8 do
      if mode ==1 then
        theMode = "fill"
      else
        theMode = "line"
      end
      mode = 1 - mode
      love.graphics.rectangle(theMode, j*tileSize, i*tileSize, tileSize, tileSize)
    end
   mode = 1 - mode
  end
end
function love.draw()
  drawBoard()
end
```

The code is quite straightforward; we are just toggling fill and line by simply using the fact that 1 – 1 = 0 and 1 – 0 = 1, so 1 - mode will help us toggle the number held in mode between 0 and 1. Then, using an if statement, we set theMode to fill if the value of mode is 1 or line if the value of mode is 0. Because we are dealing with an even number of squares, at the end of the inner loop, the value of mode will again be what we started with, so we do a toggle once again. That way, the next line will start with the alternate mode, hence the alternating pattern. To see what would happen if we did not do that, comment out mode = 1 - mode after the rectangle function and see what the code renders.

Circles

The syntax for the function to draw a circle is

```lua
love.graphics.circle(mode, x, y, radius, segments)
```

mode, as before, is either fill or line, x and y are the center points, and radius is the size of the circle. The default number of segments is 10, which draws a jagged circle, good for debugging or for systems that have low resources. For smooth good quality circles, the number of segments recommended are 100.

Let's try animating some circles:

```
local circles = {}
function love.mousepressed(x, y, button)
  if button == "l" then
    newCircle = {
      size = 0,
      n = 20,
      x = x,
      y= y
      }
    table.insert(circles, newCircle)
  end
end
function love.update(dt)
  for _, c1 in pairs(circles) do
    c1.size = c1.size + c1.n * dt
  end
end

function love.keypressed(key)
  if key == " " then
    circles = {}
  end
end
function love.draw()
  for _, c in pairs(circles) do
    love.graphics.circle( "line", c.x, c.y, c.size, 100)
  end
end
```

This code makes the circles grow indefinitely. However, we can set a limit for the maximum and minimum size of the circles.

Let's choose a maximum of 20 and a minimum of 0. To do this, we just need to change the update function, as follows:

```
function love.update(dt)
  for _, c1 in pairs(circles) do
    c1.size = c1.size + c1.n * dt
    if c1.size < 0 then
      c1.size = 0
      c1.n = c1.n * -1
    elseif c1.size > 20 then
      c1.size = 20
      c1.n = c1.n * -1
    end
  end
end
```

Polygons

Polygons are drawn using the function love.graphics.polygon, which has the following syntax:

```
love.graphics.polygon(mode, vertices)
```

The vertices make up a table with the points to draw the shape. The following example draws a triangle pointing downward:

```
love.graphics.polygon ("fill", 100,100,200,100,150,200)
```

> **Note** If you are using fill mode, the polygons must be convex and simple; otherwise, they can produce rendering artifacts.

Quads

We can also draw a quadrilateral shape (a four-sided polygon) by using the love.graphics.quad function. The syntax is

```
love.graphics.quad( mode, x1, y1, x2, y2, x3, y3, x4, y4 )
```

Though quads may seem just like polygons, they can be used for different purposes—for example, to copy a portion of a specified image onto the screen. You can create an animation from a series of images all stored on one image (texture), and then use the quads to help you display portions of the image.

We can create a quad using the newQuad function and then draw it on the screen using the drawq function. This can be very useful for creating animation sheets.

Figure 11-8. Sprite sheet to be used for animating the stick figure (courtesy of Bonzo Industries; http://bonzo_industries. webs.com/sprites.htm)

```
lg = love.graphics
sheet = lg.newImage("stick.png")
wd, ht = sheet:getWidth(), sheet:getHeight()
frameCount = 11
frameSpeed = 5
tileWd, tileHt = 39, 62
delay = 0
curr = 1
scale = 2
frames = {}
function love.load()
    for i=1, frameCount do
      frames[i] = lg.newQuad((i-1)*tileWd, 0, tileWd, tileHt)
    end
end
```

```
function love.draw()
  lg.drawq(sheet, frames[curr], (_W-(tileWd*scale))/2, (_H-(tileHt*scale))/2, 0, scale, scale)
end
function love.update(dt)
  delay = delay + 1
  if delay > frameSpeed then
    delay = 0
   curr = curr + 1
   if curr > frameCount then curr = 1 end
  end
end
```

In our love.load function, we create and store the quads, representing each frame. This helps in achieving speed and efficiency. We can simply draw any frame in the sequence after that by simply referencing the quad as stored in the table. To get the fourth frame, we simply reference the fourth quad (i.e., frames[4]). In our drawq function, we are multiplying tileWd and tileHt by the scale value and also passing the scale as a parameter. This helps to create the animation at the specified scale, which is double in our case (i.e., 2).

To make the animation visible, we slow it down by using a loop in the love.update function, where we increment a frame every 5 updates. This is just for illustration purposes; if this animation were critical, then you would have to rely on the dt (time elapsed) instead of 5 updates to achieve the same frame rate on all platforms. This could mean some skipped frames if the system you are running it on is slow.

We can see our stickman hobble, as shown in Figure 11-9.

Figure 11-9. Our stickman animation

Application Settings – conf.lua

LÖVE allows you to configure the settings for the application. To do so, you need a conf.lua file and it has to contain a love.conf function. If the conf.lua file is present, it is run before main.lua is.

We can create an application window of any size we choose. This example sets the application to a mobile-app screen size of 320×480 (see Figure 11-10).

```lua
function love.conf(t)
  t.screen.width = 320
  t.screen.height = 480
  t.title = "iPhone3"
  t.author = "Jayant C Varma"
end
```

Figure 11-10. Running the application with mobile-app dimensions

Some of the other settings that can be added to the love.conf function are t.screen.fullscreen which can be either true or false.

You can also use the module settings to enable or disable certain modules. Here are some examples:

```lua
t.modules.joystick =false
t.modules.keyboard = true
t.modules.event = true
t.modules.physics = false
```

Creating Effects

LÖVE comes prepackaged with particle effects, so you can create many spectacular effects in your app or game, including smoke trails, fog, and snow.

To create particles, we need to create a *particle emitter*—a source that will emit a particle. Then we need to set the parameters on what our particle is like (e.g., how fast it moves, its lifespan, how long it takes to decay, what kind of particle is it, etc.).

```
function love.load()
  img = love.graphics.newImage("part2.png")
  p = love.graphics.newParticleSystem(img, 256)
  -- This creates a new particle emitter that emits particles
  -- with the image img and shall have a maximum of 256 particles.
  p:setEmissionRate (20)
  p:setLifetime(1)
  p:setParticleLife(4)
  p:setPosition(50,50)
  p:setDirection(0)
  p:setSpread(2)
  p:setSpeed(10,30)
  p:setGravity(30)
  p:setRadialAcceleration(10)
  p:setTangentialAcceleration(0)
  p:setSize(1)
  p:setSizeVariation(0.5)
  p:setRotation(0)
  p:setSpin(0)
  p:setSpinVariation(0)
  p:setColor(200,200,255,240,255,255,255,10)
  p:stop()
end

function love.update(dt)
  p:start()  -- Create a particle burst
  p:update(dt) -- Update the particle's position as required
end

function love.draw()
  love.graphics.draw(p, 20, 0)
end
```

If you want to move the particle emitter with the mouse, you can simply change the love.update function to the following:

```
function love.update(dt)
  p:setLocation(love.mouse:getX(), love.mouse:getY())
  p:start()  -- Create a particle burst
  p:update(dt) -- Update the particle's position as required
end
```

This will now move the particle emitter to the location of the mouse cursor. If you want to remove the pointer, add this line to the love.load function:

```
love.mouse.setVisible(false)
```

As shown in Figure 11-11, this creates a particle emitter that spews particles. You can play with the various setGravity values; for example, a negative number will make the particles float. You can also play with setSize to make the particles bigger or smaller, and setColor to change the color of the particles.

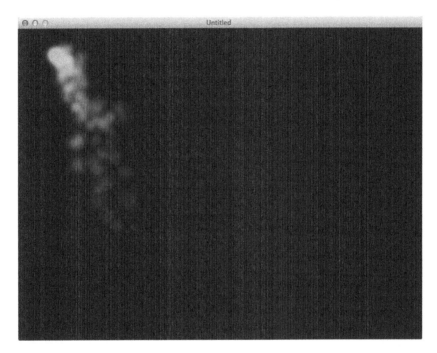

Figure 11-11. *Particle effects following the mouse pointer*

> **Tip**   If you want to visually create particle effects, there is an application written in LÖVE that allows for interactive particle creation. It can be found at https://love2d.org/forums/viewtopic.php?f=5&t=8747&sid=9bf680d6ed9857549d63fb2ba63fc078.

Physics

Box2D is the common thread across all of these frameworks when it comes to physics. As mentioned earlier, Box2D is a very complex and large library. While some frameworks wrap and offer a few functions to work with the library, LÖVE offers developers complete access, so there are a couple of extra steps involved to create a physics body.

First we need to set up the physics world, in which we define its boundaries. A good place to start is to use the screen dimensions for the world.

```
world = love.physics.newWorld(0,0,_W,_H)
```

> **Note**   In LÖVE 0.8.0, the function `love.physics.newWorld` has been changed to take the x, y components of gravity and if the bodies are allowed to sleep or not: `love.physics.newWorld( xg, yg, sleep )`.

Next we set the scaling factor of the bodies (something that is not possible in Corona SDK, which gives it some bugs regarding physics bodies):

```
world:setMeter( number )
```

All the coordinates in this physics world are divided by this `number` value. This is a convenient way to draw on the screen without the need for graphic transformations.

Next we create a physics body:

```
local body = love.physics.newBody(world, 10, 10, 0, 0)
```

The parameters that we pass are the `world` object, the x- and y-coordinates, the mass of the object, and the rotational inertia of the object.

The physics world does not automatically update itself; it is up to us to do the updating. We can ensure that it updates via the `love.update` method, as follows:

```
function love.update(dt)
  world:update (dt)
end
```

> **Note**   With LÖVE 0.8.0, this function has been modified, and it does not take the mass and inertia. Instead it takes a string that defines the body type, which can be static, dynamic, or kinematic and is defined as `love.physics.newBody( world, x, y, type )`.

After having created the body, we need to give it a shape. This is the bounding box on the physics object, which can be a rectangle, circle, polygon, edge shape, or chain shape. An *edge shape* is a line segment, while a *chain shape* is made up of multiple line segments.

```
local bodyshape = local.physics.newRectangleShape(body, 0, 0, 20, 40, 0)
```

This code gives the body a shape that is a rectangle starting at 0, 0 (relative to the body) that is 20 units in width and 40 units in height.

If we run this code at this point, it will do nothing. We still need to draw the body onto the screen. To do so, in the `love.draw()` function, we draw the shapes:

```
function love.draw()
  love.graphics.rectangle("fill", body:getX(), body:getY(), 20, 40)
end
```

You will now see the rectangle drawn at the top-left corner of the screen. It does not automatically move like a physics body should. This is because the mass is currently set to 0, which means that the body does not move, as it is weightless. If we change that and assign it a little weight, it will start to descend or ascend (depending on the gravity settings). If we give the object a positive weight value in this example, it will off the screen, as there is no other object to stop it from falling off the screen.

One of the reasons we have used a rectangle and not a polygon for the bodyShape is that since this object is going to be a dynamic object, we need it to be drawn as it moves. Using the body:getX() and body:getY() functions, we get the current x and y position of the object and draw it there. If we had used the polygon method, it would have created a static object at a fixed location.

We add these two lines in the `love.load()` function:

```
ground = love.physics.newBody(world, 400,600,0,0)
groundShape = love.physics.newRectangleShape(ground, 0,0,800,65,0)
```

This creates a static object called `ground` which is a rectangular-shaped body and then we add this line in the `love.draw()` function, which will render the shape solid:

```
love.graphics.polygon("fill", groundShape:getPoints())
```

Now we have a ground at the bottom that will prevent the smaller physics body from falling off the screen.

We can also add interactivity by adding an impulse to the object when the mouse is clicked. We do this via the `love.mousepressed` function.

```
function love.mousepressed(key, button)
  if button == "l" then
    body:addImpulse(0,-20)
  end
end
```

When we click in the window, the object jumps up and then lands on the ground again. You can change the impulse value to a larger or smaller number to vary the results.

When the object goes out of the world that we set, it gets removed, so if it jumps up too high, it will not return. If you want the object to jump off the screen and return, then you'll need to create a world that is larger than the screen size—for example:

```
world = love.physics.newWorld(-_W, -_H, _W*2, _H*2)
```

Displaying Text

In a game, we might want to display text on the screen in addition to sprites, physics bodies, and so on. We use the `print` or the `printf` function available in the `love.graphics` library. Here's an example of the `print` function:

```
love.graphics.print("Hello world", 10, 10)
```

And here's the `printf` function:

```
love.graphics.printf("Hello World finally but right aligned", 25, 45, 30, "right")
```

As mentioned, this needs to be in the `love.draw` function; otherwise, it won't be visible on the screen.

The `print` function just draws the text on the screen at the x,y-coordinates provided, whereas the `printf` function draws text that is formatted and also wrapped and aligned. The syntax for the `printf` function is

```
printf(text, x, y, width, alignment)
```

The `alignment` is a string that can be `left`, `right`, or `center`, while the `width` specifies the width of the text; any text that exceeds this value gets wrapped automatically.

As described earlier, in the "Images" section, we can set the color via the `love.graphics.setColor` function. This will set the color for all objects drawn subsequently. So, the way to manage this is to set the color for every object before it is drawn.

To print the seven colors of the rainbow, we can use

```
lg = love.graphics
lgc = love.graphics.setColor
function love.load()
  lg.setBackgroundColor(255,255,255)
end

function love.draw()
  lgc(141,56,201) -- Violet
  lg.print("Violet", 10,10)
  lgc(46,08,84) -- Indigo
  lg.print("Indigo", 10,30)
  lgc(0,0,255) -- Blue
  lg.print("Blue", 10,50)
  lgc(0,255,0) -- Green
  lg.print("Green", 10,70)
  lgc(255,255,0) -- Yellow
  lg.print("Yellow", 10,90)
  lgc(255,165,0) -- Orange
  lg.print("Orange", 10,110)
  lgc(255,0,0) -- Red
  lg.print("Red", 10,130)
end
```

Shaders

LÖVE has supported pixel shaders since 0.8.0; these are also called fragment shaders. These compute the color and other attributes for each pixel. With shaders, you can generate a variety of effects, including adding color to images.

The pixel effects are not programmed or described in Lua; they use OpenGL Shading Language (GLSL) instead, which is a subset of functions used by the pixel shaders. Note the C or JavaScript type syntax of GLSL in contrast to the Lua syntax.

Let's make a sample that colors an image black and white:

```
local image = love.graphics.newImage("myImage.png")
imagesx = image:getWidth()
imagesy = image:getHeight()

effect = {}
effect.name = "Black and White"
effect.effect = love.graphics.newPixelEffect [[
    extern number value;
    vec4 effect(vec4 color, Image texture, vec2 texture_coords, vec2 pixel_coords)
      {
        vec4 pixel = Texel(texture, texture_coords);
        float avg = max(0, ((pixel.r + pixel.g + pixel.b)/3) + value/10);
        pixel.r = avg;
        pixel.g = avg;
        pixel.b = avg;
        return pixel;
      }
]]

value = 0

function effect.func()
    effect.effect:send("value", value)
    love.graphics.setPixelEffect(effect.effect)
    love.graphics.draw(image)
end
function love.draw()
    love.graphics.setColor(255,255,255)
    effect.func()
  love.graphics.setPixelEffect()
end
```

To invert the colors of the image, we can simply change the effect as follows:

```
effect.effect = love.graphics.newPixelEffect [[
    vec4 effect(vec4 color, Image texture, vec2 texture_coords, vec2 pixel_coords)
      {
        vec4 pixel = Texel(texture, texture_coords);
        pixel.r = 1.0 - pixel.r;
        pixel.g = 1.0 - pixel.g;
        pixel.b = 1.0 - pixel.b;
```

```
        return pixel;
    }
]]
```

This also requires a slight change to the `effect.func` function:

```
function effect.func()
    love.graphics.setPixelEffect(effect.effect)
    love.graphics.draw(image)
end
```

What we have done is simply set the value of the pixel r, g, and b colors to be 1 minus the value, which is similar to inverting the image's colors. For more effects, you can read up on GLSL at http://www.opengl.org/documentation/glsl/ and also play around with the code. There are quite a few samples on the forums that you can download and study. Apple has their own documentation on GLSL at https://developer.apple.com/library/mac/#documentation/GraphicsImaging/Conceptual/OpenGLShaderBuilderUserGuide/Introduction/Introduction.html which points to the older version 1.20.8. This should be used instead of the newer versions as the version Apple has information on is what is available on the iOS devices.

Making Sound

A game framework is incomplete if you cannot play sound. With LÖVE, first we need to load the sound into memory and then play it as required.

```
popSound = love.audio.newSource("pop.ogg", "static")
```

`static` tells LÖVE that it needs to load and decode this sound entirely before it starts to play. This is different from streaming, where the sound can be played in parts as it is streamed from disk.

To play the sound, we simply use

```
love.audio.play(popSound)
```

Let's create an example that makes a popping sound each time the window is clicked:

```
function love.load()
  pop = love.audio.newSource("pop.ogg", "static")
end
function love.mousepressed(mx, my, mButton)
  if mButton == "l" then
    love.audio.play(popSound)
  end
end
```

Apart from playing a sound, LÖVE also provides functions to increase and decrease the volume. You can also change the pitch by simply using `popSound:setPitch(value)`, where value has a range between 0 and 1. The same ranges apply for `setVolume` and can be set as `popSound:setVolume(value)`.

In this sample, we'll have a bit of fun with the pitch:

```
count = 1
function love.load()
  pop = love.audio.newSource("pop.ogg", "static")
end
function love.mousepressed(mx, my, mButton)
  if mButton == "l" then
    count = count + 1
    if count>15 then count = 1 end
    pop:setPitch(count/10)
    love.audio.play(popSound)
  end
end
```

With what you have learned, try to create a grid that resembles a repeating bubble-wrap pattern, using a bubble image for each cell in the grid. When each bubble is clicked, make the image change to a popped bubble and have it make a popping sound.

If you want to play some background music—music that keeps repeating or playing for the duration of the game or till you want it to stop—you can use the function setLooping:

```
backgroundMusic = love.audio.newSource("music.mp3")
backgroundMusic:setLooping(true)
love.audio.play(backgroundMusic)
```

Sample Game Code

This final section will give an example of a game that incorporates all of the topics covered in the chapter. The example creates a picture-logic puzzle (aka nanogram puzzle), which is similar to a crossword puzzle, except the player has to fill in squares with numbers instead of letters, based on numerical clues that are provided. For example, if the clue is 2, it means that the row or column contains two filled squares that are contiguous. A clue of 1,1 means that the row or column contains two squares that are not contiguous and must have at least one blank square between them.

In our sample, we shall randomly create a puzzle for a 5×5 grid and create the clues, as shown in Figure 11-12.

```
squares = 5
_W = love.graphics:getWidth()

_H = love.graphics:getHeight()

math.randomseed(os.time())
local size = 400/squares
local boxes = {}
local solved = false

function make_board()
  solved = false
```

```
  size = 400/squares      -- Recalculate the sizes
  boxes = {}              -- Reset the array

  -- Create a random puzzle by filling the board
  for x = 1, squares do
    for y = 1, squares do
      box = {Orig = math.random(0,1), X = x, Y = y, Curr = 0}
      -- We set the value for that box randomly to on or off
      table.insert(boxes, box)
    end
  end

  -- Set the first row to be on
  for k,v in pairs(boxes) do
    if v.X == 1 then
      v.Orig = 1
    end
  end

end

make_board()

function findnumberx(x)
  -- This returns the clue for the column x
  local n = {}
  local c = 0

  for k,v in pairs(boxes) do
    if v.X == x then
      if v.Orig == 1 then
        c = c + 1
      else
        if c > 0 then
          table.insert(n, tostring(c))
        end
        c = 0
      end
    end
  end

  if c > 0 then
    table.insert(n, tostring(c))
  end

  return table.concat(n,",")
end

function findnumbery(y)
  -- This returns the clue for the row y
```

```lua
  local n = {}
  local c = 0
  for k,v in pairs(boxes) do
    if v.Y == y then
      c = c + 1
    else
      if c > 0 then
        table.insert(n, tostring(c))
      end
      c = 0
    end
  end
  if c > 0 then
    table.insert(n, tostring(c))
  end
  return table.concat(n, ",")
end

function love.load()
  button_off = love.graphics.newImage("buttonoff.png")
  button_on = love.graphics.newImage("buttonon.png")
  button_not = love.graphics.newImage("buttonnot.png")
end

function love.draw()
  love.graphics.setColor(255,255,255)   -- White
  love.graphics.setFont(love.graphics.newFont(12))   -- 12pt size
  -- Draw the appropriate image, On, Off or Not
  for k, v in pairs(boxes) do
    if v.Curr == 0 then
      love.graphics.draw(button_off, v.X*size, v.Y*size, size/30, size/30, 0, 0)
    elseif v.Curr == 1 then
      love.graphics.draw(button_on, v.X*size, v.Y*size, size/30, size/30, 0, 0)
    elsif v.Curr == 2 then
      love.graphics.draw(button_not, v.X*size, v.Y*size, size/30, size/30, 0, 0)
    end
  end

  -- Display the clues for the columns
  for x=1, squares do
    love.graphics.print(findnumberx(x), x*size, size - 40
  end

  -- Display the clues for the rows
  for y=1, squares do
    love.graphics.print(findnumbery(y), size-40, size*y
  end

  -- Show if the puzzle has been solved
  if solved then
    love.graphics.setColor(255,0,0)   -- Red
    love.graphics.setFont(love.graphics.newFont(24))   -- 24pt size
```

```lua
      love.graphics.print("You have solved the puzzle",
         size + 10, _H/2)
   end

end

function love.mousepressed(mx, my, button)
   for k, v in pairs(boxes) do
      theBox = mx > v.X * size and my > v.Y * size and
               mx < v.X * size + size and my < v.Y * size + size
      -- Check if the point where the mouse was clicked is inside
      -- and v is the current box it is inside
      if theBox then
        if mouse=="l" then
          -- If the left mouse button is clicked, set or unset the grid
          if v.Curr == 0 or c.Curr == 2 then
            v.Curr = 1
          else
            v.Curr = 0
          end
        elseif mouse == "r" then
        -- If the right mouse button is clicked, mark or unset the grid
          if v.Curr == 0 or v.Curr == 1 then
            v.Curr = 2
          else
            v.Curr = 0
          end
        end
      end
   end

   solved = true
   for k,v in pairs(boxes) do
     if v.Curr == 2 then v.Curr = 0 end
     if v.Orig == v.Curr then
       -- Do nothing, everything is fine
     else
       -- If the Orig is not equal to Curr, then the puzzle is
       -- not solved
       solved = false
       break
     end
   end
end

function love.keypressed(key)
  if key == "up" or key == "w" then
  -- If the key is w or up arrow, increase the size of the board
    if sqaures < 9 then
      squares = squares + 1
      make_board()
    end
```

```
  elseif key == "down" or key == "s" then
  -- If the key is s or dn arrow, decrease the size of the board
    if sqaures > 2 then
      squares = squares - 1
      make_board()
    end
  end
end
```

Figure 11-12. A picture-logic puzzle game

> **Note**   This code was taken from the LÖVE forums and was written by the user GijsB and can be found
> at https://love2d.org/forums/viewtopic.php?f=5&t=3391.

Summary

This chapter discussed the various functions available in LÖVE. This is a very comprehensive and powerful framework for desktop applications and can be used to integrate desktop features with your mobile applications. LÖVE is a complete framework in many regards; it is cross platform and fully functional, with physics, sound, particle systems, and drawing functions. Additionally, it is one of the very few frameworks that allows for pixel access.

In the next chapter, we shall look at Codea, which was inspired by LÖVE and is modeled on the Processing libraries.

Chapter **12**

Codea

The last of the frameworks on our list is Codea. This was created as an IDE on the iPad. The highlight of the app was and rather still is the editor, which makes editing, or rather writing, code on the iPad fun. It has autocomplete functionality and a custom keyboard that puts commonly used keys at your fingertips, rather than making you switch between layouts to reach certain numbers or symbols.

The biggest advantage of Codea is that you can test your app on the target device directly, rather than having to upload to test on the device or use a simulator, as is the case with other frameworks. In this sense, Codea is the fastest and the most accurate simulator and player that you can use.

Getting Codea

The first step for getting Codea is purchasing it from the iTunes store; it is available only for the iPad at the moment. The link for the Codea app can be found at `http://itunes.apple.com/au/app/codea/id439571171?mt=8`.

When you start Codea, you'll see the start screen, shown in Figure 12-1, which offers the option to either open some samples to study or start a new project. When a new project is created, Codea also creates a skeleton template to build upon. Clicking the Getting Started button will take you to a complete reference to Codea, including the reference manual, forums, and wiki, and the Lua reference manual.

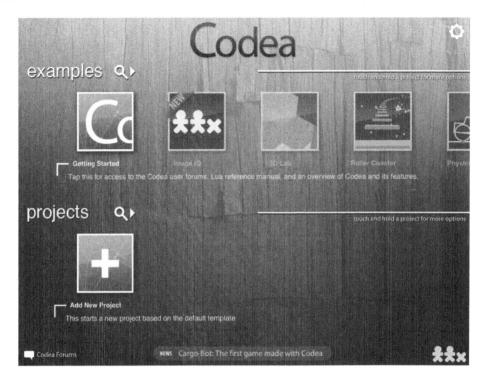

Figure 12-1. The start screen when you launch Codea

Codea Architecture

The major portion of Codea is the editor, which includes Lua syntax highlighting. The engine that powers Codea shares a lot with the Processing language (see `http://processing.org`). The concepts and APIs are taken from Processing, and Codea benefits from Processing's mature and stable API.

With the Codea runtime, your code can be compiled on the desktop using a Mac with Xcode. The code that you write with Codea can be compiled with the runtime, and the app can be uploaded to the iOS App Store. The first app that was created using the Codea runtime was Cargo-Bot, which proved that the Codea runtime was ready for use as a framework.

Hello World

Like most of the Lua-based frameworks, Codea uses `main.lua` as the entry point to the code being run. The `main.lua` file has two functions that help work with the application.

The first one is `setup`; this is the function that is run only once at the start of the application. This function can be used to run all the initialization code required for the application. The second function is `draw`; this is the function that is responsible for drawing, or rather updating, the screen at every frame. Here are the two functions:

```
function setup()
  print("Hello World")
end
```

```
function draw()
  background(100,120,160,255)
  font("Georgia")
  fill(255)
  fontSize(20)
  textWrapWidth(70)
  text("Hello World from Codea", WIDTH/2, HEIGHT/2)
end
```

When you run these functions, you'll see the text "Hello World from Codea" in the middle of the screen, as shown in Figure 12-2. The Codea run screen has two property windows on the left side, which display parameters and the console output window. The rest of the screen displays the graphical output of the code.

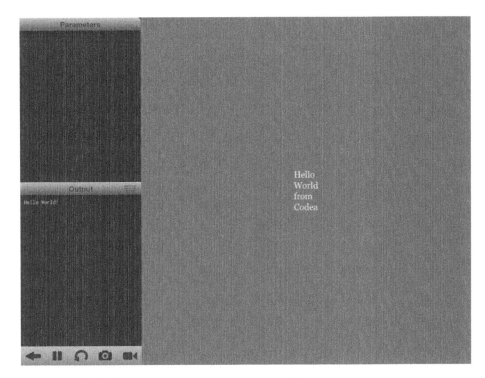

Figure 12-2. Hello World using Codea

> **Note**   You can remove the two left-hand windows by using the function displayMode(FULLSCREEN) to give yourself more screen space.

The parameters can be used for interactive input to the code. These are typically in the form of sliders that can help set ranges.

Parameters

While in interactive running mode, you might want to be able to change some of the code on the fly to see how it will alter the output. For example, say you want to alter the stroke width or the radius of a circle. Rather than setting that in the code and running it again, you can use the parameter sliders to alter it on the fly.

Parameters can be created using the `parameter` function. The `parameter` function takes three arguments: the *name* of the parameter, the *starting* range, and the *end* range. The name of the parameter is also the name of the global variable, which can be accessed in the code. Here's an example:

```
parameter("Radius", 1, 10)
```

This shall create a slider in the Parameters window that allows for choosing the radius. The best place to create the parameter sliders is in the `setup` function. The `parameter` function allows for the slider value to be changed as a floating-point number, whereas the `iparameter` function allows for selection of an integer number in the range.

```
function setup()
  parameter("Radius", 100, 500)
  iparameter("BlueAmount", 0, 255)
end

function draw()
  background(10,10,20)
  stroke(255)
  fill(255,0,BlueAmount)

  strokeWidth(1)
  ellipseMode(RADIUS)
  ellipse(0,0,Radius, Radius)
end
```

Now when we run the code, we can adjust the radius of the ellipse that we draw and also modify the blue color amount. This allows the color to change from Red to Magenta.

Note You can add a fourth argument to the `parameter` or the `iparameter` function that sets the initial value of the global variable.

Drawing with Codea

Since Codea is a GUI-based framework, we'll focus on the `draw` function, which enables us to create graphics.

On the Codea drawing surface, the screen is refreshed, or rather drawn, over 60 times a second. However, there is no certainty that the `draw` function will be called 60 times per second, as this is dependent on the time the code inside of `draw` takes to complete and return.

The screen in Codea is a bit different from other frameworks. In most frameworks, the top-left corner is the origin (0, 0), and the x-axis value increases moving right and the y-axis value increasing moving downward. In Codea, the lower-left corner is the origin, and the x-axis value increments as it moves to the right and the y-axis increases as it moves upward.

Secondly, because of the side panels, the screen is obscured, and the size reported is 750×768 in landscape mode and 494×1024 in portrait mode. You can remove this panel by calling the displayMode(FULLSCREEN) function. However, even in full-screen mode, the buttons as seen at the bottom of the screen in Figure 12-2 above, still remain. To remove the buttons as well, you can use the displayMode(FULLSCREEN_NOBUTTONS) function.

If you use the displayMode function with the FULLSCREEN_NO_BUTTONS, argument, you need to manually call the close function to return back to the editor.

Orientation

The orientation for your Codea app can be set using the supportedOrientation function. The default value for supportedOrientation is ANY, which supports all orientations. However, you can preset it to the ones that you need.

The options are

- ANY
- LANDSCAPE_ANY
- LANDSCAPE_LEFT
- LANDSCAPE_RIGHT
- PORTRAIT
- PORTRAIT_ANY
- PORTRAIT_UPSIDE_DOWN

System Keyboard

The keyboard can be displayed or hidden as needed using the showKeyboard and hideKeyboard functions. There is another keyboard-related function, keyboardBuffer, which returns the text in the keyboard buffer. Every time the keyboard is shown, the keyboard buffer is cleared. Here is an example of using the showKeyboard and keyboardBuffer functions:

```
function touched(touch)
  showKeyboard()
end

function draw()
  background(40,40,50)
  fill(255)
  textMode(CORNER)
```

```
buffer = keyboardBuffer()
_, bufferHeight = textSize(buffer)
if buffer then
text (buffer, 10, HEIGHT - 30 - bufferHeight)
end
end
```

Drawing Mode

When you draw something, it is not automatically persisted, i.e. erased and needs to be redrawn everytime. However, you can set the mode so that the previously drawn frame persists on the screen and is not erased. You can do so by setting the backingMode to RETAINED. The default mode is STANDARD.

> **Note**   When the RETAINED mode is used with the new iPad, a bug in iOS5 does not work as expected. It is however fixed by Apple in iOS6 and works as expected.

Background Color

The background color can be changed using the background function. This function takes the color in RGBA format. With the Codea editor, you can also manually select and set the color by simply tapping on the numbers, which brings up a color picker for manual selection of the color.

```
background(red, green, blue, alpha)
```

Pen Color

The pen color, or *foreground* color, that is used for all the drawing can be set using the stroke function. The parameters that the stroke function takes are also in RGBA format.

```
stroke(0,0,0,255)  -- Would set the pen color to black
```

Fill Color

The fill color can be set using the fill function. It is set in terms of arguments, similar to the preceding two color functions.

```
fill(255,164,0)  -- sets the fill color to orange
```

Line Width

The line width for the drawing can be altered using the strokeWidth function.

```
strokeWidth(3)  -- sets the stroke width to 3
```

> **Note**   While you can set the fill color by using `fill(255,164,0)` or set the pen color by using `stroke(0,0,0)` or the stroke Width by using the `strokeWidth(3)`, you can retrieve these values by passing nothing to these functions, simply as `fill()` which would return the current fill color, `stroke()` would return the stroke color and `strokeWidth()` would return the width.

Drawing Lines

The function to draw lines is the `line` function. This takes four arguments: the x- and y-coordinates of the start point and endpoint of the line. The line is drawn between these two points.

```
line(10,10,300,300)   -- draws a line between 10,10 and 300,300
```

The *line cap* mode is used to determine how the ends of the lines are drawn. There are three *line cap* modes that are used when drawing lines: ROUND, SQUARE, and PROJECT. The default mode is ROUND.

- ROUND: Draws the lines with the ends rounded off
- SQUARE: Draws the lines with the ends squared off
- PROJECT: Draws the lines with square edges, but projected out, as in ROUND mode.

Anti-Aliasing

When drawing lines, you can end up with jagged edges, which make for an unpleasant visual experience. To deal with this, Codea has a function that smoothes the edges out—what is known as *anti-aliasing*. To perform anti-aliasing, you call the `smooth` function, all subsequently drawn lines will be anti-aliased.

> **Note**   While drawing thin lines, you might want to switch to no anti-aliasing using the `noSmooth` function. Thin lines when anti-aliased would look worse than without anti-aliasing.

Drawing Circles and Ellipses

The function to draw a circle or ellipses is the `ellipse` function. This takes four parameters, which depend on the *ellipse mode* being used to draw the ellipse (discussed following). In one such mode, CENTER, the four parameters are the x,y-coordinates of the center point around which the circle is drawn, followed by the diameters—one for the x-axis and one for the y-axis. If these are the same, a circle is drawn. If these are different, an ellipse is drawn.

Here's the syntax for drawing a circle:

```
ellipse(50,50,20,20)
```

And here's the syntax for drawing a ellipse:

```
ellipse(100,100,20,50)
```

As mentioned, there are four ellipse modes that allow you to draw ellipses in various different ways:

- CENTER: In this mode, the parameters are the center x,y-coordinates, followed by the x and y diameters. This is the mode used in the previous example.

- RADIUS: This mode uses the center x,y-coordinates, followed by the x and y *radii*, instead of the diameters.

- CORNER: This mode takes the x,y-coordinates of the lower-left corner of the ellipse, followed by the width and height. The ellipse is drawn in the bounding rectangle as specified by the arguments.

- CORNERS: This mode takes the x,y-coordinates of the lower-left corner of the ellipse, followed by the upper-right corner of the ellipse. The ellipse is drawn in the bounding rectangle as specified by the arguments.

The following snippets provide examples of the preceding modes:

```
ellipseMode(CENTER)
ellipse(100,100,50,50)

ellipseMode(RADIUS)
ellipse(100,200,50,50)

ellipseMode(CORNER)
ellipse(200,100,50,50)

ellipseMode(CORNERS)
ellipse(200,200,50,50)
```

Drawing Rectangles

The function for drawing rectangles is the `rect` function. It takes four arguments, which, as with ellipses, depend on the mode in which the rectangle is being drawn. In CENTER mode, the arguments are the starting x,y-coordinates, followed by the width and height of the rectangle.

```
rect(10,10,300,100)  -- draws a rectangle that is 300x100 and positions it at 10,10
```

Following are the four modes for drawing rectangles:

- CENTER: This mode takes as parameters the center x,y-coordinates, followed by the width and the height.

- RADIUS: The mode takes the center x,y-coordinates, followed by half the width and height.

- CORNER: This mode takes the x,y-coordinates of the lower-left corner of the rectangle, followed by the width and height. The rectangle is drawn in the bounding rectangle as specified by the arguments.

- CORNERS: This mode takes the x,y-coordinates of the lower-left corner of the rectangle, followed by the absolute coordinates of the upper-right corner, rather than the width and height. The rectangle is drawn in the bounding rectangle as specified by the arguments.

The following snippets provide examples of the preceding modes:

```
rectMode(CENTER)
rect(100,100,50,50)

rectMode(RADIUS)
rect(100,200,50,50)

rectMode(CORNER)
rect(100,100,50,50)

rectMode(CORNERS)
rect(100,200,50,50)
```

Drawing Text

The function to draw text onto the screen is text. It takes three arguments: the text itself, and the position in x- and y-coordinates where the text needs to be displayed.

```
text("This is sample text", 10,200)
```

There are other functions that help to set the attributes of the text being displayed, like the font name and size. The following function creates the text and also returns the width and the height of the text that was created:

```
w, h = textSize("Hello World")
print(w, h)
```

Drawing Modes

The text function also has two drawing modes that specify how the arguments passed are parsed and the text is displayed:

- CENTER: In this mode, the text is centered around the x,y-coordinates passed to the text function for drawing. This is the default text-drawing mode.

- CORNERS: In this mode, the x,y-coordinates passed to the text function specify the lower-left corner of the text.

Text Alignment

The text when drawn can be aligned as either of the alignments, LEFT, RIGHT, or CENTER. The default text alignment setting is LEFT.

Text Wrapping

While drawing the text, you can also set the width of the text to be displayed, and any text that exceeds that width gets wrapped to the next line. If the text wrap setting is set to 0, text is not wrapped.

```
textWrapWidth(80)
text("This text would get wrapped onto multiple lines",100,100)
```

Changing the Font

The font function can be used for rendering text. The fonts that can be set on the iOS device are limited to a list of fonts available on the device, and the default font used is *Helvetica*.

Changing the Font Size

The fontSize function can be used to change the size of the font being rendered. The default size for text rendering is 17 points.

Displaying Images

Sprites in Codea are images that can be loaded and displayed on the screen using the sprite function. However, the way the architecture of Codea is defined, there are *sprite packs* from which you can use images. To load an image, you don't use the path to the image, as in other framework, but instead refer to the image as *SpritePack:SpriteName*. This function requires at least three arguments: the spriteName, or the *image handle*, and the x,y-coordinates where the sprites will be positioned. The function can also take the width and height as arguments.

```
sprite("Planet Cute:Grass Block", WIDTH/2, HEIGHT/2)
```

> **Note**   In the current version of Codea, you can also use images from the photo library or the clipboard on the device, as well as images from Dropbox and from the library of free sprites available in Codea (from Dan Cook, of http://lostgarden.com).

Images loaded from the device or an online source can be used as sprites in Codea. To determine the size of the sprites, you can use the function spriteSize, which returns the width and height of the sprite name passed to the function.

```
sprWidth, sprHeight = spriteSize("Planet Cute:Grass Block)
print(sprWidth, sprHeight)
```

You can also set the *sprite mode*, which determines how the sprite is displayed on the screen. The x,y-coordinates are used to position the sprite, just like the options for drawing. The default value for SpriteMode is CENTER. The other modes that can be set are RADIUS, CORNER, and CORNERS, which function similarly to the modes used for drawing ellipses and rectangles.

With Codea, *images* are different from sprites. Images are *canvases* that are created via code, and their bits are set using the set method with an x,y-coordinate and a color. The color of a particular pixel can be obtained by using the get method. Portions of the image can be copied to create new images using the image.copy function.

Drawing Off-screen

Most of the drawing functions as we have seen in the above paragraphs draw directly on screen. The drawing functions can be instructed to draw onto a context (a drawing area) as we specify using the setContext function. When we want the drawing to be resumed back onto the screen context, we can simply call the setContext function again without passing it any parameters.

```
myImage = image (400,400)

setContext(myImage)
ellipse(200,200,200)
rect(0,0,100,100)
setContext()

sprite(myImage, WIDTH/2, HEIGHT/2)
```

Loading Sprites into an Image

While images can be manipulated by getting or setting the pixel colors and created using the image.copy function, sprites cannot be manipulated in these ways. To be able to manipulate sprite images, you can copy or load the sprite onto an image using the readImage function, which creates an image object from the sprite, like so:

```
myImage = readImage("Planet Cute:Heart")
```

Saving Images

This saveImage function can help create and save images to the device or Dropbox. The way to save an image is by passing it the sprite pack—which is either Documents or Dropbox—followed by the file name. Note that if the file name already exists, the original file will be overwritten, and if the image is set to nil, then the file specified will be deleted.

```
saveImage("Documents:theSprite", image)
```

> **Note** If the device is a retina device, it will save two files when using this function: a retina-sized image with a @2x suffix and a non-retina image scaled to 50 percent.

Saving Data

When working with an application, you might want to save the data so that it persists. The data can be saved either locally, making it available to only the current Codea project, or globally, making it available to all Codea projects on the device. Here's an example of saving data locally:

```
local theName = (readLocalData("username"))
if theName == nil then
  theName = "Default"
  saveLocalData("username", theName)
end
print(theName)
```

If you run this code, "Default" will be printed to the output console.

If you want to start afresh and remove all of the values stored, you can use the clearLocalData function.

Drawing Without Color

There are times when you might want to draw something with a clear color—for example, if you want a nonfilled (transparent) shape or a shape with no outline. This can be done with the sample functions that have the prefix no. These are described in the following subsections.

noFill

The noFill function sets the fill color to transparent, drawing a shape that has no fill (but could have an outline). Figure 12-3 demonstrates drawing a rectangle with and without a fill.

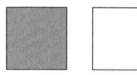

```
rect(10,10,50,50)

noFill()

rect(10,100,50,50)
```

Figure 12-3. *A rectangle with a fill (left) and one without (right)*

noStroke

The noStroke function sets the color used for drawing to transparent. This function removes the outline from a shape. (See Figure 12-4.)

```
rect(10,10,50,50)

noStroke()

rect(10,100,50,50)
```

Figure 12-4. *A rectangle with a stroke (left) and one without (right)*

noTint

The tint function changes the color of the sprite according to the multiply effect in image-processing packages. The noTint function removes all of the tinting while drawing the sprites.

Transformation Functions

The display objects that we can create can be transformed in various ways, including rotating and scaling, with functions like rotate, scale, translate, and zLevel (what a lot of developers refer to as the z-Index). These functions apply the respective transformations to all subsequent drawings, not just an individual display object.

Rotate

The rotate function takes the angle arguments in degrees.

```
rotate(30)
rect (226,226,52,52)
```

Scale

The scale function takes the scaling parameters either as a single scaling factor that is applied to all the axes, or as individual axes.

```
scale(amount)
scale(xScale, yScale)
scale(xScale, yScale, zScale)
```

Translate

The translate function specifies an amount to displace the subsequent drawings. *Displacement* is like an offset that is added to the coordinates.

```
rect(0,0,50,50)
translate(20,20)
rect(0,0,50,50)
translate(40,40)
rect(0,0,50,50)
```

> **Note**   All of the transformation functions are relative, which means that they will perform the operations of the given value from the current value. For example, rotate(10) will rotate the object 10 degrees from its current position.

Transform functions change the *display matrix*. The display matrix is like a stack, where the current settings can be saved using the pushMatrix function and the original settings can be restored using the popMatrix function. In certain cases, you can also reset the entire display matrix to its default values using the resetMatrix function.

Recording Video

Codea has built-in functions for recording video. The functions for working with video recording are simple:

- ▨ startRecording: You can start the recording by calling this function. Do not call this function from within the setup function.

- ▨ stopRecording: You can stop recording by calling this function. When we stop recording, the video is saved to the device's camera roll.

- ▨ isRecording: With this function, you can query if something is currently being recording.

Touch

Codea runs on the iPad, which is a touch device, so the way to get input other than from the keyboard is via touches.

The function that manages when the screen is touched is the touched function. Each touch point generates a touch object, which has the following members:

- ▨ id: The unique identifier for the touch

- ▨ x: The x position of the touch on the screen

- ▨ y: The y position of the touch on the screen

- ▨ prevX: The x position from the previous frame of the touch

- ▨ prevY: The y position from the previous frame of the touch

- ▨ deltaX: The amount the touch has moved on the x-axis

- ▨ deltaY: The amount the touch has moved on the y-axis

- ▨ state: The state of the touch, which can be BEGAN, MOVING, or ENDED

- ▨ tapCount: The number of times the touch point has been tapped

There is a global variable called CurrentTouch that contains the most recent touch on the screen. Here's an example of its use:

```
function draw()
  background(0)
  fill(255)
  ellipse(CurrentTouch.x, CurrentTouch.y, 300)
end
```

This code produces a white circle on the screen that looks like a spotlight and moves with the touch as you glide the finger across the screen.

Drawing with Touch

I previously discussed how you can move the display object based on the touch point. If you create an array of touch points, you can render them to generate interesting results. Here's an example:

```
points = {}
index = 0
maxPts = 99

function setup()
  watch("index")
end

function touched(touch)
  index = index + 1
  if index > maxPts then
    index = maxPts
    table.remove(points, 1)
  end
  table.insert(points, touch)
end

function draw()
  background(40,40,50)

  strokeWidth(3)
  lineCapMode(ROUND)

  if index > 1 then
    ptx, pty = points[1].x, points[1].y

    for i=2, index do
      sx, sy = points[i].x, points[i].y
      line(ptx,pty, sx, sy)
      ptx, pty = sx, sy
    end
  end
end
```

For some variety, you can also play with maxPts variable and see the results.

> **Note** To watch a variable, simply use the function watch but remember to enclose the variable name in quotes for it to work. If the variable is a table, it displays as Table and an address to the memory, while the internal objects created by Codea can be watched without specifying the individual components, like watch("Gravity") can be used to watch all of the three axis data instead of each individual axis as watch("Gravity.x"), watch("Gravity.y") and watch("Gravity.z")

Multitouch

Multitouch is supported on the iPad, but it is not handled automatically. You can handle multitouch by saving the touches into an array and iterating through them between the time that the BEGAN and ENDED states are triggered. Here's an example:

```
touches = {}
function touched(touch)
  if touch.state == ENDED then
    touches[touch.id] = nil
  else
    touches[touch.id] = touch
  end
end

function draw()
  background(0)
  for k,v in pairs(touches) do
    math.randomseed(v.id)
    fill(math.random(255), math.random(255), math.random(255))
    ellipse(v.x, v.y, 100, 100)
  end
end
```

> **Caution**   If you have system-wide multigestures enabled, then you might also want to turn them off on the iPad from Settings, as they take precedence and interfere with touches if there are more than two-finger touches.

Making Sound

While other frameworks play WAV or MP3 files, Codea allows for playing dynamically created waveforms. This has the advantage of taking up less space in the final distribution and also allows you to create dynamic sounds.

Here's an example of how to create a jump sound:

```
function touched(touch)
  sound(SOUND_JUMP, 1234)
end
```

Now when you touch the screen, it plays a sound.

Following are the types of predefined built-in sounds in Codea, each one of these have various settings that can be used as in the example above we use setting #1234:

- SOUND_BLIT
- SOUND_EXPLODE
- SOUND_HIT

- SOUND_JUMP

- SOUND_PICKUP

- SOUND_POWERUP

- SOUND_RANDOM

- SOUND_SHOOT

- DATA

The Codea editor also allows you to fine-tune the different parameters for a sound as a Base64-encoded string, which can be passed to a function to play sound based on the encoded characters in the string. The custom sound is typically of type DATA followed by the string that specifies the settings.

```
sound(DATA, "ZbBAJgBAQEBAQEBAQEBAMqqQPXtbpz3NzMw+QABAfOBAQEBAQEBA")
```

Alternatively, synthesizer waveforms can be used to make sound. Following are the types of waveforms that Codea has in-built support for:

- SOUND_NOISE

- SOUND_SAWTOOTH

- SOUND_SINEWAVE

- SOUND_SQUAREWAVE

These waveforms can be fine-tuned by passing the parameters to the sound function:

```
function touched(touch)
  sound({
    Waveform = SOUND_NOISE,
    AttackTime = 1.2,
    SustainTime = 1
  })
end
```

The other settings that can be fine-tuned are

- AttackTime

- SustainTime

- SustainPunch

- DecayTime

- StartFrequency

- MinimumFrequency

- Slide

- DeltaSlide

- VibratoDepth

- VibratoSpeed

- SquareDuty

- DutySweep

- RepeatSweep

- PhaserSweep

- LowPassFilterCutOff

- LowPassFilterCutOffSweep

- LowPassFilterResonance

- HighPassFilterCutOff

- HighPassFilterCutOffSweep

- Volume

iOS Hardware

One of the advantages of iOS devices is the inclusion of an accelerometer and a gyroscope. As mentioned previously, a great thing about Codea is that since you code and run the app on the device, you can actually test on the device as well, and you can get actual data feedback from the hardware.

The accelerometer returns the gravitational acceleration. The data from the accelerometer can be obtained from the Gravity variable, which has x, y, and z as its members.

```
ht = HEIGHT - 20
function draw()
  text(Gravity.x, 100,ht)
  text(Gravity.y, 200,ht)
  text(Gravity.z, 300,ht)
end
```

Now you can watch the numbers change as you tilt the iPad around.

```
GravityX = 0
GravityY = 0

supportedOrientation(LANDSCAPE_LEFT)

function setup()
  watch("Gravity")
end

function draw()
  GravityX = Gravity.x
  GravityY = Gravity.y

  background(127,127,127,255)
  stroke(255,255,255,255)
```

```
strokeWidth(15)
lineCapMode(ROUND)
pushMatrix()
translate(WIDTH/2, HEIGHT/2)

grav = vec2(Gravity.x * 300, Gravity.y * 300)

line(0,0,grav.x, grav.y)

down = vec2(1,0)
orient = down:angleBetween(grav)

pushMatrix()
resetMatrix()

translate(WIDTH/2, HEIGHT/2)
translate(grav.x, grav.y)
rotate(math.deg(orient))

line(0,0,-25,-20)
line(0,0,-25,20)

popMatrix()

popMatrix()
end
```

The preceding code is from the Codea sample project; it measures the tilt of the device. As shown in Figure 12-5, the code draws an arrow that demonstrates the tilt of the device.

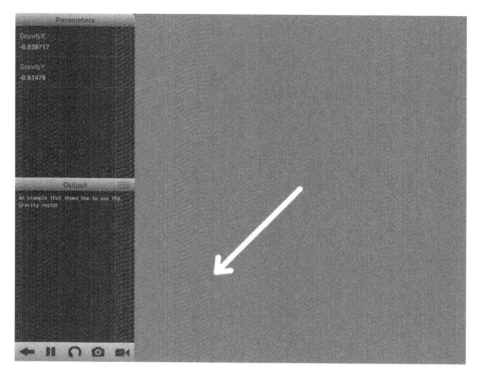

Figure 12-5. The accelerometer application running in Codea

Downloading Data

In your app, you may want to download data from the Internet while it's running—this might be data, graphics, or news. The LuaSocket Library is integrated into Codea providing functions to work with network data and functionality. The http class has a request function that allows for downloading the data from the Internet.

```
function done(theData, status, headers)
  data = theData
  if status == 200 then
    print("YAY!! Done")
    print(theData)
  else
    print("Error downloading the file")
  end
end

http.request("http://www.oz-apps.com", done)
```

When we call the request function, we pass it the URL of the data we want to download and a function that is called when the download completes. The function gets three parameters: theData, status, and the headers table. The status is the http code, which is 200 when it succeeds, 404 when the page cannot be found, 403 for forbidden, and so on.

Displaying Web Pages

In some apps, you might want to browse a web page rather than just download data or a file. In such a scenario, we use the openURL function. This starts the mobile Safari browser and opens the URL passed.

```
openURL("http://www.oz-apps.com")
```

Physics

Like all of the frameworks covered in the book, Codea uses Box2D for physics. The following example shows how to create a physics body and then update a display object based on the position of the physics object:

```
bouncy = 0.5

function createPhysicsObj(x1, y1, x2, y2)
  local temp = physics.body(EDGE, vec2(x1,t1), vec2(x2,y2))
  temp.type = STATIC
  temp.restitution = bouncy
 return bouncy
end

function setup()
ball.physics.body(CIRCLE, 50)
  ball.x = WIDTH/2
  ball.y = HEIGHT/2
  ball.restitution = bouncy
ball.sleepingAllowed = false

  createPhysicsObject(0,0,0,HEIGHT)
  createPhysicsObject(0,0,WIDTH,0)
  createPhysicsObject(WIDTH,0,WIDTH,HEIGHT)
  createPhysicsObject(WIDTH,HEIGHT,0,HEIGHT)
end

function draw()
  background(40,40,50)
  strokewidth(0)
  fill(255)

  physics.gravity(Gravity)
  ellipse(ball.x, ball.y, ball.radius*2)
end
```

Now as you tilt the device, you can see the ball moving around (see Figure 12-6).

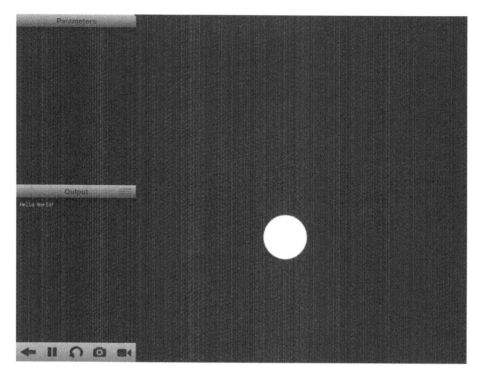

Figure 12-6. The ellipse moves as you tilt the device and bounces off the sides of the screen

As discussed, we can place a display object at the coordinates of the physics object at every frame as the positions are updated. In the preceding example, we used an ellipse. Here, we can simply replace the line that draws the ellipse with one that draws a sprite:

```
sprite("Planet Cute:Character Boy", ball.x, ball.y, ball.radius*2)
```

Not all of the physics functions are available in Codea. The following list describes those that Codea allows us to work with:

- body.applyForce: This function applies force to the physics body as a vector.
- body.applyTorque: This function applies torque to the physics body.
- body.destroy: This function destroys the physics body, which is then garbage-collected.
- body.getLinearVelocityFromLocalPoint: This function gets the linear velocity of the body at a given point in local space.
- body.getLinearVelocityFromWorldPoint: This function gets the linear velocity of the body at a given point in world space.
- body.getLocalPoint: This function returns the point of the physics body in local coordinates.
- body.getWorldPoint: This function returns the point of the physics body in world coordinates.

- body.testOverlap: This function tests if the physics body intersects with a given physics body.

- body.testPoint: This function can be used to determine if a world point is inside of the body.

Vector Math

Codea has built-in vector math functionality. There are two types of vector structures: vec2 and vec3. The vec2 structure has functions for 2D vector math, and vec3 has functions for 3D math. The functions available are similar, but vec2 takes two arguments while vec3 takes three arguments.

angleBetween

The angleBetween function returns the angle in radians, and it takes the other point to determine the angle between the two points, as a vec2 point.

```
v1 = vec2(100,100)
angle = math.deg(v1:angleBetween(vec2(100,200)))
print(angle)
```

cross

The cross function returns the cross product between two vec2 types.

```
v1 = vec2(1,1)
vec = v1:cross(vec2(2,5))
print(vec)
```

dist

The dist function returns the distance between the two vectors.

```
v1 = vec2(1,1)
vec = v1:dist(vec2(2,5))
print(vec)
```

distSqr

The distSqr function returns the squared distance between two vectors.

```
v1 = vec2(1,1)
vec = v1:distSqr(vec2(2,5))
print(vec)
```

dot

The dot function returns the dot product of two vectors.

```
v1 = vec2(1,1)
vec = v1:dot(vec2(2,5))
print(vec)
```

len

The len function returns the length of the vector.

```
v1 = vec2(1,1)
print(vec:len())
```

lenSqr

The lenSqr function returns the squared length of the vector.

```
v1 = vec2(1,1)
vec = v1:lenSqr()
print(vec)
```

normalize

The normalize function returns the normalized version of the vector.

```
v1 = vec2(1,1)
vec = v1:normalize()
print(vec)
```

rotate

The rotate function returns a rotated copy of the vector. The angle has to be in radians.

```
v1 = vec2(1,1)
vec = v1:rotate(math.rad(45))
print(vec)
```

rotate90

The rotate90 function returns a copy of the vector rotated by 90 degrees.

```
v1 = vec2(1,1)
vec = v1:rotate90()
print(vec)
```

Summary

As discussed in this chapter, Codea is the only Lua framework as of now that runs on the device itself. This makes it the most accurate simulator of all the existing frameworks. The API is based on Processing and covers most of the functions required for mobile app development. It has some additional functions that were out of the scope of this chapter, but help in rendering complex 2D and 3D graphics. One of the functions that allows for advance effects is the mesh object.

This chapter also discussed how to create videos and generate sound with Codea. Codea offers complete access to the iPad hardware, provides you with a substantial subset of Box2D physics functionality, and includes built-in 2D and 3D graphics capabilities. With the Codea runtime, apps can now be compiled and be uploaded for sale to the Mac App Store. Finally, Codea includes the entire API reference and IDE on the device itself, making it a great solution for the mobile developer on the move.

Chapter 13

Libraries

While these frameworks discussed in this book are complete in their own respects, developers always require a little bit more. This subtle demand generally translates into libraries and tools that are created for internal use. Some people also share these tools and libraries, either commercially or under the MIT license. The use of these third-party libraries does not undermine the power of these frameworks, but instead works to enhance the frameworks further. In this chapter, we shall look at some libraries that are useful when developing—some of which can be adapted for use with frameworks other than the one they were initially developed for.

This chapter doesn't present an all-inclusive list of libraries, as there are many talented developers that keep creating newer libraries. Many of them are variants of a previous library. For example, there are several particle engine libraries for Corona SDK, not all of which can be covered.

Particle Candy

- *URL*: www.x-pressive.com/ParticleCandy_Corona/index.html
- *Price*: € 39.95
- *Platforms*: Corona SDK

This is a popular and extremely useful particle generator library written in Lua, from www.x-pressive.com. It is specific to Corona SDK. Because Corona SDK code has to be distributed in plain-text form, this is available as full source code, which allows you to study the way it works. It is expected that you do not redistribute the code or resell it in any modified form. The library comes with several very useful and impressive examples. It makes so many effects look easy and abstracts the calculations required to achieve them. Apart from standard smoke- and fire-type effects, it allows you to create more advanced effects, and provides access to things like attractors (as shown in Figure 13-1), repellers, and emission shapes.

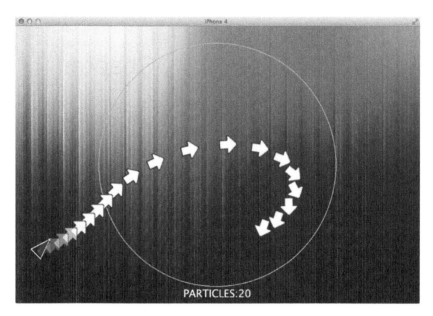

Figure 13-1. Particle Candy emitter running the attractor sample

> **Note**   Chapter 14 will discuss a related tool, Particle Designer, which can be used to visually create particle effects and export the settings to Particle Candy.

Sample Code

```
Particles.CreateEmitter("E1", screenW*0.05, screenH*0.5, 45, true, true)
-- DEFINE A PARTICLE TYPE
Particles.CreateParticleType ("Test",
    {
    imagePath     = "arrow.png",
    imageWidth    = 32,    -- PARTICLE IMAGE WIDTH  (newImageRect)
    imageHeight   = 32,    -- PARTICLE IMAGE HEIGHT (newImageRect)
    velocityStart = 150,   -- PIXELS PER SECOND
    alphaStart    = 0,     -- PARTICLE START ALPHA
    fadeInSpeed   = 2.0,   -- PER SECOND
    fadeOutSpeed  = -1.0,  -- PER SECOND
    fadeOutDelay  = 3000,  -- WHEN TO START FADE-OUT
    scaleStart    = 1.0,   -- PARTICLE START SIZE
    weight        = 0,  -- PARTICLE WEIGHT (>0 FALLS DOWN, <0 WILL RISE UPWARDS)
    bounceX       = false, -- REBOUND FROM SCREEN LEFT & RIGHT BORDER
    bounceY       = false, -- REBOUND FROM SCREEN TOP & BOTTOM BORDER
    bounciness    = 0.75,  -- REBOUND ENERGY
    emissionShape = 0,     -- 0 = POINT, 1 = LINE, 2 = RING, 3 = DISC
    emissionRadius= 140,   -- SIZE / RADIUS OF EMISSION SHAPE
    killOutsideScreen  = true,  -- PARENT LAYER MUST NOT BE NESTED OR ROTATED!
    lifeTime      = 4000,      -- MAX. LIFETIME OF A PARTICLE
```

```
autoOrientation     = true,   -- AUTO-ROTATE INTO MOVEMENT DIRECTION
useEmitterRotation = true,   --INHERIT EMITTER'S CURRENT ROTATION
    } )

-- FEED EMITTERS
-- (EMITTER NAME, PARTICLE TYPE NAME, EMISSION RATE, DURATION, DELAY)
Particles.AttachParticleType("E1", "Test", 10, 9999,0)
-- TRIGGER THE EMITTERS
Particles.StartEmitter("E1")
local Emitter1 = Particles.GetEmitter("E1")
-- ATTRACTION FIELD
Particles.CreateFXField("A1", 0, screenW*0.5,screenH*0.5, 1.5, 140, true)
```

Text Candy

▩ *URL*: www.x-pressive.com/TextCandy_Corona/index.html

▩ *Price*: €39.95

▩ *Platforms*: Corona SDK

This is another offering by X-Pressive.com, which works with text. It offers special effects that can be used to rotate, animate, and otherwise play with text (see Figure 13-2). For example, it can be used to create '80s-style sine-scrollers with literally one line of code.

Figure 13-2. Text Candy animating text

The code that runs the preceding animation is pretty simple, and is shown following:

Sample Code

```
local MyText = TextCandy.CreateText({
    fontName    = "FONT1",
    x           = screenW*.5,
    y           = screenH*.5,
    text        = "ARE YOU READY TO ROCK? ",
    originX     = "CENTER",
    originY     = "CENTER",
    textFlow    = "CENTER",
    charSpacing = -5,
    lineSpacing = -4,
    showOrigin  = false,
    })

MyText:applyDeform({
    type          = TextCandy.DEFORM_CIRCLE,
    radius        = 120,
    autoStep      = true,
    ignoreSpaces  = false,
    })

MyText:applyAnimation({
    startNow        = true,
    restartOnChange = true,
    charWise        = true,
    frequency       = 60,
    alphaRange      = 0.5,
    })
```

Widget Candy

- *URL*: www.x-pressive.com/WidgetCandy_Corona/index.html
- *Price*: € 39.95
- *Platforms*: CoronaSDK

This is a third offering from X-Pressive.com. This library deals with creating GUIs using visual elements. It has functionality for using themes, which means that you can not only create custom widgets, but you can *skin* them (change their appearance) on the fly. It provides for most of the commonly used widgets, including list boxes, radio buttons, check boxes, buttons, and sliders. One of the salient features of Widget Candy is its ability to scale widgets. You can set the widget to be a percentage (as in HTML) so that if you run it on a different device, the display element will scale accordingly. This feature eliminates having to design your UI specifically for every new device. Figure 13-3 displays some of the UI elements that can be created using Widget Candy.

Figure 13-3. Widget Candy, displaying various widgets on the device

Sample Code

```
_G.GUI.NewList(
    {
    x            = "center",
    y            = "center",
    width        = "80%",
    height       = "90%",
    scale        = _G.GUIScale,
    parentGroup  = nil,
    theme        = "theme_1",
    name         = "LST_MAIN",
    caption      = "WIDGET CANDY SAMPLES:",
    list         = ListData,
    allowDelete  = false,
    readyCaption = "Quit Editing",
    border       = {"shadow", 8,8, 64},
    onSelect     = function(EventData) _G.LoadSample(EventData) end,
    } )
```

Corona AutoLAN

- *URL*: www.mydevelopersgames.com/AutoLAN/

- *Price*: Free

- *Platforms*: Corona SDK

This library is a Lua sockets implementation that allows for multiplayer communication over wireless using a combination of UDP and TCP socket communications. It features automatic network discovery and integration, which can be achieved with just a couple of lines of code. Because AutoLan uses plain Lua socket communications, it can be adapted to work with frameworks other than Corona SDK. It also has file transfer and flow control functionality.

Sample Code

```
local client = require "Client"
client:start()
client:autoconnect()
```

On the server side, it is as simple as this:

```
local server = require "Server"
server:start()
```

And transferring files is as easy as this:

```
client:sendFile(filename, srcPath, destFile)
```

Corona Profiler

- *URL*: www.mydevelopersgames.com/site/
- *Price*: $9.99
- *Platforms*: Corona SDK

This is perhaps the only analyzer available that goes about its business while you run the app in the CoronaSDK simulator. This can help determine how your code is performing. The profiler can be started and stopped via Lua commands in your app. While it is running, it creates analysis data on a line-by-line basis, inspecting the time taken for each line or function to run. While it is specifically created for Corona SDK, it relies on pure Lua for functioning. With a few minor changes, it can be adapted to work with any framework. Sample output from Corona Profiler is shown in Figure 13-4.

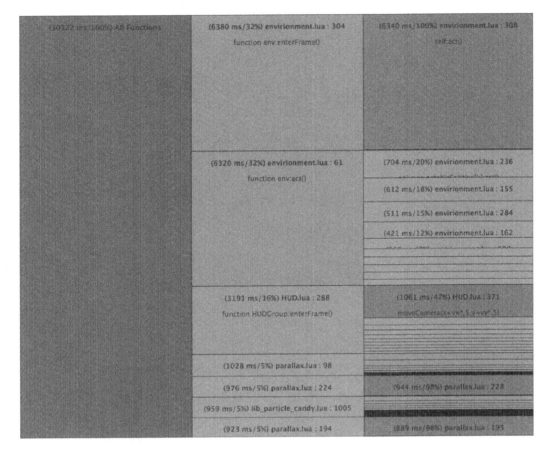

Figure 13-4. The visual analysis/results of your app after running Corona Profiler

Sample Code

```
profiler = require "Profiler"
profiler.startProfiler()
```

Director

- *URL*: http://rauberlabs.blogspot.com.au/2011/08/director-14-books.html
- *Price*: Free
- *Platforms*: Corona SDK

Director is a scene-manager library available that—while very useful and popular—is being phased out, as Corona Labs is replacing it with its own version, called Storyboard. There was a time when Director was more popular than Corona SDK itself. However, because Storyboard is officially supported by Corona Labs and offers similar options, it is advised that you use Storyboard (although Director is still widely used in a lot of e-books and games).

Sample Code

```
director = require("director")
local mainGroup = display.newGroup()

mainGroup :insert(director.directorView)
director:changeScene("Screen1")
```

Note that Screen1.lua contains the code and display logic for screen1.

Lime

- *URL*: www.justaddli.me

- *Price*: £20.00

- *Platforms*: Corona SDK

Lime is a library that provides functions to load maps created with the tile editor Tiled. Gideros Studio and Moai have built-in functions to load Tiled maps, so this is most applicable for Corona SDK only. The sample code following can display a map like that shown in Figure 13-5.

Figure 13-5. Map displayed using Lime

Sample Code

```
local lime = require("lime")
local map = lime.loadMap("platform.tmx")
local visual = lime.createVisual(map)
```

RapaNui

- *URL*: https://github.com/ymobe/rapanui
- *Price*: Free
- *Platforms*: Moai

RapaNui is a high-level Moai-only library that sits on top of the Moai SDK and offers easy-to-use syntax, similar to that of Corona SDK. While in Moai it would take a couple of lines of code to load and display an image on the screen, with RapaNui it takes literally a line of code.

Sample Code

```
ball = RNFactory.createImage("ball.png")
ball.x = 10
ball.y = 10
```

Gideros Illustrator (SVG Library)

- *URL*: http://go.to/gideros-illustrator
- *Price*: Free
- *Platforms*: Gideros Studio

If you create your designs with Adobe Illustrator or a similar app, you can make much crisper graphics and art than with scaled bitmaps. This library works with Gideros Studio and can currently parse SVG files exported from Adobe Illustrator. Currently this library is free and has functions that facilitate working with vector graphics. You can load SVG images and render them to the device using just one line of code. The graphic shown in Figure 13-6 is drawn using vector objects in Gideros with the help of the SVG library.

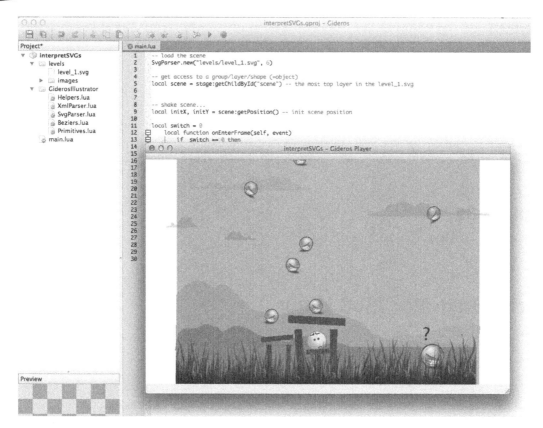

Figure 13-6. An SVG image displayed in the Gideros Player

Sample Code

```
SvgParser.new("myFile.svg")
```

TNT Particles Library

- *URL*: www.tntparticlesengine.com/
- *Price*: Free
- *Platforms*: Gideros Studio

This is the only library offering for Gideros Studio for working with particles. Best of all, it's free.

Sample Code

```
local particleGFX = (Texture.new("smoke.png"))
local cloud1 = CParticles.new(particleGFX, 5, 12, 12, "screen")
cloud1:setSpeed(10, 40)
cloud1:setSize(3, 5)
```

```
cloud1:setAlpha(0)
cloud1:setRotation(0, -10, 360, 10)
cloud1:setAlphaMorphIn(20, 3)
cloud1:setAlphaMorphOut(0, 3)

local emitter1 = CEmitter.new(cloud1)
emitter1:start()
```

Busted

- *URL*: https://github.com/Olivine-Labs/busted/
- *Price*: Free
- *Platforms*: All Lua-based platforms

One common complaint from developers is that Lua does not enable unit-testing functionality. Unit testing is quite an important concept, especially when working with abstract and predisplay rendered classes. This library is not tied to any framework, but instead uses pure Lua functions. The specs for Busted test scripts read naturally, like English. The output is quite easy to understand and visually comprehensible, as shown in Figure 13-7.

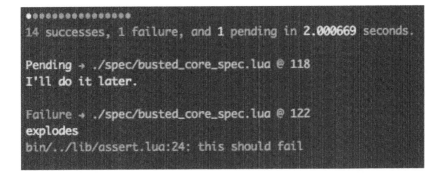

Figure 13-7. Busted running unit tests

Sample Code

```
require ("busted")
describe("Busted unit testing framework", function()
  describe("should be awesome", function()
    it("should be easy to use", function()
      assert.truthy("Yup.")
    end)

    it("should have lots of features", function()
      -- deep check comparisons!
      assert.same({ table = "great"}, { table = "great" })
      -- or check by reference!
      assert.is_not.equals({ table = "great"}, { table = "great"})
      assert.true(1 == 1)
```

```
      assert.falsy(nil)
      assert.error(function() error("Wat") end)
    end)

    it("should provide some shortcuts to common functions", function()
      assert.unique({{ thing = 1 }, { thing = 2 }, { thing = 3 }})
    end)
    it("should have mocks and spies for functional tests", function()
      local thing = require("thing_module")
      spy.spy_on(thing, "greet")
      thing.greet("Hi!")

      assert.spy(thing.greet).was.called()
      assert.spy(thing.greet).was.called_with("Hi!")
    end)
  end)
end)
```

Moses

■ *URL*: https://github.com/Yonaba/Moses/

■ *Price*: Free

■ *Platforms*: All Lua-based platforms

The Moses library, created by Roland Yonaba, helps manage tables in Lua, and includes functionality for popping and pushing, slicing, returning the first item, and returning the next item. Moses doesn't have any dependencies on other functions or classes, and can be used across frameworks.

Sample Code

```
local moses = require("moses")
local list = moses.range(10)
-- => {0,1,2,3,4,5,6,7,8,9,10}
list = moses.map(list, function(_,value) return value*10+value end)
-- => {0,11,22,33,44,55,66,77,88,99,110}
list = moses.filter(list,function(i,value) return value%2==0 end)
-- => {0,22,44,66,88,110}
moses.each(list,print)
-- =>   1    0
-- =>   2    22
-- =>   3    44
-- =>   4    66
-- =>   5    88
-- =>   6    110
```

Allen

- *URL*: https://github.com/Yonaba/Allen/
- *Price*: Free
- *Platforms*: All Lua-based platforms

Allen is another offering from Roland Yonaba. It provides string-related functions for tables—that is, while Moses works on tables, Allen works on strings.

Sample Code

```
local allen = require("allen")
local lyrics = 'hey I just met you\nand this is crazy\nbut here is my number\nso call me maybe'
lyrics = allen.lines(lyrics)
for i,line in ipairs(lyrics) do
  line = allen.capitalizeFirst(line)
end
```

BhWax

- *URL*: https://github.com/bowerhaus/BhWax
- *Price*: Free
- *Platforms*: Gideros Studio

BhWax is a plug-in for Gideros and is based on Corey Johnsons' Wax library for Objective-C. This exposes the iOS API to Lua and more specifically to Gideros. With this plug-in one can create native UIKit elements and UIWindow, UIViews, etc.

Sample Code

```
require "wax"
function show()
    print("Down")
end
function hide()
    print("Up")
end
btn = UIButton:buttonWithType(UIButtonTypeRoundedRect)
btn:setFrame(CGRect(110,110,100,37))
btn:setTitle_forState("Press Me", UIControlStateNormal)
btn:setTitle_forState("Pressed", UIControlStateHighlighted)
getRootViewController():view():addSubview(btn)
btn:addTarget_action_forControlEvents(self,"hide", UIControlEventTouchDown)
btn:addTarget_action_forControlEvents(self,"show", UIControlEventTouchUpInside)
```

This plug-in can offer the features that would enable developers to integrate the new iOS API into their apps without having to wait for the framework developers to add the functionality.

Interestingly, to have complete twitter functionality in your app, it takes 3 lines of code with this Plug-in to have the twitter UI interface as seen in Figure 13-8 below.

```
twit = TWTweetComposeViewController:init()
twit:setInitialText("The tweet here")
getRootViewController():presentModalViewController_animated(twit, true)
```

Figure 13-8. Composing a tweet using the native Twitter UI running in Gideros Player

Summary

This chapter covered many of the libraries that are commonly used with Lua. For more information, you can also consult the lua-users wiki (http://lua-users.org/wiki/), which provides many Lua snippets that aim to resolve specific issues, and also includes attempts by the community to extend Lua and its functionality.

Chapter 14

Third-Party Applications

While the journey toward making a game is one that is filled with learning, it is also one where there is a constant need to have tools to automate or take away the drudgery from various tasks, so that you can focus your time and energy on coding. Now that you are reading this, either you have jumped forward or you have read this far in the book. In either case, this chapter should stand alone in presenting some valuable tools that can help make your development work much easier. This chapter introduces a selection of third-party tools that work for a variety of frameworks.

IDEs

The IDE (integrated development environment) is perhaps the most important part of the entire process of development. It is a combination of a few things: the text editor, the simulator, the asset manager, and the error and runtime messages console. Typically, when you start to work with a framework for the first time, you expect to see something tangible be seen on screen that you can interact with. In the case of Corona SDK, Moai, and LÖVE, there is no supplied IDE, so it may be a bit unsettling and difficult to determine what to do next. However, there are plenty of third-party IDEs that help bridge this gap. This section will discuss some of them.

Glider

- *URL*: www.mydevelopersgames.com/CIDER/
- *Price*: $39.99
- *Platforms*: Mac OS X, Windows

This is a wonderful feature-rich cross-platform IDE (initially called Cider) from M.Y. Developers. The newer version (is shown in Figure 14-1) has support for Corona SDK, Gideros Studio, and Moai. It features a preview functionality that lists out the functions and variables from a Lua file, along with their class type and inherited members. It also features smart class-aware autocompletion functionality that will give the most relevant items in a given context. It has advanced debugging features like step-in, step-out, step-over, run to cursor, call stacks, and more. Variables can be watched and even changed dynamically while running. Ultimote in Glider presently has functionality to simulate Corona SDK hardware events in the IDE. It even has integrated versioning support for Git, Subversion, and Mercurial and also includes a local file history, which retains every change made on the file.

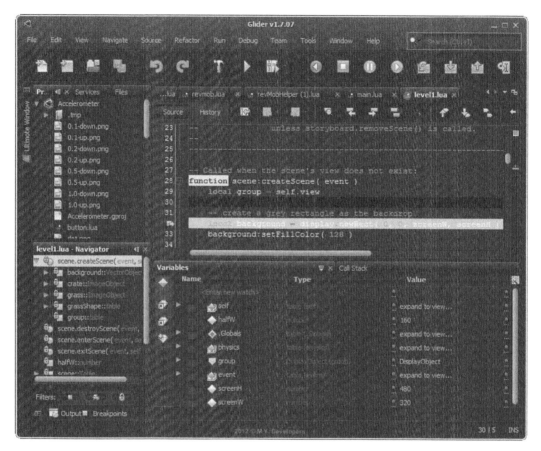

Figure 14-1. The Glider IDE

CoronaComplete

- *URL*: http://coronacomplete.com
- *Price*: $26.99 ($29.99 on the Mac App Store)
- *Platforms*: Mac OS X

CoronaComplete is a Mac OS X–only IDE (that currently only works with Corona SDK). It was created by Vladu Bogdan, who is also the author of the wonderful utilities SpriteHelper and LevelHelper (mentioned later in this chapter). CoronaComplete includes functionality for viewing assets, and has smart arguments so you can use autocomplete to select a function. It even has built-in documentation added by the author, so you do not have to go online to the web site to get

API documentation. It integrates with the Corona debugger and offers functionality for displaying variables and stepping through or over code while debugging. One if its best features is its ability to record your running app and create a video, which can be placed on a web site or used for promotional activities. A screenshot of CoronaComplete is shown in Figure 14-2.

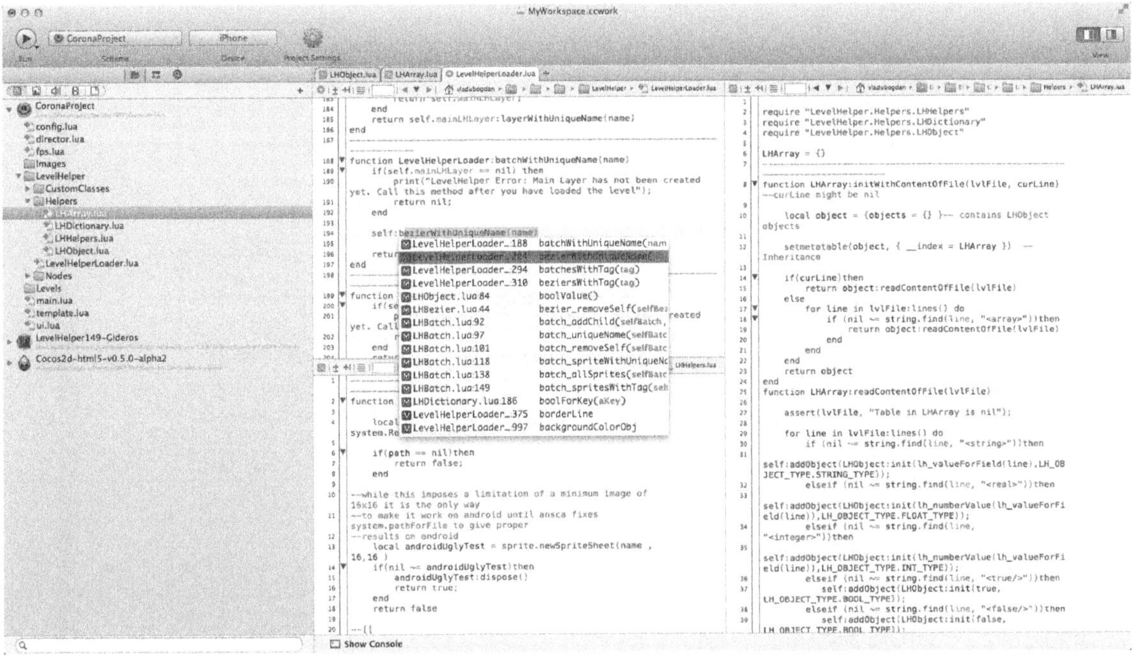

Figure 14-2. CoronaComplete, displaying the project assets

Note   CoronaComplete is now superceeded by CodeHelper Pro.

Lua Studio

- *URL*: http://lua-studio.luaforge.net
- *Price*: Free
- *Platform*: Windows

This is a Windows-only application and is a complete IDE for Lua. It does not cater to Lua-based frameworks. Lua Studio is a well-integrated Lua IDE; it displays a list of local and global variables, along with information about the calling stack (see Figure 14-3). It even allows for step-in, step-out, and step-over functionality while debugging.

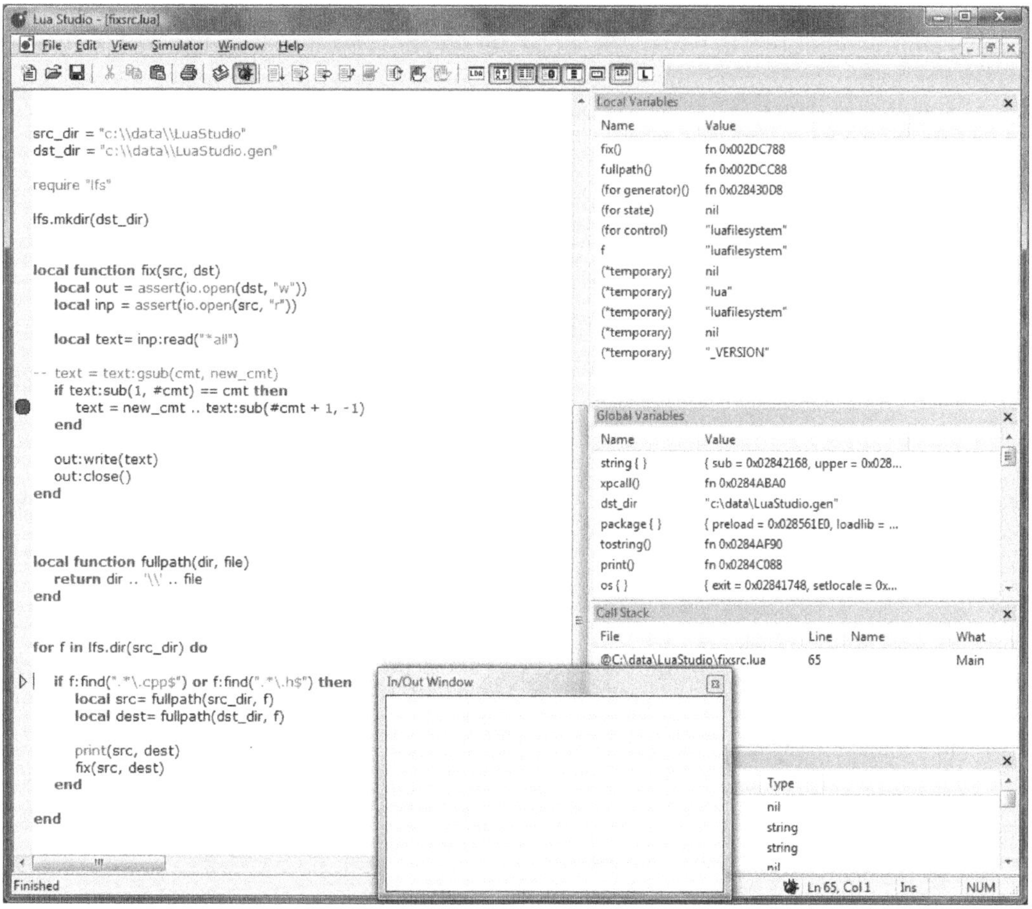

Figure 14-3. Lua Studio for Windows running a debug session with Lua code

ZeroBrane Studio

- *URL*: http://studio.zerobrane.com/

- *Price*: Free

- *Platform*: Windows, Mac OS X, Linux

This is the only IDE for Lua written in Lua and it has support for most of the frameworks we discussed, including Gideros, Moai and LÖVE. It has a small footprint and is easy to use, providing most of the professional features that developers expect from an IDE, including syntax highlighting, a remote debugger, a code analyzer, live coding, and debugging. It also supports auto complete and a scratch pad for running and testing Lua code snippets. This is available from the author's site in binary format or as source code from his GitHub account at https://github.com/pkulchenko/zerobranestudio/.

Text Editors

While IDEs offer a complete environment, as you develop, your reliance on IDEs may vary. Many people reach a point where they feel that they no longer require an IDE, but a very good text editor instead. There are some wonderful free and paid text editors for both Mac OS X and Windows. Since Lua is such a simple language, in theory, a very simple Notepad-like text editor is all you need to write code. However, it always helps to have syntax highlighting, code folding, and ability to jump between functions, dynamic debugging, and so on.

Notepad++

▦ *URL*: http://notepad-plus-plus.org

▦ *Price*: Free

▦ *Platforms*: Windows

This is a Windows-only editor; it is open source and quite powerful, and is updated on a regular basis. It features syntax highlighting, code folding, and multitab editing (as shown in Figure 14-4). It has support for several languages other than Lua, and it can be extended with plug-ins.

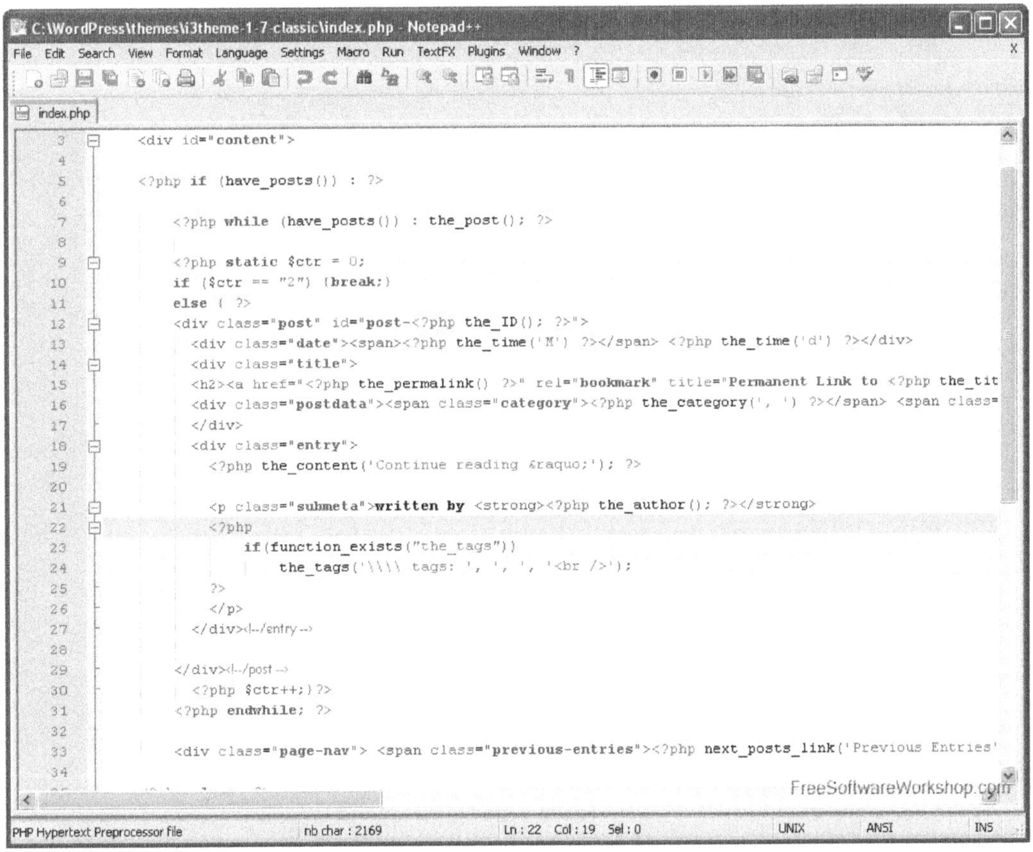

Figure 14-4. Notepad++

TextMate

- *URL*: http://macromates.com/

- *Price*: $50

- *Platforms*: Mac OS X

TextMate is one of the few text editors for the Mac that has bundles (for syntax, functions, etc.) to help extend the functionality of TextMate. The earlier version, 1.5.x, is a paid app, whereas the newer version, TextMate 2.0 is open source and freely available. It includes bundles created for Corona SDK and Gideros Studio, in addition to basic Lua. Figure 14-5 shows a Lua file being edited in TextMate.

Figure 14-5. Editing a Lua file in TextMate 1.5

TextWrangler

- *URL*: http://barebones.com/products/TextWrangler
- *Price*: Free
- *Platforms*: Mac OS X only

TextWrangler is a free text editor, available from Bare Bones Software. It has many features, including code folding, syntax highlighting, and project browsing. Text Wrangler is free, and is basically a lite version of BBEdit (described next). Some of the features of TextWrangler are shown in Figure 14-6.

Figure 14-6. TextWrangler

BBEdit

- *URL*: http://itunes.apple.com/us/app/bbedit/id404009241?mt=12

- *Price*: $49.99

- *Platforms*: Mac OS X

BBEdit is a full-featured text editor, also from Bare Bones Software. It includes all of the features of TextWrangler, along with autocomplete and some additional SSH-related functionality. Figure 14-7 shows many of the features available in BBEdit.

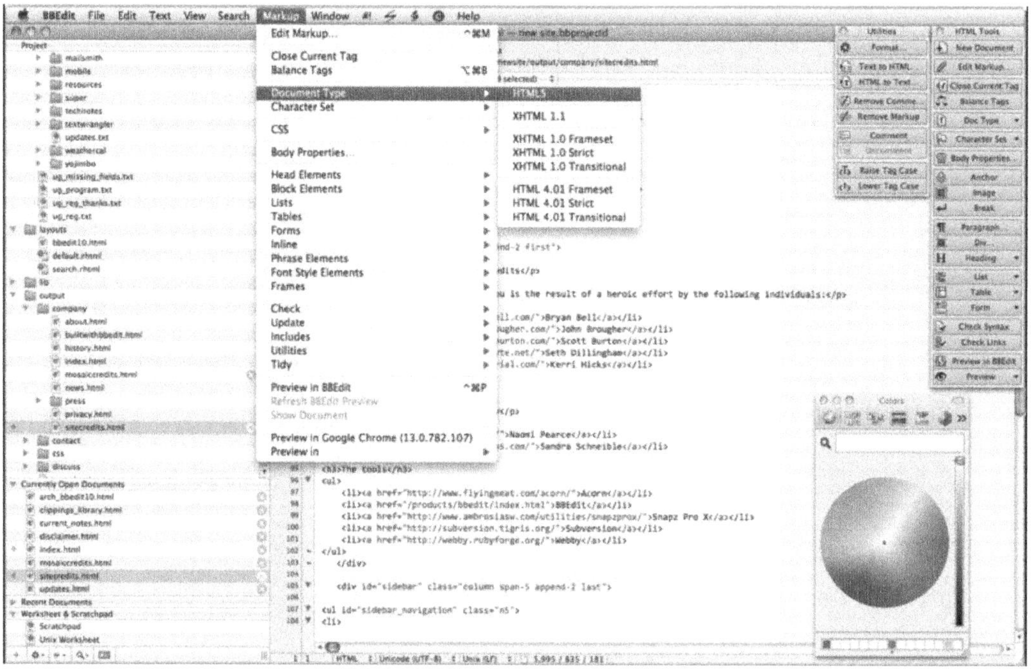

Figure 14-7. BBEdit and its features

Sublime Text 2

- *URL*: www.sublimetext.com

- *Price*: $59

- *Platforms*: Mac OS X only

Like TextMate and BBEdit, Sublime Text 2 is a modern text editor that includes functionality like syntax highlighting, code folding, and so on. It is a bit expensive comparatively, but it allows for unlimited usage without disabling any features, so in effect it can be used as free software. (However, it is *not* free, and if you use it on a continual basis, then you should purchase a license for it.) Figure 14-8 shows Lua code being edited with syntax highlighting and line numbers.

Figure 14-8. Editing a Lua file in Sublime Text 2

Textastic Code Editor

■ *URL*: http://itunes.apple.com/us/app/textastic-code-editor/id383577124?mt=8

■ *Price*: $9.99

■ *Platforms*: iOS

This is currently the only recommendable option for writing code on the iOS platform. It can be used to save documents on the device or via a network or Wi-Fi. It has support for WebDAV, FTP servers, and even Dropbox. It supports syntax highlighting for over 80 languages. It also supports TextMate themes and definitions. The functions in the file can be browsed and jumped to via the list in the symbol browser. It includes autocomplete for HTML and CSS keywords only (at the moment) It also provides an onscreen cursor that can help in navigation and selection, as shown in Figure 14-9.

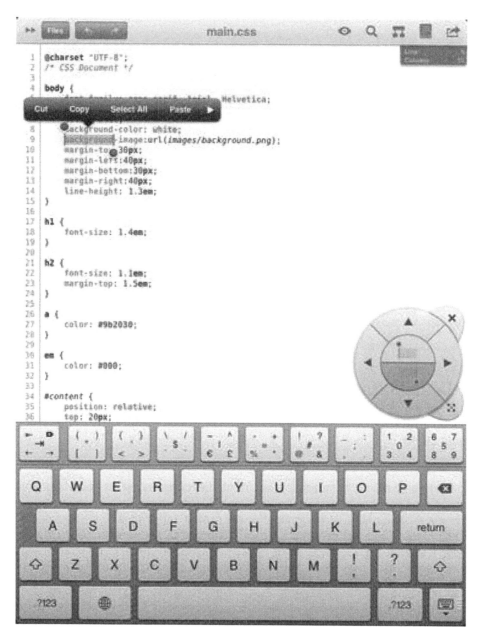

Figure 14-9. Textastic Code Editor on the iPad

Snippets Collectors

Every now and then you might come across some function or routine that is interesting, but might not be related to your project at that moment. Later, when you might need it, it's possible that you might draw a blank on the function code. In these cases, a snippet collector is always a good tool to have. This section describes two useful ones.

CodeBox

- *URL*: http://itunes.apple.com/us/app/codebox/id412536790?mt=12
- *Price*: $4.99
- *Platforms*: Mac OS X

This is an unstructured snippet collector. It allows for snippets to be added to a data file. Each of the snippets can have multiple tables, which can each have a different syntax language highlighting. You can mix web pages and text files, as shown in Figure 14-10. This is a particularly useful tool for developers, as it does not suffer from the one-file-per-snippet problem; instead, it can store an entire project per snippet entry.

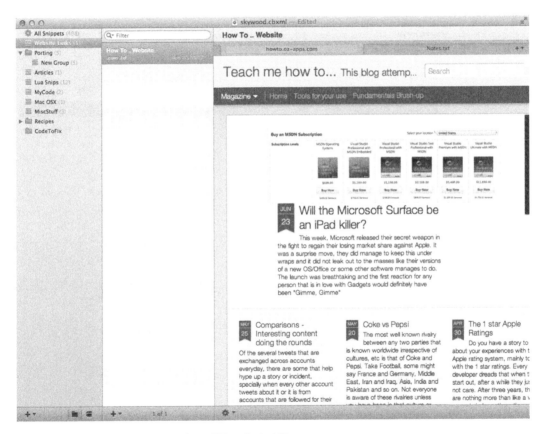

Figure 14-10. CodeBox with snippets, including a URL and a text file

Code Collector Pro

- *URL*: www.mcubedsw.com/software/codecollectorpro/
- *Price*: Free (soon to be open source)
- *Platforms*: Mac OS X

This is one of the earlier offerings and has a bit of structure to it; it looks similar to an e-mail client—that is, it includes folders, each containing a snippet, and the snippet can be previewed in the bottom pane (as shown in Figure 14-11). Each snippet has only one text box or tab, and it can be set to be of a particular language.

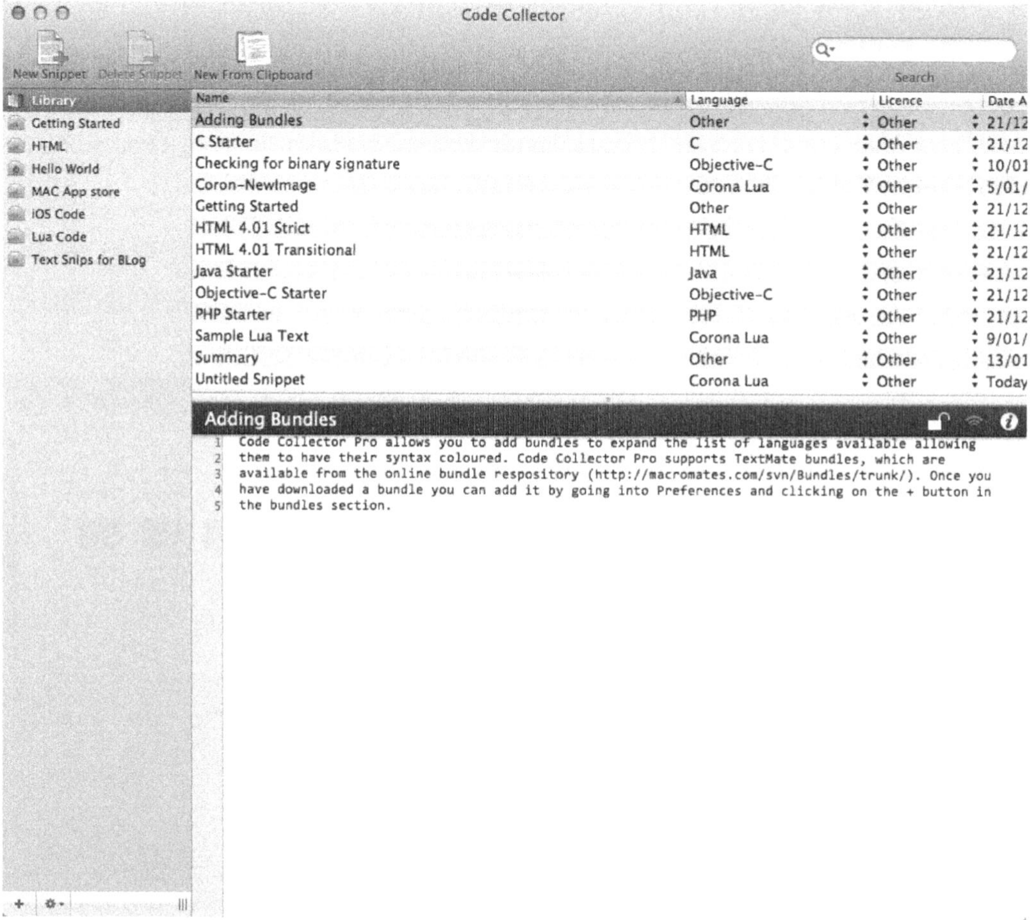

Figure 14-11. Snippets in Code Collector Pro

Versioning

Code is ever evolving—you often have to add or alter data in a file while developing or while testing. For this reason, it's good to have some form of versioning so that you can keep track of changes and switch back and forth between code versions. While you can choose between CVS, Subversion, Mercurial, and Git, I find that Git works best as a stand-alone versioning system with the ability to extend to a team repository. There are plenty of Git clients that can help with managing the Git repository both on the desktop and online. For online repositories, you can start by creating a repository on GitHub or Bitbucket.

Bitmap Editors

The selling point of most non-3D games is generally the graphics—the majority of users' decisions to purchase games are made based on the screenshots in the App Store. Now, graphics of course don't make themselves, but not everyone can afford (or even needs) Photoshop (although it has become the de facto standard as the software for creating graphics). This section describes some alternative software products you can use to create your graphics, depending on your requirements.

Pixen

- *URL*: http://pixenapp.com/

- *Price*: $9.99 if purchased from the Mac App Store

- *Platforms*: Mac OS X

If you are creating 8-bit graphics or pixel graphics, then you need tools that are well suited for the task; zooming in onto the canvas and using the grid is one approach, but bitmap editors are made for the specific tasks of pixel art manipulation, as shown in Figure 14-12. Pixen a tool for Mac OSX is now available on the Mac App Store and is priced at $9.99; the free version has been taken down from the website. However, the source is still available on GitHub.

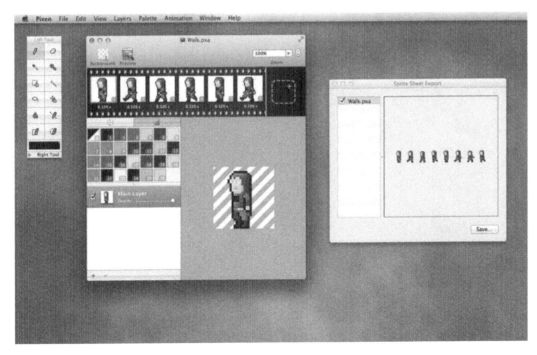

Figure 14-12. Editing a sprite or image using Pixen

GraphicsGale

- *URL*: www.humanbalance.net/gale/us/

- *Price*: ¥1995 (approximately $25; also available in a free edition)

- *Platforms*: Windows only

GraphicsGale is wonderful tool available on the Windows platform for working with 8-bit or pixel graphics. While you could use Microsoft Paint for certain tasks, such as magnifying and setting a grid, the additional features available in GraphicsGale make it a tool of choice. It has onion-skinning to aid in cell animation, and it has functionality to export and import between several formats. It is a single tool that can help create animated cursors, icons, and so on. Figure 14-13 shows GraphicsGale in action.

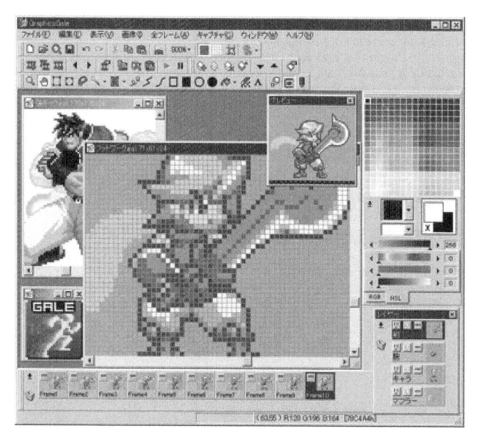

Figure 14-13. Editing a pixel sprite in GraphicsGale

Pixelmator

- *URL*: http://itunes.apple.com/us/app/pixelmator/id407963104?mt=12

- *Price*: $14.99 (launch price)

- *Platforms*: Mac OS X

Pixelmator, which has evolved over the past few years, is a painting application that runs on the Mac. It is a beautiful application in terms of its UI, and offers many features such as layers, effects, handling multiple file formats, brushes, etc., that you might only expect from a more advanced program, like Photoshop, for a fraction of the cost. The new version, dubbed Cherry, is a workhorse, offering a visual repository of over 150 effects that are much faster and more responsive than similar features in to Photoshop (one of which—a kaleidoscope effect—is shown in Figure 14-14). It can handle RAW files as well as many other file formats.

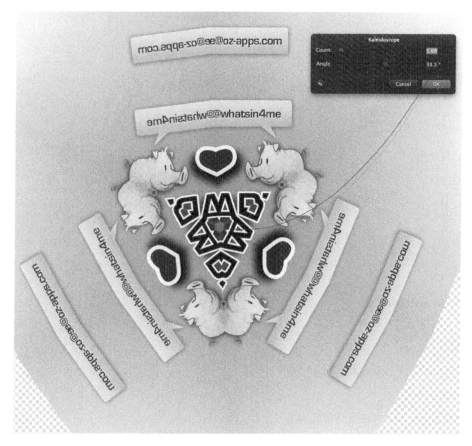

Figure 14-14. An image in Pixelmator with a kaleidoscope effect applied

Axialis IconWorkshop

- *URL*: www.axialis.com/iconworkshop/
- *Price*: $69.95
- *Platforms*: Windows

This is a Windows-only application designed primarily as an icon-creating tool. It has some lovely visual templates you can use to create great-looking results. The icons can be used as images for the tab bars, and so on. The image packs even include things like shine and highlighting so you can create icons that have the same glossy feel as professionally made ones. Figure 14-15 highlights some of the features available.

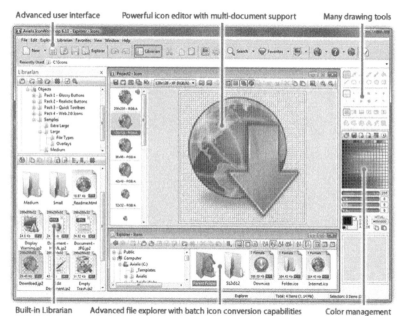

Figure 14-15. Axialis IconWorkshop

Inkscape

- *URL*: http://inkscape.org/
- *Price*: Free
- *Platforms*: Mac OS X, Windows

With the retina display, Apple has expected that the assets be created in different resolutions: normal, @2x (for retina devices), and now @HD or @4x (retina iPads). The raster or bitmap graphics can be scaled only so much from normal resolution to large HD graphics before you notice the scaling and pixelation. With vector graphics, the image can be scaled to suit various resolutions without significant loss of detail. Adobe Illustrator and Corel Draw have set the standards in this space; however, Inkscape has a large set of tools and is comparable to these programs (as shown in the sample image in Figure 14-16). Even better, it is open source and free.

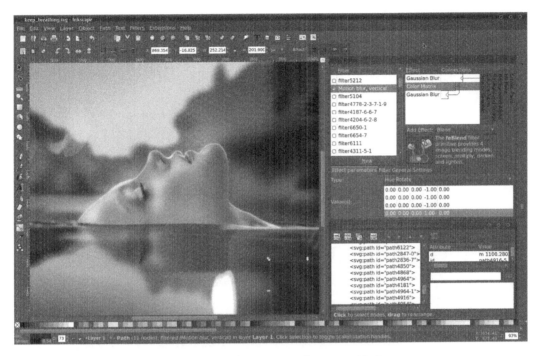

Figure 14-16. An example of art that can be produced with Inkscape using vector objects

Paint.NET

- *URL*: www.getpaint.net
- *Price*: Free
- *Platforms*: Windows

This open source paint software for Windows offers layers and functionality like Photoshop, but at no price. Paint.NET offers most of the features of Photoshop, including the ability to edit multiple images at the same time. It features layers that allow for compositing effects and editing. It has an unlimited undo history. It runs on the Windows platform and is quite fast. It also has support for plug-ins. Figure 14-17 shows Paint.NET in action.

Figure 14-17. An image in Paint.NET

iConify

■ *URL*: http://itunes.apple.com/us/app/iconify/id416289784?mt=12

■ *Price*: Free

■ *Platforms*: Mac OS X only

When you've finished creating your game or app, you need to create the icons and assets for packaging the app. Apple, in particular, requires you to use a couple of icons of specific sizes before you can make your app available in the App Store. iConify is one of the many utilities available that can help you create icons of the various required sizes. Figure 14-18 shows the simple interface of iConify.

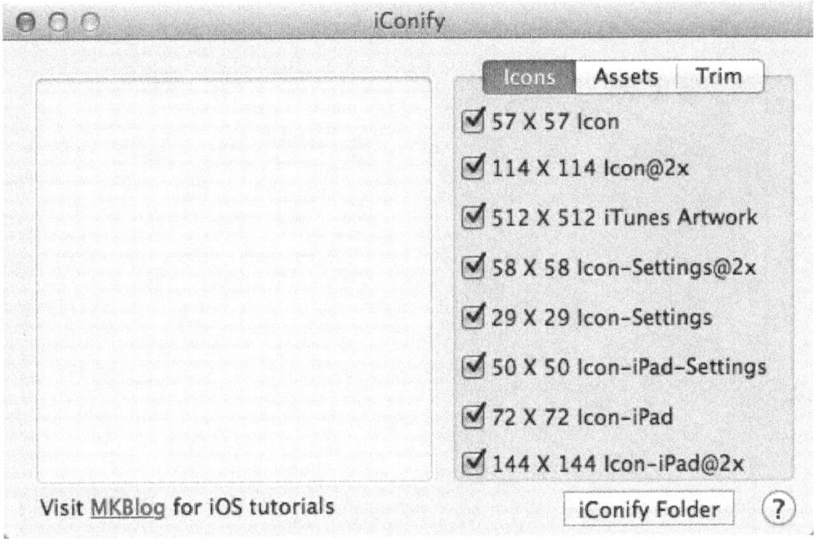

Figure 14-18. Using iConify to create appropriately sized icons for iOS devices

Here are some of its key features:

- The application is simple to use.
- You can drag 512×512-pixel or 1024×1024-pixel icons to the canvas and have all the necessary smaller icons are created for you automatically.

Sprite Animation and Level Creation Tools

This section describes a variety of tools for creating sprite animations and levels in your own games to give them that extra polish and visual appeal.

SpriteHelper

- *URL*: http://itunes.apple.com/us/app/spritehelper/id416068717?mt=12
- *Price*: $12.99
- *Platforms*: Mac OS X

This is a tool that takes individual frames and creates a single sprite sheet texture that contains these frames. SpriteHelper goes a little beyond by also including the ability to set the physics object properties to the frame, as shown in Figure 14-19. Corona SDK is presently the only framework that SpriteHelper natively supports. However, it is rather easy to adapt SpriteHelper for use with Gideros Studio or Moai. SpriteHelper is available only via the Mac App Store. It's also available as a free lite version that has limited functionality, but is good enough for testing out the product.

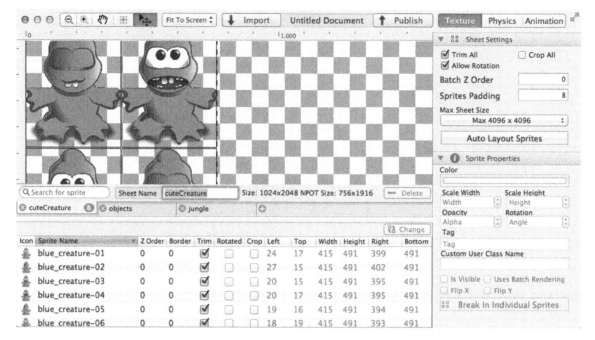

Figure 14-19. Editing the physics boundary of a sprite with SpriteHelper

LevelHelper

■ *URL*: http://itunes.apple.com/us/app/levelhelper/id421740820?mt=12

■ *Price*: $19.99

■ *Platforms*: Mac OS X

Complementary to SpriteHelper, this app helps you create levels for your game. It is similar to a tile-based editor, but with the difference that it also allows for adding physics objects and shapes to the levels, as shown in Figure 14-20. It can currently output levels for cocos2D and Corona SDK only. Like SpriteHelper, LevelHelper is also available via the Mac App store only and offers a free lite version.

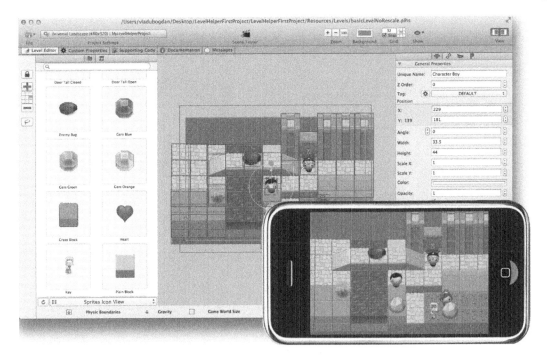

Figure 14-20. LevelHelper, with a level on the screen and simulated on the device

Tiled

- *URL*: www.mapeditor.org/
- *Price*: Free
- *Platforms*: Mac OS X, Windows, *nix

Tiled is a recommended and widely used open source editor for creating tile maps. It works by generating TMX files that contain map definitions. Gideros Studio has a native API to read this format. The generated tile maps can be read in other frameworks and used for RPG-style or tile-based games. Figure 14-21 shows an RPG map being created in Tiled.

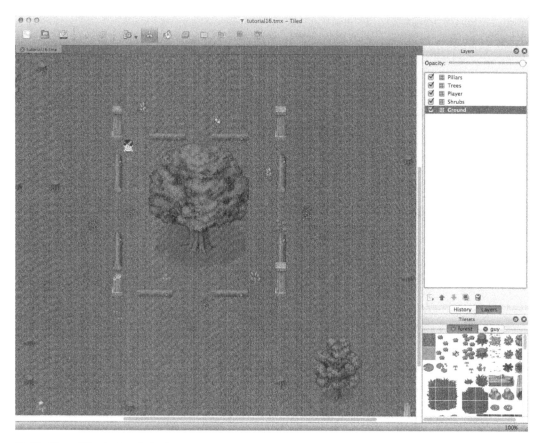

Figure 14-21. Map editing in the Tiled editor

TexturePacker

- *URL*: www.codeandweb.com/texturepacker
- *Price*: $24.84
- *Platforms*: Mac OS X, Windows, Ubuntu

This utility helps create sprite sheets and texture maps. It can even create sprite sheets from PSD and SWF files. It has versatile output and supports Corona SDK, Gideros Studio, and Moai, in addition to some other frameworks, and even supports the generic JSON format, which can be used in any framework when parsed. The TexturePacker web site has some interesting information about texture packaging, plus tutorials and articles to help you understand how to use TexturePacker. TexturePacker can also be used to automate with the build process using Xcode, Ant, CMake, and so on. Figure 14-22 shows a sprite sheet being created from a Flash animation (SWF) in TexturePacker.

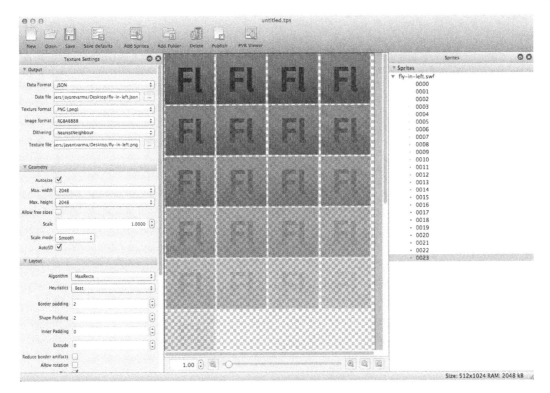

Figure 14-22. TexturePacker creating a sprite sheet from a Flash animation (SWF)

PhysicsEditor

- *URL*: www.codeandweb.com/physicseditor
- *Price*: $19.87
- *Platforms*: Mac OS X and Windows

PhysicsEditor is the complementary app from the author of TexturePacker. PhysicsEditor is a tool for defining physics objects for your graphics to include in your game framework. It allows you to create realistic collisions and other physics events. It even has the facility to create collision masks between objects, and it works with a variety of frameworks, including Corona SDK, Gideros Studio, and Moai. The author of PhysicsEditor is quite proactive in adapting the tools to work with as many frameworks as possible. Figure 14-23 shows an example of PhysicsEditor at work.

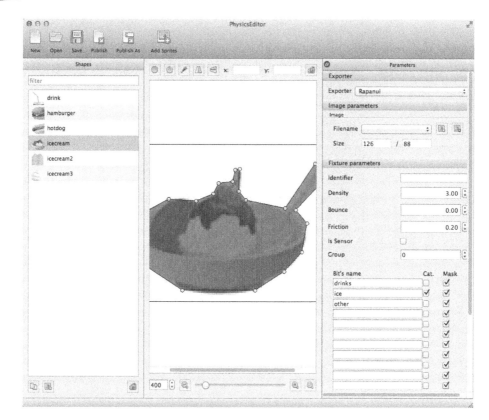

Figure 14-23. Outlining an image for use with physics engines in PhysicsEditor

Particle Designer

- *URL*: http://particledesigner.71squared.com/

- *Price*: $7.99

- *Platforms*: Mac OS X

With the advent of modern devices, gamers are no longer satisfied with simple effects. Developers are creating games that are increasingly realistic, and a big part of that comes from the use of particle engines. Particle Designer is a visual tool for creating particle effects. Particle Designer allows you to experiment and tweak the parameters of your particles, and even save your settings as presets (in PEX files) to reuse. Moai in particular has API functions for loading and using PEX files directly. Figure 14-24 shows some of the wide variety of effects you can create with Particle Designer.

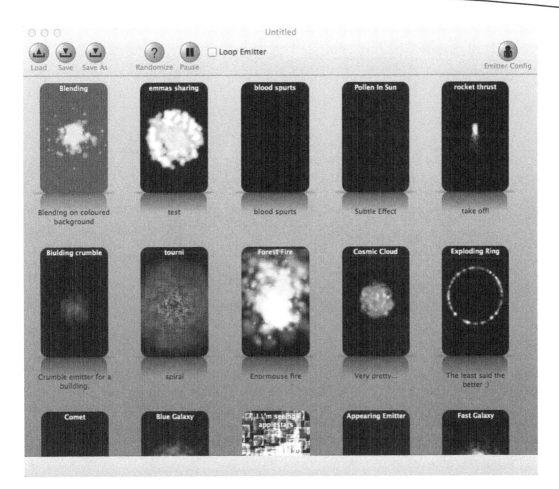

Figure 14-24. Various effects you can create with Particle Designer

Glyph Designer

- *URL*: http://glyphdesigner.71squared.com/
- *Price*: $29.99
- *Platforms*: Mac OS X

This is another app from the author of Particle Designer. Glyph Designer facilitates creating bitmap fonts. In a couple of clicks, you can generate amazing-looking font sheets for use in your apps. Bitmap fonts are supported in most of the frameworks. Figure 14-25 shows a bitmap font sheet created using Glyph Designer. Corona SDK requires the Text Candy library (discussed in Chapter 13) to use fonts created via Glyph Designer. While Gideros and Moai have built-in API to handle bitmap or glyph fonts, Glyph Designer has the advantage of being able to create gradient fills, apply shadows, and create font textures almost instantly.

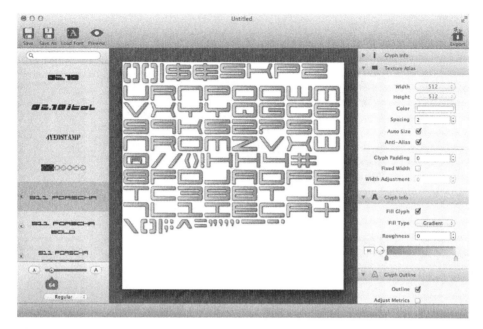

Figure 14-25. Creating a bitmap font in Glyph Designer

Spriteloq

■ *URL*: www.loqheart.com/spriteloq

■ *Price*: $49 or $99 (includes 2 hours of premium support)

■ *Platforms*: Mac OS X

This is another tool that helps create sprite sheets from Flash SWF movies. If you create some of your animations in Flash, you can use Spriteloq to very easily convert them into sprite sheets for animating in your app, as shown in Figure 14-26. Though the Spriteloq output is specific to Corona SDK, the generated files can be parsed and used with any framework.

> **Note**   Lanica has purchased Spriteloq and is now called Animo
> (http://lanica.co/about/animo/) and the price has gone up to $149.

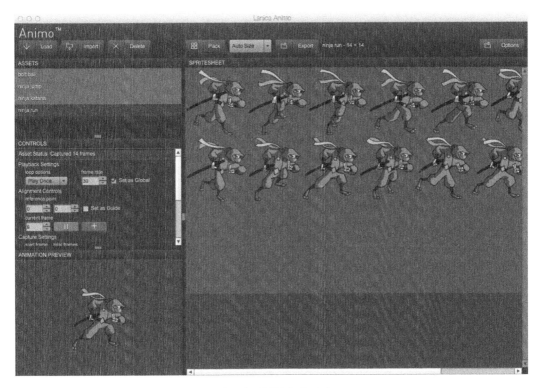

Figure 14-26. *Creating a sprite sheet from a Flash animation (SWF) in Spriteloq*

Zoë

- *URL*: http://easeljs.com/zoe.html

- *Price*: Free

- *Platforms*: Mac OS X

Zoë is a free program for creating sprite sheets from Flash movies. The options available with Zoë are limited in comparison to those of Spriteloq and TexturePacker, but the advantage is that it's free. Figure 14-27 shows Zoë in action playing an SWF animation frame by frame.

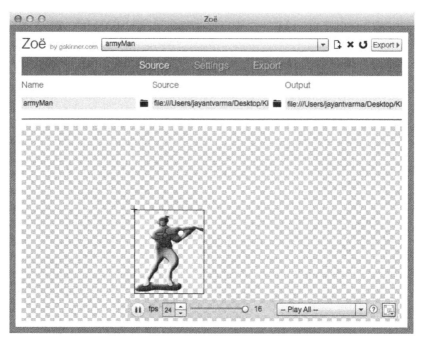

Figure 14-27. Zoë playing a Flash animation

TNT Animator Studio

- *URL*: www.tntparticlesengine.com

- *Price*: Free

- *Platforms*: Mac OS X, Windows

While most of the utilities mentioned previously generate sprite sheets from individual images, TNT Animator Studio is a tool that generates animations from these sprite sheets. The application is currently aimed for use with Gideros Studio and includes a Lua API to load and use these animations. The generated TAN files are XML files and therefore can be parsed and used with any other framework. Figure 14-28 shows the simplistic UI of TNT Animator Studio.

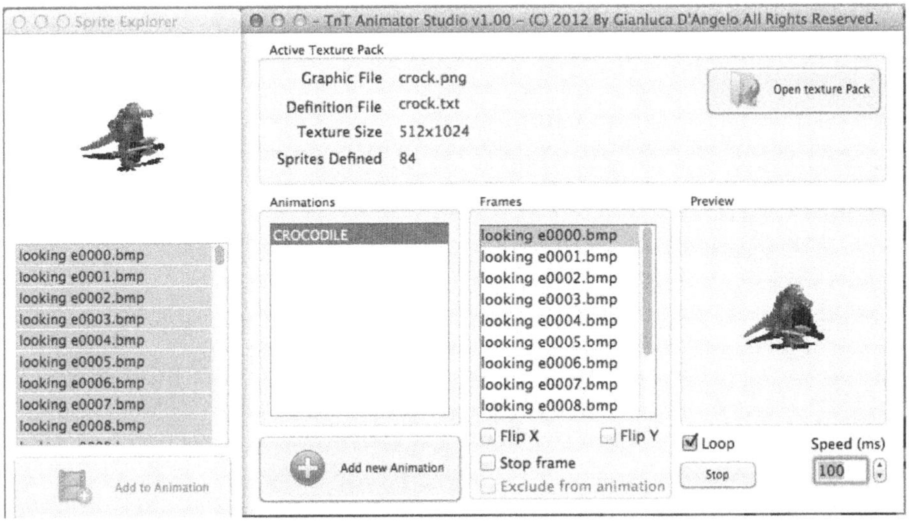

Figure 14-28. Creating animations using TNT Animator Studio

Sound Tools

A game without sound is just incomplete. Even the most brilliant-looking fireworks animation would seem dull if there were no accompanying whiz, bang, pop, and crackle sounds. By complementing your graphics, sound plays an important role in the success of an app. This section describes some apps that can help you create and manipulate sound and effects for your apps.

Audacity

- *URL*: http://audacity.sourceforge.net/
- *Price*: Free
- *Platforms*: Mac OS X, Windows

This is an open source and multiplatform waveform editor. It allows for manipulating sound files in various ways, including trimming, extending, adding effects, slowing or speeding up the playback, and changing the pitch. Audacity is used by many for creating audio file markers which are used in audio books. Figure 14-29 shows an audio waveform being edited in Audacity.

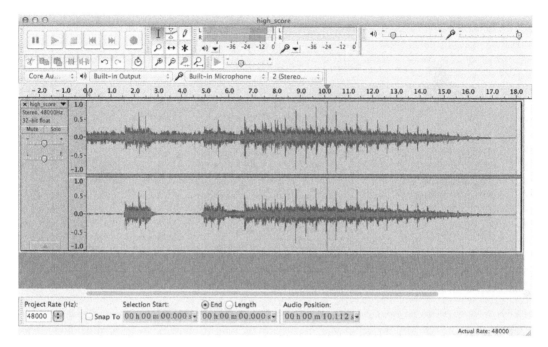

Figure 14-29. Editing a waveform in Audacity

Bfxr

■ *URL*: www.bfxr.net/

■ *Price*: Free

■ *Platforms*: Web browser, Adobe Air–based desktop version

This utility allows you to create 8-bit sounds that you can manipulate by tweaking various parameters. The resulting sounds can be used for various sound effects in your games. Bfxr provides a very easy and economical way to create interesting sound effects for your games. Figure 14-30 shows the Bfxr interface and the various settings that can be set for your sound effects.

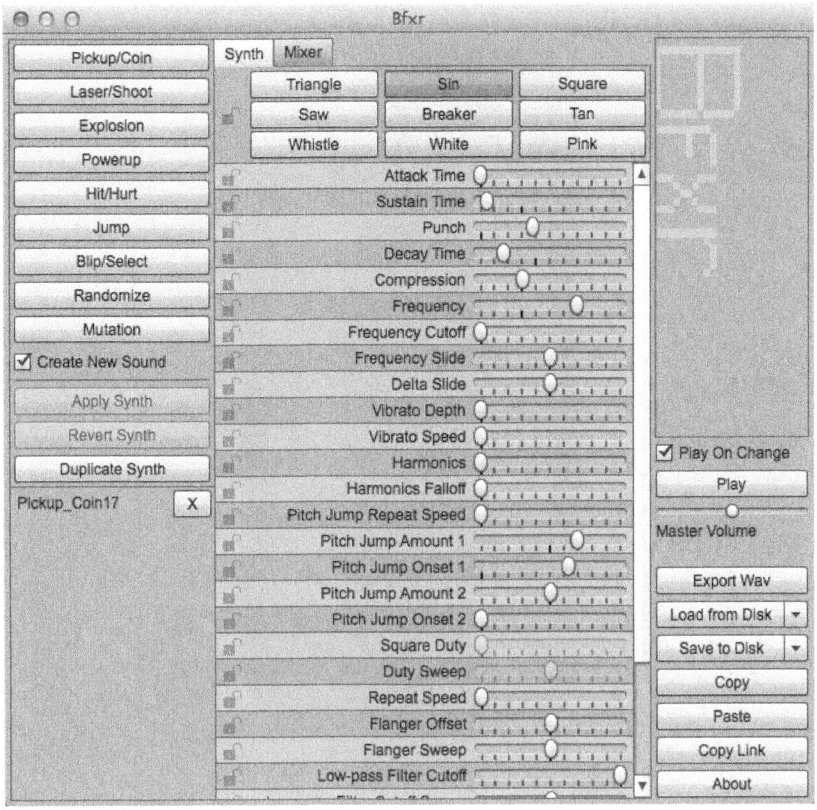

Figure 14-30. Bfxr—useful for creating 8-bit sounds

NodeBeat

- *URL*: http://itunes.apple.com/us/app/nodebeat/id428440804?mt=8
- *Price*: $0.99
- *Platforms*: iOS 4.2+

NodeBeat is an app that runs on iOS and can be used to create random yet interesting music. While many musical instrument apps require various amounts of skill and knowledge to create music, NodeBeat lets you generate random music that you can change dynamically while app is playing it. Figure 14-31 shows a composition in NodeBeat. The composition can be recorded to a wav file and exported via iTunes or email. There is also a free Flash version of NodeBeat with limited features compared to the iOS version that works for all Windows, Mac OS X and Linux. It is available at http://nodebeat.com/.

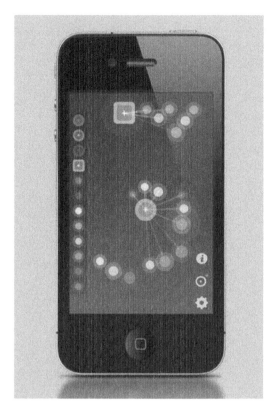

Figure 14-31. *NodeBeat, an iOS app that allows you create music visually*

Summary

This chapter presented various third-party tools that can help you in creating your app or game. Most of the tools I presented have been tested by many developers (or are among the few available for a particular framework). You'll come across many other third-party tools you can experiment with yourself as well. This chapter by no means presented a comprehensive list of available tools, and more tools and utilities are released every day.

Chapter 15

Sample Source Code

You have nearly come to the end of this book; I hope you have had a good read and learned a lot. In the first part of the book I introduced you to Lua and its functions, and in the second part I introduced you to the various Lua-based frameworks that you can use to develop for iOS devices. This chapter will provide the complete source code for an application called Chopper Rescue, which you can use as a base for creating your own games.

In Chopper Rescue, you are in control of a rescue chopper, with the goal of saving survivors. As your chopper moves, you'll need to avoid various obstacles that can cause you to crash. When survivors appear, your job is to collect them. In certain situations, you'll need to tap the screen to shoot bullets; you can only shoot a certain number of bullets at any given time, so you must use this feature carefully. The game is controlled using the accelerometer on the device.

This chapter contains details on how the game works. The complete source code can be downloaded from the book's page on apress.com. This source code is specifically designed for Corona SDK and Gideros Studio only.

Graphics

When you begin designing a game, the second thing after coming up with a wonderful idea is creating graphics. For the Chopper Rescue game, I had an idea of what I needed, but not having access to a graphic artist, I drew some images by hand and scanned them. Figure 15-1 shows what I came up with, and Figure 15-2 shows the resulting sprite sheet.

Figure 15-1. *The hand-drawn scanned images before being converted into sprites*

Figure 15-2. *The sprite sheet created for the graphics used in Chopper Rescue*

Setting Up the Environment

Our code will need to constantly calculate positions. Unless we make the app for a specific resolution, we will never know what resolutions the app will be running at. Therefore, we set up our environment and collect these bits of information, which will be useful later and save us from having to calculate them again.

To get the width and height of the device, you can use the following in Corona SDK:

```
local  _W, _H = display.contentWidth, display.contentHeight
```

and the following in Gideros Studio:

```
local _W, _H = application:getDeviceWidth(), application:getDeviceHeight()
_H, _W = _W, _H
```

> **Note**   Under Gideros, the height and width of the device is always returned in reference to the Portrait orientation. Because this game is going to run in Landscape orientation, we need to swap the height and width.

We also set up a few other variables that will be useful throughout the game:

```
local MAX_BULLETS = 5    -- the maximum number of bullets you can shoot
local MAX_FUEL = 500     -- the amount of fuel that you get when you refuel
local MAX_LIVES = 3      -- the maximum number of lives
local lives = MAX_LIVES -- the maximum number of tries
local fuel = MAX_FUEL    -- the maximum amount of fuel available
local score = 0
local distance = 0
local hiscore = 0
local collected = 0
local filter = 0.8
local gameover = false
```

We set the following for Corona SDK:

```
local NORMAL = 6   -- the normal speed for things that move
local FAST = 12    -- the speed of things that move fast
```

and the following for Gideros Studio:

```
local NORMAL = 3   -- the normal speed for things that move
local FAST = 6     -- the speed of things that move fast
local TOPLINE = 100
local BOTTOMLINE = 500

local random = math.random
local floor = math.floor
local background
```

We also set the following for Corona SDK:

```
local performAfter = timer.performWithDelay
background = display.newRect(0,0,_W,_H)
background:setFillColor(255,255,255)
```

```
-- Corona SDK has a black background, so we need to have a white rectangle
-- till it is replaced with a background image.
```

and the following for Gideros Studio:

```
local performAfter = Timer.delayedCall
local bullets = {}        -- container to hold the bullets fired
local scenery = {}        -- the objects that make up the scenery
local sounds = {}         -- the array that holds all the sounds in it
local restartGame = nil -- the handler function
local survivor, tanker
local waiting = 0
local baseLine = 578

local wTime = 0
local fwait = false
local fx, fy = 0,0
```

Making the Chopper Fly

With the graphics ready, placing the chopper on the screen is an easy task. Keeping with the idea of keeping the app portable, we rely on having generic functions that can be swapped out to accommodate another framework.

Here's the code for Corona SDK:

```
function loadImage(imageName, x, y)
    local x = x or 0
    local y = y or 0
    local image = display.newImage(imageName, x, y)
    return image
 end
```

And with Gideros Studio, we use the following:

```
function loadImage(imageName, x, y)
  local x = x or 0
  local y = y  or 0
  local image = Bitmap.new(Texture.new(imageName))
  stage:addChild(image)
  image:setPosition(x,y)
  image.width = image:getWidth()
  image.height = image:getHeight()
  return image
end
```

We simply create a generic function called loadImage that takes the imageName and the x,y-coordinates and loads the image for us. If you decide to switch your code to another framework, you will only need to address this function, and the rest of your code will work fine. Using this function, we display our helicopter in the middle of the screen:

```
local heli = loadImage("_chopper.png", _W/2, _H/2) -- middle of the screen
```

In order to position our items, as we'll do later, we create a generic function called position and pass it the object to position followed by the x,y-coordinates.

Here's the code for Corona SDK:

```
function position(theObj, x, y)
  if theObj == nil then return end
  theObj:setReferencePoint(display.TopLeftReferencePoint)
  theObj.x = x
  theObj.y = y
end
```

And here's the code for Gideros Studio:

```
function position(theObj, x, y)
  if theObj ~= nil then
    theObj:setPosition(x,y)
  end
end
```

Using the Accelerometer

We can plug into the accelerometer to move the helicopter on the screen as follows.

Here's the code for Corona SDK:

```
local isSimulator = system.getInfo("environment") == "simulator"
local _hasAccel = not isSimulator
```

And here's the code for Gideros Studio:

```
require ("accelerometer")
local _hasAccel = accelerometer:isAvailable()
if _hasAccel then
  accelerometer:start()
end
```

There is no function equivalent to accelerometer:start() in Corona SDK. To deal with this, we have to set an EventListener that listens to the events; the events are then fired based on the update frequency set.

```
function onAccelerometer(event)
  -- capture the events here
end
Runtime:addEventListener("accelerometer", onAccelerometer)
```

Moving the Helicopter

Now that we've set up the accelerometer, we can move the helicopter based on the data returned from the accelerometer. We set up an enterFrame event that runs 30 or 60 times per second (depending on the fps setting and the responsiveness of your code).

Here's the code for Corona SDK:

```
Runtime:addEventListener("enterFrame", update)
```

And here's the code for Gideros Studio:

```
stage:addEventListener(Event.ENTER_FRAME, update)
```

The update is a function defined as follows:

```
function update(event)
 -- check if the game is over
  if gameOver == true then return end
  fWait = (wTime > 0)
  if fWait then
    wTime = wTime - 0.01
    if wTime < 0 then
      wTime = 0
    end
    return
  end

  if _hasAccel==true then
    local gx, gy = getAcceleration()
    fx = gx * filter + fx * (1-filter)
    fy = gy * filter + fy * (1-filter)
    updatePlayer(fx, fy)
  end
end
```

We use the generic function getAcceleration() because Corona SDK returns the acceleration to the function onAccelerometer. In Gideros, we need to poll the data when we need it.

Here's the code for Corona SDK:

```
local gpx, gpy, gpz
function onAccelerometer(event)
  -- capture the events here
  gpx, gpy, gpz = event.xGravity, event.yGravity, event.zGravity
end
```

```
function getAcceleration()
    return gpx, gpy, gpz
end
```

And here's the code for Gideros Studio:

```
function getAcceleration()
  local px, py = accelerometer:getAcceleration()
  return py, px -- note the swap order, because our app is in landscape orientation
end
```

If we move the helicopter to the bottom of the screen, it will crash into the ground, so we need a function that handles a crash. This function reduces the lives value by 1, and when the lives value reaches 0 (i.e., no lives are left), the game is over.

```
function reduceLife()
  lives = lives - 1
  fuel = MAX_FUEL  -- reset the fuel to max with every new start

  gameOver = lives <= 0
  if lives <= 0 then
    -- game over
    print("Game Over")
  else
    position(heli, _W/2, _H/2)
    wTime = 2
  end
end
```

The player can be updated with the data returned from the accelerometer in the function updatePlayer, as follows:

```
function updatePlayer(theX, theY)
  local PLAYERSPEED = FAST * 2 -- twice as fast as the fastest item
  local  px, py = getPosition(heli)
  px = px - (theX * PLAYERSPEED)
  py = py - (theY * PLAYERSPEED)

  if px < 0 then px = 0 end
  if px > _W - heli.width then
    px = _W - heli.width
  end
  if py < TOPLINE then py = TOPLINE end
  if py > BOTTOMLINE + 10 then
    -- crash into the ground reduceLife() return
  end
  position(heli, px, py)
end
```

The function getPosition returns the current position of the image.

Here's the code for Corona SDK:

```
function getPosition(theObj)
  if theObj == nil then return end
  theObj:setReferencePoint(display.TopLeftReferencePoint)
  return theObj.x, theObj.y
end
```

And here's the code for Gideros Studio:

```
function getPosition(theObj)
  if theObj == nil then return end
  return theObj:getPosition()
end
```

Now when you run the code on the device (in Corona SDK) or the device player (in Gideros Studio), the helicopter moves on the screen when the device is tilted. If you let the helicopter go to the bottom of the screen, it will reappear in the middle of the screen. After all the lives are exhausted, the program will stop and print the message "Game Over" to the terminal/console.

Making Sound

No game is complete unless there are at least some sound effects. In the preceding code, we have a function called playSound that plays sound as required.

Here's the Corona SDK version:

```
function playSound(theSound)
  audio.play(handle)
end
```

And here's the Gideros Studio version:

```
function playSound(theSound)
  local channel = theSound:play()
  return channel
end
```

We will have to change the way we set up the sounds array because of the way we index the sounds when playing them.

Here's what we need to use in Corona SDK:

```
function setupSound()
  sounds = {
    explosion      = audio.loadSound("_001.wav"),  -- explosion
    shoot          = audio.loadSound("_002.wav"),  -- shoot bullet
    collectSurvivor = audio.loadSound ("_003.wav"),  -- collect survivor
    collectFuel    = audio.loadSound ("_004.wav"),  -- collected fuel
    crash          = audio.loadSound ("_005.wav"),  -- crash
  }
end
```

And here's the Gideros Studio version:

```
function setupSound()
  sounds = {
    explosion      = Sound.new("_001.wav"),  -- explosion
    shoot          = Sound.new("_002.wav"),  -- shoot bullet
    collectSurvivor = Sound.new("_003.wav"),  -- collect survivor
    collectFuel    = Sound.new("_004.wav"),  -- collected fuel
    crash          = Sound.new("_005.wav"),  -- crash
  }
end
```

Since we wrap all of our sounds in the setupSound function, we need to call this once at the start, like so:

```
setupSound()
```

Shooting Bullets

To enable the helicopter to shoot bullets, we set an event listener to capture the taps or touches to trigger a shot.

In Corona SDK, we use this:

```
Runtime:addEventListener("tap",shoot)
```

And in Gideros Studio, we use this:

```
stage:addEventListener(Event.TOUCHES_END, shoot)
```

In the shoot function, we check if the number of bullets on the screen is less than the MAX_BULLETS value, and only then spawn a new bullet. When we shoot, we shall also play a shooting sound; this is achieved via our playSound function.

```
function shoot()
  if gameOver == true or wTime > 0 then return end
  if #bullets < MAX_BULLETS then
    local hx, hy = getPosition(heli)
    local spr = loadImage("_bullet.png", hx+heli.width, hy + (heli.height/2))
    blt = {
      sprite = spr,
      x = hx + heli.width,
      y = hy + (heli.height/2),
      wd = spr.width,
      ht = spr.height,
    }
    table.insert(bullets, blt)
    playSound(sounds.shoot) -- play the shooting sound
  end
end
```

Moving the Bullets

After we shoot the bullets, we also need to move them; otherwise, they'll be stuck in place on the screen, as shown in Figure 15-3. When a bullet reaches the end of the screen or collides with an object, we need to remove it from the screen and make space for a new one.

```
function moveBullets()
  local blt
  for i = #bullets, 1, -1 do
    blt = bullets[i]
    blt.x = blt.x + FAST -- bullets move fast
    position(blt.sprite, blt.x, blt.y)

    -- check for collision
    if blt and blt.x > _W then
      destroyObject(blt.sprite)
      table.remove(bullets,i)
      blt = nil
    end
  end
end
```

Figure 15-3. The bullets frozen where they were fired

This moveBullets function needs to be called as many times as required to keep the bullets moving. We do this inside of the update function, which allows us to call the moveBullets function repeatedly. Figure 15-4 illustrates how this is represented on the screen.

Figure 15-4. Bullets now moving from the helicopter toward the right of the screen

We use another generic function, destroyObject, to remove the object from the screen. It's defined differently depending on the framework.

Here's the Corona SDK version:

```
function destroyObject(theObj)
  if theObj == nil then return end
  display.remove(theObj)
end
```

And here's the Gideros Studio version:

```
function destroyObject(theObj)
  if theObj == nil then return end
  if theObj.removeFromParent then theObj:removeFromParent() end
end
```

Spawning Enemies

We now have a helicopter that can move on the screen and shoot bullets that disappear once they reach the edge of the screen. Next, we'll randomly spawn some items that will be used as enemies. We'll spawn items of the following types:

- Plane
- Balloon
- Flower
- Grass
- Lamppost
- House
- Tall house
- Cloud 1
- Cloud 2
- Cloud 3
- Angry cloud

The images for these items were shown previously in Figures 15-1 and 15-2.

Instead of using absolute numbers, we create a table list to refer to these items using the enumerate function, as follows:

```
function enumerate(theTextArray)
  local returnVal = {}
  for i,j in pairs(theTextArray) do
    returnVal[j] = i
  end
```

```
  return returnVal
end

local objects = enumerate{"plane","balloon","flower","grass","lamppost","house","tallHouse","cloud1"
,"cloud2","cloud3","angryCloud"}
function spawnEnemies()
  waiting = waiting + 1            -- counter to slow down the spawn speed
  if waiting < 60 then return end -- hopefully an item per second
  waiting = 0
  local spr = nil
  local yDir = 0
  local speed = NORMAL
  local rnd = random(1,11) -- get an item between 1 and 11
  local xPos, yPos = 0,0

  if rnd == objects.plane then        -- spawn a new plane
    spr = loadImage("_plane.png")
    yPos = random(2,5) * spr.height
    speed = FAST
  elseif rnd == objects.balloon then -- spawn a balloon
    spr = loadImage("_balloon.png")
    yPos = random(2,5) * spr.height
    yDir = 1
  elseif rnd == objects.flower then  -- spawn flower
    spr = loadImage("_flower.png")
    yPos = BOTTOMLINE - spr.height
  elseif rnd == objects.grass then   -- spawn grass
    spr = loadImage("_grass.png")
    yPos = BOTTOMLINE - spr.height
  elseif rnd == objects.lamppost then -- spawn a lamppost
    spr = loadImage("_post.png")
    yPos = BOTTOMLINE - spr.height
  elseif rnd == objects.house then   -- spawn a house
    spr = loadImage("_house.png")
    yPos = BOTTOMLINE - spr.height
  elseif rnd == objects.cloud1 then  -- spawn cloud1
    spr = loadImage("_cloud1.png")
    yPos = TOPLINE + random(1,5) * spr.height
    speed = random(NORMAL, FAST)
  elseif rnd == objects.cloud2 then  -- spawn cloud2
    spr = loadImage("_cloud2.png")
    yPos = TOPLINE + random(1,5) * spr.height
    speed = random(NORMAL, FAST)
  elseif rnd == objects.cloud3 then  -- spawn cloud3
    spr = loadImage("_cloud3.png")
    yPos = TOPLINE + random(1,5) * spr.height
    speed = random(NORMAL, FAST)
  elseif rnd == objects.tallHouse then -- spawn tallHouse
    spr = loadImage("_tallhouse.png")
    yPos = BOTTOMLINE - spr.height
  elseif rnd == objects.angryCloud then -- spawn an angry cloud
    spr = loadImage("_cloud.png")
```

```
    yPos = TOPLINE + random(1,5) * spr.height
    speed = random(NORMAL, FAST)
  end
  xPos = _W + random(3,8) * spr.width
  position(spr, xPos, yPos)
  table.insert(scenery,{
    sprite = spr,
    speed = speed,
    x = xPos,
    y = yPos,
    dir = yDir,
    wd = spr.width,
    ht = spr.height,
    objType = rnd
  })
end
```

Moving the Scenery Objects

In the previous section, we spawned the 11 objects, but set their x positions to a position off the screen. In this way, the items will start from a location off the screen and scroll in gradually, rather than suddenly appearing on the screen. However, we have not written the code to scroll the scenery as yet. In our update function, we need to add moveScenery() after the moveBullets function. The idea is similar to that of the moveBullets function. In this function, however, in addition to moving the items to provide the illusion of our helicopter moving through the sky as the objects pass by, we also update the distance travelled and the fuel used. When we reach a critical reserve of 100 fuel units, we display the tanker, which can be collected to refuel.

```
function moveScenery()
    for i = #scenery, 1, -1 do
        local nme = scenery[i]
        nme.x = nme.x - nme.speed
        nme.y = nme.y + nme.dir

        if nme.y < TOPLINE or nme.y > BOTTOMLINE then
            nme.dir = -nme.dir
        end

        local rnd = random(1,10)
        if rnd > 3  and rnd < 4 then
            nme.dir = -nme.dir
        end

        position(nme.sprite, nme.x, nme.y)
        if nme.x < -nme.wd then
            destroyObject(nme.sprite)
            table.remove(scenery, i)
        end
    end
```

```
  fuel = fuel - 0.1
  distance = distance + 0.1

  -- updateAllText() -- update the HUD
  -- if out of fuel, lose a life
  if fuel <= 0 then
    reduceLife()
    return
  end
end
```

Now we can see the scenery scroll by as the chopper moves in the sky, as shown in Figure 15-5. Later, we'll also call the checkCollision function from this moveScenery function.

Figure 15-5. *The scenery objects scrolling from right to left*

Losing a Life

When you crash into the ground or another object, or run out of fuel, you lose a life. This involves reducing the number of lives, and when the number of lives reaches zero, the game is over. We created the reduceLife function earlier; now let's add some more functionality to that function.

```
function reduceLife()
  lives = lives - 1
  fuel = MAX_FUEL -- a fresh start with every life

  -- updateAllText() -- Update the HUD
  playSound(sounds.crash) -- Crash Sound
  wTime = 2
  performAfter(1000, -- perform this after a second
    function()
      -- remove all scenery items
      for i=#scenery, 1, -1 do
        destroyObject(scenery[i].sprite)
        table.remove(scenery, i)
      end
      -- remove all bullets
      for i = #bullets, 1, -1 do
```

```
        destroyObject(bullets[i].sprite)
        table.remove(bullets, i)
      end
      wTime = 2
      position(heli,_W/2,_H/2)
      gameOver = lives <= 0
      setVisible(heli, not gameOver)
      setVisible(txtGameOver, gameOver)
      setVisible(txtTapAgain, gameOver)

      setVisible(tanker, false)
      position(tanker, _W + random(3,5) * tanker.width, baseLine - tanker.height)
      if gameOver == true then
        if floor(distance) + score > hiscore then
          hiscore = floor(distance) + score
        end

        -- showReplayScreen()
      end
    end)

end
```

Since we need to create a generic set of functions to accommodate several frameworks, we have a couple of new functions like setVisible and bringToFront, which allows us to show or hide the objects or re-order the display of the objects.

Here's the code for Corona SDK:

```
function setVisible(theObject, setHow)
    if theObject == nil then return end
  theObject.isVisible = setHow or false
end
```

And here's the code for Gideros Studio:

```
function setVisible(theObject, setHow)
    if theObject == nil then return end
  local setHow = setHow or false
  theObject:setVisible(setHow)
end
```

The bringToFront function is defined as follows in Corona SDK:

```
function bringToFront(theObject)
    if theObject == nil then return end
  theObject:toFront()
end
```

and as follows in Gideros Studio:

```
function bringToFront(theObject)
    if theObject == nil then return end
  stage:addChild(theObject, 1)
end
```

Let There Be Some Color

The graphics that we created for the game are all black and white. To add some variety, we can colorize the objects by giving them particular RGB values in our code. We can set up a table of basic colors, which can be then used to colorize the graphics.

```
Local Colors = {
  {0,   0,   255},    -- blue
  {255, 0,   0},      -- red
  {0,   255, 0},      -- green
  {255, 0,   255},    -- magenta
  {0,   255, 255},    -- cyan
  {255, 255, 0},      -- yellow
  {255, 255, 255},    -- white
  {179, 115, 255},    -- orange
}
```

Here's the code specific to Corona SDK:

```
Function Colorize(Theobject, Thecolor)
  If Thecolor < 1 Or Thecolor > #Colors Then
    Return
  End
  Local R, G, B, A = Unpack(Colors[Thecolor])
  A = A Or 255
  Theobject:Setfillcolor(R, G, B, A)
End
```

And here's the code specific to Gideros Studio:

```
Function Colorize(Theobject, Thecolor)
  If Thecolor < 1 Or Thecolor > #Colors Then
    Return
  End
  Local R, G, B, A = Unpack(Colors[Thecolor])
  A = A Or 255
  R = R / 255
  G = G / 255
  B = B / 255
  A = A / 255

  Theobject:Setcolortransform(R, G, B, A)
End
```

We can colorize the enemies we spawn by adding the color attribute when we spawn them, as follows:

```
  Clr = Random(1,7)
If Rnd == Objects.Plane Then         -- spawn a new plane
  Spr = Loadimage("_Plane.Png")
  Ypos = Random(2,5) * Spr.Height
  Speed = FAST
  Clr = Colors.
Elseif Rnd == Objects.Balloon Then -- spawn a balloon
  Spr = Loadimage("_Balloon.Png")
  Ypos = Random(2,5) * Spr.Height
  Ydir = 1
  Clr = 8 -- overrride the random color
End
```

After the If...Then block, we call the colorize method and pass it the color index.

```
Colorize(Spr, Color)
```

We could set up the colors with named references instead of using a numeric index, but since we want to give the objects a random color within a particular range, a numeric index is better. If we wanted to use named colors instead, we could use the following:

```
Colors = {
  Red = {255, 0, 0},
  Blue = {0, 0, 255},
  Green = {0, 255, 0},
  -- and so on...
}
```

Displaying Information

We also need to display information to the player about how many survivors were saved, how much fuel is left, how much distance covered, and so on. To display this information, we use text objects.

Here's the code for Corona SDK:

```
function newText(theText, xPos, yPos, theFontName, theFontSize)
  local xPos, yPos = xPos or 0, yPos or 0
  local theFontSize = theFontSize or 14
  local theFontName = theFontName or native.systemFont
  local _text = display.newText(theText, xPos, yPos, font, 24)
  position(_text, xPos, yPos)
  _text:setTextColor(0,0,0)
  return _text
end
```

And here's the code for Gideros Studio:

```
function newText(theText, xPos, yPos, theFontName, theFontSize)
  local xPos, yPos = xPos or 0, yPos or 0
  local theFontSize = theFontSize or 24
  local theFontName = theFontName or "Helvetica.ttf"
  local _font = TTFont.new(theFontName, theFontSize)
  local _text = TextField.new(_font, theText)
  _text.width = _text:getWidth()
  _text.height= _text:getHeight()

  stage:addChild(_text)
  position(_text, xPos, yPos - _text.height) -- Gideros uses baseline font
  return _text
end
```

Now that we have the newText function, which creates our text items, we can create the function to update the text on the text object.

Here's the code for Corona SDK:

```
function updateText(theObject, theNewText)
  if theObject == nil then return end
  theObject.text = theNewText or ""
end
```

And here's the code for Gideros Studio:

```
function updateText(theObject, theNewText)
  if theObject == nil then return end
  theObject:setText(theNewText or "")
end
```

Next we can create the HUD items.

Here's the Corona SDK code:

```
local textLine = baseLine + 10
```

And here's the Gideros Studio code:

```
local textLine = baseLine + 55
local txtLives, txtFuel, txtSaved, txtScore, txtGameOver, txtTapAgain
function createHUDItems()
  -- create the items lives, fuel, saved, score, and game-over text

  txtLives = newText(lives, 170, textLine)
  txtFuel = newText(fuel, 610, textLine)
  txtSaved = newText(collected, 840, textLine)
  txtScore = newText(score, 410, textLine)
  txtGameOver = newText("G a m e  O v e r", 0, 0)
```

```
  position(txtGameOver, (_W - txtGameOver.width)/2, _H/2)
  txtTapAgain = newText("Tap to play again", 0, 0)
  position(txtTapAgain, (_W - txtGameOver.width)/2, _H/2 + 40)
end
```

To create these text objects, we first need to call `createHUDItems`, and then we can toggle their visibility as required:

```
createHUDItems()
```

The game-over text remains on the screen right in the middle. We want to display that only when the game is actually over, not while it is in progress. To do this, we can simply set the *visibility* of that text to `false`—that is, hide it using the `setVisible` function:

```
setVisible(txtGameOver, false)
setVisible(txtTapAgain, false)
```

When the game is over and we need to display the game-over text, we simply set the *visibility* to `true`.

To update all of the text in the text objects that we created, we use the `updateAllText` function:

```
function updateAllText()
  updateText(txtLives, lives)
  updateText(txtFuel, fuel)
  updateText(txtScore, score)
  updateText(txtSaved, collected)
end
```

At the start, we call the `createHUDItems` function to initially display the text objects, and then we add the `updateAllText` function in our `update` function loop so that it keeps updating the amount of fuel left, the number of survivors collected, and the number of lives remaining.

Game Over; Play Again?

When the number of lives reaches zero, we display the message "Game Over" and offer the user the choice to play again. Then the program simply waits for the player to tap the screen to play again.

To handle taps or touches on the screen, event listeners have to be set. We can add or remove `eventHandlers` as follows in Corona SDK:

```
function addHandler(theEventName, theHandler, theObject)
  local theObject = theObject or Runtime
  theObject:addEventListener(theEventName, theHandler)
end
function removeHandler(theEventName, theHandler, theObject)
  local theObject = theObject or Runtime
  theObject:removeEventListener(theEventName, theHandler)
end
```

and like so Gideros Studio:

```
function addHandler(theEventName, theHandler, theObject)
  local theObject = theObject or stage
  theObject:addEventListener(theEventName, theHandler)
end

function removeHandler(theEventName, theHandler, theObject)
  local theObject = theObject or stage
  theObject:removeEventListener(theEventName, theHandler)
end
```

Now we've added handlers, we need to set up a listener for taps on the screen.

Here's the code for Corona SDK:

```
tapEvent = "tap"
```

And here's the code for Gideros Studio:

```
tapEvent = Event.TOUCHES_END
```

With this we can create a generic handler:

```
function showReplayScreen()
  removeHandler(tapEvent, shoot)
  addHandler(tapEvent, restartGame)
end
```

And the *tapped* handler can be defined as follows:

```
function restartGame(event)
  -- restart the game by setting most of the values to defaults
  wTime = 2
  -- we can set the reinitialization code here; e.g., setting the values, repositioning elements, etc.
  setVisible(txtGameOver, false)
  setVisible(txtTapAgain, false)
  score = 0
  distance = 0
  collected = 0
  fuel = MAX_FUEL
  lives = MAX_LIVES
  setVisible(heli,true)

  updateText(txtFuel, fuel)
  updateText(txtScore, score)
  updateText(txtSaved, saved)
  updateText(txtLives, lives)

  -- remove the handler that will restart the game removeHandler(tapEvent, restartGame) gameOver = false
  -- add the handler to shoot bullets when tapped addHandler(tapEvent, shoot) end
```

Collisions

The last thing left in the grand scheme of things is to detect when the helicopter collides with any of the scenery items, which will crash it, and when the helicopter collides with a survivor, which will save the survivor.

```
function checkCollisions()
  -- create the player rect local hx, hy = getPosition(heli) pRect = {
    x = hx,
    y = hy,
    wd = heli.width,
    ht = heli.height,
  }

  -- find if the helicopter collided with a scenery object
  for i = #scenery, 1, -1 do
    local nme = scenery[i]
    if nme.objType == objects.plane or nme.objType == objects.balloon or
      nme.objType == objects.lamppost or nme.objType == objects.house or
      nme.objType == objetcs.tallHouse or nme.objType == objects.angryCloud then
      hx, hy = getPosition(nme.sprite)
      nRect = {
        x = hx,
        y = hy,
        wd = nme.sprite.width,
        ht = nme.sprite.height,
      }

      if collides(nRect, pRect) == true then
        reduceLife()
        break
      end
    end
  end
  hx, hy = getPosition(survivor)
  sRect = {
    x = hx,
    y = hy,
    wd = hx + survivor.width,
    ht = hy + survivor.height,
  }

  -- check if we have collected the survivor
  if collides(sRect, pRect) == true then
    collected = collected + 1
    updateText(txtSaved, collected)
    setVisible(survivor, false)
    score = score + 100
    updateText(txtScore, score)
    playSound(sounds.collectSurvivor)
  end
```

```
    -- check if we have collected the fuel
    if tanker~= nil then
      hx, hy = getPosition(tanker)
      tRect = {
        x = hx,
        y = hy,
        wd = hx + tanker.width,
        ht = hy + tanker.height,
      }
      if collides(tRect, pRect) == true then
        fuel = MAX_FUEL
        updateText(txtFuel, fuel)
        setVisible(tanker, false)

        -- reposition the tanker off the screen
        position(tanker, _W + random(3,5) * tanker.width, baseLine - tanker.height)
        playSound(sounds.collectFuel)
      end
    end
end
```

The function collides is a simple function that checks if the rectangles bounding the sprites overlap. This is similar to the *overlappingRectangle* function called rectOverlaps, which is discussed in Chapter 7.

```
function collides(rect1, rect2)
  local x,y,w,h = rect1.x,rect1.y, rect1.wd, rect1.ht
  local x2,y2,w2,h2 = rect2.x,rect2.y, rect2.wd, rect2.ht

  return not ((y+h < y2) or (y > y2+h2) or (x > x2+w2) or (x+w < x2))
end
```

To make things interesting, we can also show/hide the crash graphic in place of the helicopter every time it crashes into an object or the ground, as follows:

```
hx, hy = getPosition(heli)
setVisible(heli, false)
position(crash, hx, hy)
setVisible(crash, true)
```

Later, in the replay screen displayed by the showReplayScreen function, we can remove the crash graphic and set the helicopter back to visible, as follows:

```
setVisible(crash, false)
setVisible(heli, true)
position(heli, _W/2, _H/2)
```

Shooting Planes and Balloons

Earlier, we spawned bullets and made them move toward the right side of the screen. Now we have to handle cases in which the bullets hit something, in which case we remove the objects that are hit.

This game only allows us to shoot down planes and balloons, so in our moveBullets function, we check if the bullet has collided with any object; if it hits the angryCloud or the tallHouse they are absorbed.

```lua
local function moveBullets()
  local blt
  for i=#bullets,1,-1 do
    blt = bullets[i]
    blt.x = blt.x + FAST
    position(blt.sprite, blt.x, blt.y)

    tRect = {
      x=blt.x,
      y=blt.y,
      wd=blt.wd,
      ht=blt.ht,
      }

    for j = #scenery, 1, -1 do
      local nme = scenery[j]
      if nme.objType == objects.plane or nme.objType == objects.balloon then
        hx, hy = getPosition(nme.sprite)
        nRect = {
          x = hx,
          y = hy,
          wd = nme.sprite.width,
          ht = nme.sprite.height,
          }

        if collides(nRect, tRect) == true then
          -- increment score
          if nme.objType == objects.plane then score = score + 50 end
          if nme.objType == objects.balloon then score = score + 30 end
      updateText(txtScore, score)
          destroyObject(blt.sprite)
          table.remove(bullets,i)
          blt = nil

          destroyObject(nme.sprite)
          table.remove(scenery,j)
          nme=nil

          return
        end
      elseif nme.objType == objects.angryCloud or
             nme.objType == objects.tallHouse then
        hx, hy = getPosition(nme.sprite)
        nRect = {
          x = hx,
          y = hy,
          wd = nme.sprite.width,
          ht = nme.sprite.height,
          }
```

```
        if collides(nRect, tRect) == true then
          destroyObject(blt.sprite)
          table.remove(bullets,i)
          blt = nil
        end
    end
    if blt and blt.x > _W then
      -- remove it if it is beyond the right-hand side of the screen
      destroyObject(blt.sprite)
      table.remove(bullets, i)
      blt = nil
    end
  end
end
```

The collisions are based on overlapping rectangles, which means that in some cases, the helicopter will crash in the air if it's close to—but doesn't necessarily appear to be touching—another object. Figure 15-6 illustrates this. There are ways to perform more precise collision checking, but they're beyond the scope of this chapter. See Chapter 7 for some of the functions that can help with this.

Figure 15-6. Collisions occur when the helicopter's rectangle overlaps with one of the scenery objects' rectangles

Saving Survivors and Refueling

We also need to test for the condition when the helicopter comes in contact with a survivor or the fuel tanker. In the case of these two objects, rather than spawn tankers and survivors every so often, as we do with the scenery objects, we simply hide the objects and display them as needed. In this way, it becomes important to check for the visibility of the object, as this will be key in our collision calculations.

Here's how we check the visibility in Corona SDK:

```
function isVisible(theObject)
  if theObject == nil then return false end
  return theObject.isVisible
end
```

And here's how we do it in Gideros Studio:

```
function isVisible(theObject)
  if theObject == nil then return false end
  return theObject:isVisible()
end
```

In our moveScenery function, we can include checking for the tanker and survivor, and display them as follows:

```
if tanker~= nil and isVisible(tanker) then
  local tx, ty = getPosition(tanker)
  tx = tx - NORMAL
  ty = baseLine - survivor.height
  position(tanker, tx, ty)
  if tx < - tanker.width then
    setVisible(tanker, false)
    position(tanker, _W + random(5,10) * tanker.width, ty)
  end
elseif tanker ~= nil and fuel <=100 then
    setVisible(tanker, true)
end
if survivor ~= nil then
  if isVisible(survivor) then
    position(survivor, _W+random(5,10)*survivor.width, ty)
    setVisible(survivor, true)
  else
    local tx, ty = getPosition(survivor)
    tx = tx - NORMAL
    ty = baseLine - survivor.height

    position(survivor, tx, ty)
    if tx < - survivor.width then
    position(survivor , _W + random(5,10) * survivor.width, ty)
      score = score - 50  -- penalty for not collecting a survivor
      if score < 0 then score = 0 end
    end
  end
end
```

Putting It All Together

The preceding code works, but some of the functions need to be initialized. To do this, we place the code below into the init function:

```
function init()
  background = loadImage("background.png")
  heli = loadImage("_chopper.png", _W/2, _H/2) -- middle of the screen
  objects =    enumerate{"plane", "balloon", "flower", "grass", "lamppost",
   "house", "tallHouse", "cloud1", "cloud2", "cloud3", "angryCloud"}
  survivor = loadImage("_man.png")
```

```
tanker   = loadImage("_tanker.png")
setupSound()

colors = {
  {0,   0,   255},      -- blue
  {255, 0,   0},        -- red
  {0,   255, 0},        -- green
  {255, 0,   255},      -- magenta
  {0,   255, 255},      -- cyan
  {255, 255, 0},        -- yellow
  {255, 255, 255},      -- white
  {179, 115, 255},      -- orange
}

createHUDItems()
setVisible(txtGameOver,false)
setVisible(tanker,     false)
setVisible(survivor,   false)
setVisible(txtTapAgain,false)
end
```

Figure 15-7 shows the final version of the game.

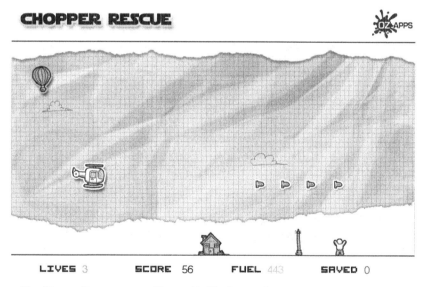

Figure 15-7. *The working Chopper Rescue game, with an added background*

> **Note**   The preceding code is only an excerpt of the full source code. While it will run and demonstrate
> the features described in this chapter, it isn't fully functional. To enjoy the full game, download the
> complete source code from the Apress web site and run it.

Summary

This chapter walked you through the process of creating a game that can be ported between frameworks with very little alteration. There are plenty of optimizations you can apply to the code, but I'll leave that as an exercise for you as you learn more about Lua and the frameworks covered in this book. Most of the logic is written in Lua, and the framework-specific functions are abstracted into functions that can be altered to suit different SDKs.

Lua's flexibility and ease of use can help you develop games quite quickly, and Lua makes your games easy to test, debug, and implement.

This brings us to the end of our journey. Looking forward to seeing the games you've created with Lua.

Index

N

O

W, X, Y, Z

CPSIA information can be obtained at www.ICGtesting.com
Printed in the USA
LVOW021837211212

312798LV00003B/11/P